*Faulkner's Short Fiction*

*Faulkner's Short Fiction*

James Ferguson

*The University of Tennessee Press*
KNOXVILLE

Copyright © 1991 by The University of Tennessee Press / Knoxville.
All rights reserved. Manufactured in the United States of America.
Cloth: 1st printing, 1991; 2nd printing, 1992.

The paper in this book meets the minimum requirements of the American
National Standard for Permanence of Paper for Printed Library Materials.
∞
The binding materials have been chosen for strength and durability.

Library of Congress Cataloging in Publication Data

Ferguson, James, 1928-
    Faulkner's short fiction / James Ferguson. — 1st ed.
        p.     cm.
    "Bibliography of Faulkner's short fiction": p.
    Includes bibliographical references and index.
    ISBN 0–87049–695–6 (cloth: alk. paper)
    1. Faulkner, William, 1897–1962—Criticism and interpretation.
2. Short story.     I. Title.
PS3511.A86Z78323        1991
813'.52—DC20                                         90-49655     CIP

For Lori

*With much love and gratitude*

# Contents

# Acknowledgments

William Faulkner produced a large body of short fiction: works that are not only significant in their own right but can also reveal a great deal about what made Faulkner the artist he was. This study is an attempt, by means of a topical approach, to examine the short fiction in a somewhat more comprehensive and systematic manner than has previously been employed. It is addressed to all readers who have some interest in Faulkner, ranging from those who have read only the great novels and a few of the most widely anthologized stories to those who have devoted much of their lives to Faulkner scholarship. Its intent is to serve as a guide to the study of the short fiction.

This book, which has been in preparation more years than I care to admit, owes a great deal to many people. Most obviously, I am indebted to the vast body of Faulkner scholarship, some of it of very high quality indeed, which I have acknowledged in the documentation throughout this volume. My interest in Faulkner was greatly intensified through my contacts with Joseph Blotner, his friend and biographer, whom I met in 1974 at the first annual conference on Faulkner and Yoknapatawpha at the University of Mississippi, and who subsequently visited Hanover College on two occasions. I am grateful to Professor Blotner for his friendship, encouragement, and advice. I am also greatly indebted to James Meriwether, who read two drafts of the manuscript and made some most significant suggestions about needed revisions, without which the book would surely not have been published. Thomas L. McHaney also read a late draft with the most scrupulous care and in his reader's report gave me some excellent advice, much of which I have been able to incorporate into this study. Needless to say, these distinguished Faulkner scholars are not responsible for any factual errors or discrepancies, the blame for which should be solely mine.

I am also grateful for the unfailingly efficient and courteous help I received from the staffs of the Alderman Library of the University of Virginia and the New York Public Library. I did much of my research at the Duggan

Library of Hanover College, where I became aware of the wonders of inter-library loan service. Many thanks to Walter Morrill, Director of Libraries at Hanover; Walter Mann; Robert Zilliox; Steven Sowards; Larry Baerveldt; Grace Ireland; all the other members of the staff of the Duggan Library; and, especially, my wife, Lorice Ferguson.

It would have been impossible to complete this study without the more than generous assistance of Hanover College. I am grateful to all those who made it possible for me to work on this project. My thanks to the Board of Trustees of the College; President Emeritus John E. Horner; President Russell Nichols; Stanley Caine, former Vice President for Academic Affairs, now President of Adrian College; Dean Charles Flynn; and especially the Faculty Development Committee (formerly the Research Committee) of Hanover College, which approved my plans for two sabbatical leaves and also approved my requests for several badly needed grants. I am also most grateful for the interest and encouragement of my faculty colleagues, par-ticularly my good friends in the English Department: Charles Fox, George Clark, Jonathan Smith, Margaret E. Stewart, Margot Tomsen, and Marsha Dutton. I owe a great deal to my students, notably those who have been enrolled in my Faulkner classes and who have shared my enthusiasm for and commitment to one of the most extraordinary literary achievements of our age.

I am sure that everyone who has worked with The University of Tennes-see Press will agree with me that it is truly a superb press. I am grateful to all the members of the staff who have contributed to the making of this book, but particularly to Carol Orr, Director, whose interest, encouragement, and judicious advice have truly meant a great deal to me.

Because I have a large family, it is impossible to thank here all those rela-tives whose love and encouragement have done so much to make this book possible. But I do want to thank my mother, Helen Briggs; my daughters, Kathleen and Lynne Chapman; and their husbands, David and Paul Chap-man, for their enthusiastic interest in this project for many years. Finally, it is impossible for me to express in any remotely adequate way my gratitude to my wife, Lorice, who, in spite of a severe and debilitating illness, has committed herself with unstinting faith and wholehearted devotion to this book. Had it not been for her, it is likely that I would have given up on it long ago. In a very real sense, it is as much her book as it is mine.

I wish to thank the University of Virginia Library (William Faulkner Collections [#6084], Manuscripts Division, Special Collections Depart-ment) for permission to quote from manuscripts and typescripts of the following Faulkner short stories: "Moonlight," "Carcassonne," "Miss Zil-phia Gant," "Artist at Home," "Drouth," "Victory," and "A Point of Law."

My thanks to the University of Mississippi Library for permission to quote from a typescript of "The Brooch." I am grateful also to W. W. Norton, Inc., the owner of the copyright to the above materials, for permission to quote from them.

I also wish to thank Random House, Inc., for permission to quote from the following copyrighted works of William Faulkner: *Collected Stories of William Faulkner*. New York: Random, 1950; *Essays, Speeches & Public Letters*. Ed. James B. Meriwether. New York: Random, 1966; *Go Down, Moses*. New York: Vintage-Random, 1973; *Knight's Gambit*. New York: Random, 1949; *The Marble Faun and A Green Bough*. New York: Random, 1965; *New Orleans Sketches*. Ed. Carvel Collins. New York: Random, 1968; *Selected Letters of William Faulkner*. Ed. Joseph Blotner. New York: Random, 1977; *Uncollected Stories of William Faulkner*. New York: Random, 1979; *The Unvanquished*. New York: Vintage-Random, 1966; *The Wishing Tree*. New York: Random, 1967.

I am grateful to the University Press of Virginia for permission to quote from *Faulkner in the University* (Frederick L. Gwynn and Joseph Blotner, eds., University Press of Virginia, 1977).

# A Note on Documentation and Related Matters

For parenthetical citations to Faulkner's books and miscellaneous collections of writings, I have employed the standard abbreviations recommended by *The Faulkner Journal*. 3.1 (1987), 85–86. Whenever possible I have also used the texts recommended in that journal, as noted in the next section, "Abbreviations for Faulkner's Texts." See also James Meriwether, "The Books of William Faulkner," *Mississippi Quarterly* 35 (1982): 265–81. Because Faulkner's *Collected Stories* is more readily available than his earlier collections, *These 13* and *Doctor Martino and Other Stories*, I have generally used the texts of the stories in the former volume except when referring specifically to the two earlier books.

A number of Faulkner's stories have variant titles. In most contexts I have preferred to use the most familiar titles, i.e., those Faulkner employed in the *Collected Stories* (if the works in question can be found in that volume). However, when referring to the genetic history of these stories or their original publication, I have, for the sake of accuracy, used other appropriate titles. For example, I generally call Faulkner's bizarre early tale of the supernatural "The Leg," but when I discuss its inclusion in *Doctor Martino and Other Stories*, I use the title "Leg," which Faulkner assigned it in that volume.

In parenthetical citations to the manuscripts and typescripts of Faulkner's stories, I have cited the number of pages in the manuscript or typescript and the specific page or pages where I found the passage in question. I have also cited, whenever possible, the appropriate page or pages in the volumes of the Garland Faulkner listed in the next section, "Abbreviations for Faulkner's Texts." For instance, "16–pp. ts. 6; *WFM 15* 19)" refers to page six of a 16-page typescript of the story under consideration and to the facsimile of that page in *William Faulkner Manuscripts 15*. If additional information is necessary, I have supplied it in the parenthetical citations or the notes. Unless otherwise indicated, the manuscripts and typescripts are in the William Faulkner Collection of the Alderman Library at the University of Virginia. For further information, the reader should refer to the Bibliography of Faulkner's Short Fiction in this book.

In quoting from unpublished material by Faulkner, I have made no attempt to correct his spelling, typographical errors, punctuation, etc. I have not used *sic* to indicate my awareness of Faulkner's errors.

# Abbreviations for Faulkner's Texts

The editions cited below have been employed. The abbreviations, those recommended by *The Faulkner Journal* 3.1 (1987): 85–86, are as follows:

| | |
|---|---|
| *AA* | *Absalom, Absalom! The Corrected Text*. New York: Vintage-Random, 1987. |
| *AILD* | *As I Lay Dying. The Corrected Text*. New York: Vintage-Random, 1987. |
| *BW* | *Big Woods*. New York: Random, 1955. |
| *CS* | *Collected Stories of William Faulkner*. New York: Random, 1950. |
| *DRM* | *Doctor Martino and Other Stories*. New York: Harrison Smith and Robert Haas, 1934. |
| *ELM* | *Elmer. Mississippi Quarterly* 36 (1983): 337–460. |
| *EPP* | *Early Prose and Poetry*. Ed. Carvel Collins. Boston: Little, 1962. |
| *ESPL* | *Essays, Speeches & Public Letters*. Ed. James B. Meriwether. New York: Random, 1966. |
| *FA* | *Father Abraham*. Ed. James B. Meriwether. New York: Random, 1984. |
| *FAB* | *A Fable*. New York: Random, 1954. |
| *FD* | *Flags in the Dust*. Ed. Douglas Day. New York: Random, 1973. |
| *FU* | *Faulkner in the University*. Eds. Frederick L. Gwynn and Joseph L. Blotner. Charlottesville: UP of Virginia, 1977. |
| *GB* | *The Marble Faun and A Green Bough*. New York: Random, 1965. |
| *GDM* | *Go Down, Moses*. New York: Vintage-Random, 1973. |
| *H* | *The Hamlet*. New York: Vintage-Random, 1973. |
| *ID* | *Intruder in the Dust*. New York: Vintage-Random, 1972. |
| *KG* | *Knight's Gambit*. New York: Random, 1949. |
| *LA* | *Light in August. The Corrected Text*. New York: Vintage-Random, 1987. |
| *LG* | *Lion in the Garden: Interviews with William Faulkner 1926–1962*. Eds. James B. Meriwether and Michael Millgate. New York: Random, 1968. |
| *M* | *The Mansion*. New York: Vintage-Random, 1965. |
| *MAR* | *Marionettes* (Ms. facsimile). Charlottesville: Published by the UP of Virginia for the Bibliographical Society of the University of Virginia, 1977. |
| *MAY* | *Mayday*. Ed. Carvel Collins. Notre Dame: U of Notre Dame P, 1977. |

| | |
|---|---|
| MF | *The Marble Faun.* See *GB* above. |
| MOS | *Mosquitoes.* New York: Liveright, 1951. |
| NH | *Notes on a Horsethief.* Greenville, Miss.: Levee Press, 1951. |
| NOS | *New Orleans Sketches.* Ed. Carvel Collins. New York: Random, 1968. |
| P | *Pylon.* New York: Harrison Smith and Robert Haas, 1935. |
| R | *The Reivers.* New York: Vintage-Random, 1966. |
| RN | *Requiem for a Nun.* New York: Vintage-Random, 1975. |
| S | *Sanctuary.* New York: Modern Library, 1932. |
| SAR | *Sartoris.* New York: Random, 1961. |
| SF | *The Sound and the Fury. New, Corrected Edition.* New York: Random, 1984. |
| SL | *Selected Letters of William Faulkner.* Ed. Joseph Blotner. New York: Random, 1977. |
| SP | *Soldiers' Pay.* New York: Liveright, 1951. |
| T | *The Town.* New York: Vintage-Random, 1961. |
| T13 | *These 13.* New York: Jonathan Cape and Harrison Smith, 1931. |
| U | *The Unvanquished.* New York: Vintage-Random, 1966. |
| US | *Uncollected Stories of William Faulkner.* Ed. Joseph Blotner. New York: Random, 1979. |
| WP | *The Wild Palms.* New York: Vintage-Random, 1966. |
| WT | *The Wishing Tree.* New York: Random, 1967. |

Below are the abbreviations for the volumes of *William Faulkner Manuscripts* (New York: Garland, 1987) that I have consulted. James B. Meriwether is the Senior Consulting Editor for the series.

| | |
|---|---|
| WFM 1 | *William Faulkner Manuscripts 1:* Elmer *and "A Portrait of Elmer": Typescripts, Manuscripts, and Miscellaneous Pages.* Ed. Thomas L. McHaney. |
| WFM 2 | *William Faulkner Manuscripts 2:* Father Abraham: *Holograph Manuscripts and Typescripts; and* The Wishing Tree: *Ribbon and Carbon Typescripts.* Ed. Thomas L. McHaney. |
| WFM 4 | *William Faulkner Manuscripts 4:* Mosquitoes: *The Ribbon Typescript and Miscellaneous Typescript Pages.* Ed. Joseph Blotner. |
| WFM 9 | *William Faulkner Manuscripts 9:* These 13: *Holograph Manuscripts and Typescripts.* Ed. Noel Polk. |
| WFM 11 | *William Faulkner Manuscripts 11:* Doctor Martino and Other Stories: *Holograph Manuscripts and Typescripts.* Ed. Thomas L. McHaney. |
| WFM 15 | *William Faulkner Manuscripts 15:* The Hamlet: *Miscellaneous Typescripts and Manuscripts.* Vol. 1. Ed. Thomas L. McHaney. 2 vols. |
| WFM 16 | *William Faulkner Manuscripts 16:* Go Down, Moses: *Typescripts and Miscellaneous Typescript Pages.* Vol. 1. Ed. Thomas L. McHaney. 2 vols. |

| | |
|---|---|
| *WFM 18* | *William Faulkner Manuscripts 18:* Knight's Gambit: *Typescript and Miscellaneous Typescript Pages.* Ed. Thomas L. McHaney. |
| *WFM 21* | *William Faulkner Manuscripts 21:* The Town: *Miscellaneous Material.* Vol. 1. Ed. Michael Millgate. 2 vols. |
| *WFM 22* | *William Faulkner Manuscripts 22:* The Mansion: *The Early Typescript: Part 1.* Vol. 1. Ed. Michael Millgate. 4 vols. |
| *WFM 24* | *William Faulkner Manuscripts 24: Short Stories: Holograph Manuscripts and Typescripts.* Ed. Joseph Blotner. |
| *WFM 25* | *William Faulkner Manuscripts 25: "Unpublished" Stories: Typescripts and Manuscripts.* Ed. Thomas L. McHaney. |

Abbreviations for other frequently cited works are:

| | |
|---|---|
| *FB* | Blotner, Joseph. *Faulkner: A Biography.* 2 vols. New York: Random, 1974. |
| *FB* rev. | Blotner, Joseph. *Faulkner: A Biography.* One-volume ed. New York: Random, 1984. |
| *FM* | *A Faulkner Miscellany.* Ed. James B. Meriwether. Jackson: Published for the *Mississippi Quarterly* by the UP of Mississippi, 1974. |

# Introduction

No one who is interested in the achievement of William Faulkner can complain that his works have been neglected by scholars and critics. It is now very difficult for even the most dedicated of Faulknerians to keep up with the vast amount of new material on the subject being produced every year. And yet there have been, until quite recently, curious lacunae, strangely neglected areas on which little important work has been done. The most obvious of these gaps, until about 1980, has been the short fiction.

Over a span of forty years Faulkner published about 100 works of fiction that were shorter than full-length novels and wrote a number of others that he was unable to sell.[1] During his most productive period, the late twenties and the early thirties, he probably expended almost as much time and effort on the short stories as on the novels. He published several important collections of stories to which he devoted much attention. And he often spoke more highly of the craft of short fiction than of that of the novel. Yet it has been only within the past decade that the stories have begun to receive their due. Hans Skei's *William Faulkner: The Short Story Career*, the first full-length study of the subject, was not published until 1981. Many of the standard general assessments of Faulkner's achievement devote relatively little attention to the stories.[2] There are, in comparison to the several thousand articles on the novels, still surprisingly few on the short fiction. Moreover, some of the very best of Faulkner's stories—"Mountain Victory," to cite one striking example—have been largely ignored by critics.[3]

Fortunately, this curious neglect is being rectified. Faulkner scholarship has become more responsible, more systematic, thanks, in no small measure, to the pleas of people like James Meriwether and Michael Millgate. Nevertheless, one wonders why it has taken so long for scholars to delve into an area that is so rich. How can this neglect be explained? Why, at least until recently, has more significant work been done on the stories of Faulkner's chief rival, Hemingway? Perhaps the most obvious answer to such questions is Meriwether's simple assertion that "Faulkner was primarily a novelist" ("Short Fiction" 293). Indeed he was—unlike Hemingway, who surely did his very best work in the stories. So extraordinary is the power of the Mississippian's greatest novels, so hypnotic is their effect, so challenging are their complexities that they have, quite naturally and properly, been the subject of the bulk of significant Faulkner scholarship. Because of their density, their mystery, their "modernity," they have tended to overshadow the seemingly far more conventional short stories.

We can speculate that many Faulkner specialists became interested in the subject in the same way. As undergraduates they were introduced to Faulkner by reading one or two of the most widely anthologized stories: "A Rose for Emily," "That Evening Sun," or perhaps the version of "The Bear" that appears in *Go Down, Moses*. But while they may have been intrigued by such pieces, it was not until they read one of the great novels— probably *The Sound and the Fury*—that they "discovered" Faulkner. After reading, with mounting excitement, several of the other novels, they may have decided to do graduate work, culminating in a thesis, on some aspect of Faulkner's work. Eventually, in the course of their studies, they probably tackled the *Collected Stories*. And it is very likely that they were disappointed.

For the *Collected Stories* is a most uneven volume, far more so than the comparable collection of Hemingway's stories. While it contains some work of the very first rank, many of the stories are mediocre or quite weak. To move within a space of about one hundred pages from the majestic solemnity of "Barn Burning" to the bathos of "Two Soldiers" or "Shall Not Perish" is something of a shock, as is the qualitative gap between the marvelously realized Indian pieces, particularly "Red Leaves" and "A Justice" in the third section of the book and the often pretentious and turgid war stories in the fourth section. Any collection that contains side by side such works as "Wash" and "Honor" or "Mountain Victory" and "Beyond" can certainly be called uneven. Therefore, while our hypothetical young scholars will be impressed by eight or ten of these pieces and will dutifully read the entire volume and the other readily available stories of Faulkner, they will ultimately, with a sense of profound relief, turn their attentions back to the great novels. Something like this has, I suspect, been the experience of a number of serious and dedicated students of Faulkner.

Perhaps another reason why Faulkner's stories have been relatively neglected is the failure of modern literary criticism, for the most part, to give the short story as a genre the kind of theoretical criticism it deserves. There are, of course, some general studies of the art of short fiction, and critics during the last half century have done distinguished work in the explication of many individual stories. Yet I cannot help but believe that the short story as an art form is still somewhat suspect. No one seems to know what a short story *is*. No study of the genre even pretends to be definitive. There is something about the weight, the bulk, the solidity of the novel that makes it far more "comfortable" to our theoreticians of fiction, far easier to handle and to make generalizations about than the curiously indefinable genre of short fiction. Hence, those critics who devote their attention to a writer like Faulkner may feel more secure in examining his novels because they have solidly based criteria by which to judge them, and they may shy away from the stories because they are uncertain as to what standards to apply in making their evaluations.

However, this hesitancy about subjecting Faulkner's short fiction to a close, detailed, and intensive scrutiny has not prevented many critics from generalizing about these works. Not surprisingly, there has been anything but unanimity in these assessments. Millgate argued in 1961 that Faulkner's powers are more consistently realized in the short fiction than in the novels (*William Faulkner* 65).[4] On the other hand, such critics as Irving Howe, Alfred Kazin, and Hyatt Waggoner have maintained that Faulkner had serious deficiencies as a writer of short stories, that he had the kind of imagination that could not be confined by the limitations and strictures of short fiction.[5]

Yet whatever one's opinions about the worth of Faulkner's total achievement in the genre, no one who is seriously interested in his fiction will deny that much more attention must be paid to this aspect of his work. Even those who have the strongest reservations about Faulkner's abilities in this area will surely concede that at least several of the stories—"Red Leaves," "That Evening Sun," "Barn Burning"—are among the best produced by any American writer in this century and that many others have very real worth. Such stories rate careful consideration for their intrinsic merits as serious works of art and deserve the kind of meticulous scrutiny that the great novels have been receiving for four decades. Furthermore, we can learn a great deal about Faulkner and about the genre of the short story by examining those stories that are merely mediocre or are downright failures for the light they throw on Faulkner's general strengths and weaknesses. His techniques and thematic concerns are clearer, more overt in the stories than they are in the novels. In striving to understand Faulkner's art, we must never forget that he was, above all else, a *storyteller*. Underlying even the most radical experiments of his mature fiction (in contrast to, say, the Joyce of *Dubliners* or the Hemingway of *In Our Time*, with their emphasis on the creation of mood, atmosphere, and epiphanic effects) is Faulkner's delight in narrative. In many of his stories, we can see that delight manifested in its purest form.[6]

Furthermore, even the most casual examination of the novels from structural and genetic perspectives should make us more aware of the very close and significant relationships between Faulkner's short fiction and his longer works. As several critics have noted, Faulkner tended to construct his novels out of blocks of somewhat discrete material.[7] Most obviously, this tendency is manifested in such hybrids as *The Unvanquished* and *Go Down, Moses*, once believed to be collections of stories but now generally assumed to be novels. This principle is also obvious in such contrapuntal works as *The Wild Palms* and *Requiem for a Nun*, but it can also be discerned in more subtle form in *Flags in the Dust*, *The Sound and the Fury*, and *Light in August*, among others. Hence, in one rather loose sense, many of Faulkner's longer works of fiction are "collections" of shorter pieces.

Moreover, as such studies as Joseph Blotner's biography have suggested, the creative impulses that led to the writing of many of the novels can be traced back to shorter works of fiction. Faulkner tells us that *The Sound and the Fury* began as a short story (*LG* 146–47; *FB* 1: 566–70), as did *The Wild Palms*. Much of the story line and thematic matter of *Absalom, Absalom!* can be discerned in rudimentary form in "Evangeline," "Wash," and "The Big Shot." On the other hand, there are several stories whose genesis can be traced to novels: such works as "There Was a Queen," "All the Dead Pilots," and "With Caution and Dispatch," which are concerned with the Sartorises; and "A Portrait of Elmer," a recasting of Faulkner's abortive second novel, *Elmer*. Thus, it seems clear that a thorough understanding of the short fiction will greatly aid any attempt to assess Faulkner's novels or his total achievement as an artist. This study is an attempt to provide some of that understanding.

But any attempt to deal with Faulkner's short fiction must immediately confront a problem of definition suggested by the very close relationship in his career between the longer and shorter forms of fiction. What, then, in the Faulkner canon *is* a work of short fiction? What are we to do with those extracts from the novels such as "The Waifs" or "The Education of Lucas Priest," which were separately published in magazine form? And, more important, how should we handle the stories—or "chapters," as some prefer to call them—in the "story-novels,"[8] *The Unvanquished* and *Go Down, Moses?*

Here I think we must be guided by the good sense of James Meriwether and by the intentions of Faulkner himself. Meriwether suggests that the most valid distinction we can make between excerpts from novels and short stories should be based on *identity*. There is no difference, for example, between "The Waifs," the piece published in *The Saturday Evening Post*, and the ending of *The Town*, and hence the former cannot really be considered a short story. On the other hand, there is a substantial difference between the version of "The Bear" that appeared in *The Saturday Evening Post* and the version from which it was extracted in *Go Down, Moses*; hence, the *Post* "Bear" does qualify as a short story ("Short Fiction" 294–96). This distinction is valid for my purposes. While extracts from the novels can certainly be categorized in one sense as works of short fiction, I will not deal with them in any substantial manner in this study.

Nor will I assume that *The Unvanquished* and *Go Down, Moses* are essentially collections of short stories, although the insistence of some Faulknerians that they are novels seems a bit simplistic.⁹ Of course, most of the material in these two volumes was originally separately published as short stories, and Faulkner at least attempted to sell virtually all of it. These stories, *in their original form,* should indeed be dealt with as autonomous works of short fiction. But when Faulkner revised them for incorporation into *The Unvanquished* and *Go Down, Moses*, it is clear that he intended that they be read as parts of a greater whole. The assumption of many critics and anthologists until fairly recently that the version of "The Bear" appearing in *Go Down, Moses*, for example, is a novella that we can readily separate from its original context is obviously fallacious. However, such confusion about these works can be partially blamed on Faulkner himself, who did not strongly object to the publication of the five-part "Bear," "Raid," and "An Odor of Verbena" in *The Portable Faulkner*. Nor was Faulkner altogether consistent in his public pronouncements about how to regard *The Unvanquished* or *Go Down, Moses*. (His memory was notoriously fallible, his treatment of his works after their original publication somewhat cavalier, and his publicly expressed opinions about his own career often erroneous or even mendacious.) Nevertheless, we must be guided here by the information we have about Faulkner's initial intent in the publication of this material. Therefore, I shall treat the original stories as autonomous, but not the versions that appear in *The Unvanquished* or *Go Down, Moses*. In any case, these distinctions are somewhat academic, since I will be concerned not only with the short stories as self-sufficient works of art but also with their relationship to Faulkner's novels and his career as a whole. Obviously, no study of Faulkner's short fiction can simply ignore *The Unvanquished* or *Go Down, Moses*.

The allusions to "autonomy" and "self sufficiency" in the preceding paragraphs suggest another problem that beset Faulkner criticism for a long time: the "saga" theory. Malcolm Cowley's famous introduction to *The Portable Faulkner* and his remarkable job of editing that volume had considerable influence on the early stage of Faulkner studies—particularly in terms of Cowley's belief that Faulkner had set out, more or less consciously, to write a relatively coherent and consistent chronicle of Yoknapatawpha County, a linked sequence of novels and stories in the tradition of Balzac and Zola. There *is* evidence from fairly early in Faulkner's career, from not long after he had discovered Yoknapatawpha, that he did have some sense that he was creating a saga and therefore some concern about the need for consistency.[10] Furthermore, it seems evident that he was himself influenced by Cowley's views in his later works; the allusions in *The Mansion* and *The Reivers* to characters and situations in the earlier novels seem, if anything, rather obvious and forced.

But the saga theory has now been largely discredited.[11] The creation of Yoknapatawpha County was simply a means to an end; Faulkner was far more concerned about the integrity of his individual works than about any attempt to write a chronicle. One of the most fundamental errors that can be made in Faulkner studies is to assume a greater degree of consistency from work to work than the writer intended. It is dangerous to explicate a Faulkner novel or story by using material drawn from any of his other works. For Faulkner was not as concerned about consistency as he was about his immediate problems in writing a specific piece—the best strategy to be employed in composing any one novel or story. In a new work he did not hesitate to make rather basic changes in characters or situations that he had previously employed. While Faulkner was careless about details, it would be naive to assume that the many inconsistencies we can find in the oeuvre are necessarily mistakes. As the preface to *The Mansion* suggests, he simply did not care much about consistency.

But Faulkner scholars have. Some of them have wanted—almost desperately, it would seem—to see the world of Yoknapatawpha County as a coherent whole and have therefore made questionable assumptions about specific works from evidence acquired from other works. Of course, this kind of thing can be helpful if it is done judiciously, since any argument for autonomy can be pushed much too far.[12] There is no great harm in reading "There Was a Queen," for example, in the light of what one knows about *Sartoris* or *Sanctuary*, as long as one realizes that Faulkner knew that most readers of the story would probably not have read those novels. But to assume, as even so distinguished a critic as Olga Vickery does, that Nancy's fears in "That Evening Sun" are foolish (301) because Faulkner employs the character again in *Requiem for a Nun* is, I think, to misread the story in a very fundamental way. The same thing is true of the rather ingenious arguments of at least two critics, on the basis of the other Indian stories, that the real father of Sam Fathers in "A Justice" is Doom (Howell, "Sam Fathers"; Bradford, "Patriarchy"); there is no convincing evidence in the work itself that such is the case.

I shall try to avoid such errors in discussing the stories and shall treat these works as largely self-sufficient entities. But in order to assess Faulkner's achievement as a writer of short fiction, we must obviously relate individual stories to each other, to the novels, and to the total oeuvre. Before we can examine the parts, we must have some sense of the whole. I shall therefore begin this study with an overview of Faulkner's career as a short-story writer: with a survey of his opinions about the genre and the conclusions we can draw from them, and with some attempts to establish *why* Faulkner wrote such a large body of short fiction and why he was more productive in the genre in certain periods of his life than in others.

In the succeeding chapters I shall look more closely at various aspects of Faulkner's handling of the genre. A chapter will be devoted to certain patterns and motifs that recur with some regularity in many of the stories. I shall be concerned in two chapters with Faulkner's management of the craft of short fiction: with his approach to point of view and with other technical considerations. Finally, I shall examine in some detail the complex relationships between the individual stories and Faulkner's books—both the collections of stories and the novels.

At this point another caveat may be necessary. In order to make reasonably valid assumptions about the place of the short stories in Faulkner's career, we must, of course, attempt to establish approximately when they were written. But in spite of the arduous efforts for several decades of any number of distinguished scholars, it seems likely now that we will never have conclusive evidence about the dates of some stories. While we do have at hand considerable information—the original dates of publication, the "sending schedule" (a record of submissions to magazines that Faulkner kept for a while), his letters, those of his publishers, recollections of his family and of friends, what the manuscripts and typescripts reveal, and some internal evidence—it is impossible to be confident about some dates. Moreover, we must ask ourselves what we mean when we attempt to establish these dates, for Faulkner sometimes worked on an individual story over a period of many years. Consider, for example, the extremely complex histories of the stories that came to be called "Spotted Horses" and "Lizards in Jamshyd's Courtyard" and were incorporated in their final forms into *The Hamlet*; or of such works as "Beyond" or "Pennsylvania Station" or "Knight's Gambit." Clearly our dating of some stories must be tentative, but we can certainly make many reasonably valid assumptions.[13]

# CHAPTER I

# The Career

## Faulkner on Short Fiction

On the several occasions when he commented on the craft of the short story, Faulkner always spoke highly of the genre, comparing it favorably to the novel. These statements, most of which were made during the last decade of his life, seem a bit repetitious and formulaic. Invariably, Faulkner made the point that, while the literary art of arts is poetry, the short story must take precedence over the novel because the novelist can afford to be more "careless." Representative of that point is the answer he gave at the University of Virginia when someone asked whether it was easier to write a novel than a short story:

> Yes sir. You can be more careless, you can put more trash in it [the novel] and be excused for it. In a short story that's next to the poem, almost every word has got to be almost exactly right. In the novel you can be careless but in the short story you can't. I mean by that the good short stories like Chekhov wrote. That's why I rate that second—it's because it demands a nearer absolute exactitude. You have less room to be slovenly and careless. There's less room in it for trash. (*FU* 207)

Such statements may strike us as being somewhat disingenuous. For there is ample evidence throughout most of Faulkner's career that he devoted more attention and concern to his novels than to his short stories, that he did most of his really serious work in the longer fictional modes, and that at certain periods he wrote short fiction only because of a pressing need for money. Furthermore, when he made this statement and similar ones at Virginia and at West Point, he had stopped writing short stories and had, indeed, done very little work in the genre since 1942. There was surely very little doubt in Faulkner's mind that he would be remembered primarily as a novelist. We are tempted to think that there is a trace of false modesty in these assertions about the short story—the same quality we can discern in his repeated statements that he was a "failed poet."

But there is probably also a vein of real sincerity here. For Faulkner expressed comparable sentiments in a letter to Joan Williams several years before he began to make his classroom pronouncements, and, considering the context in which he expressed his views to Williams—his advice to her about her writing and the closeness of his relationship with her—there is little reason to doubt the genuineness of his views: "Who told you you cant write short stories? A short story is a crystallised instant, arbitrarily selected, in which character conflicts with character or environment or itself. We both agreed long since that, next to poetry, it is the hardest art form" (*SL* 345). It would seem that here Faulkner is implicitly conceding his limitations as an artist, is acknowledging that his own art is essentially expansive, as opposed to the focused intensity required of the very best short stories. Faulkner had as great a respect for the craft of fiction, for the ideal of formal perfection as anyone, and he knew that that ideal, although never fully attainable, could be more closely approached in short fiction than in the novel. Perhaps the most interesting and suggestive thing about this letter to Joan Williams is the phrase "crystallised instant," which Faulkner used to define the short story. For in these two words we have a kind of microcosmic summation of Faulkner's aesthetic credo: his belief that the function of art is to arrest motion, which he was to express more fully three years later in the famous *Paris Review* interview with Jean Stein:

> The aim of every artist is to arrest motion, which is life, by artificial means and hold it fixed so that 100 years later when a stranger looks at it, it moves again since it is life. Since man is mortal, the only immortality possible for him is to leave something behind him that is immortal since it will always move. This is the artist's way of scribbling "Kilroy was here" on the wall of the final and irrevocable oblivion through which he must someday pass. (*LG* 253)

Perhaps Faulkner believed that this goal, which had been the basis of his art from its beginnings, could be more readily achieved within the briefer compass of short fiction than in the inevitably less cohesive and looser form of the novel.[1]

In any case, it took him considerably longer to attain real mastery of the short story—a mastery that he only occasionally achieved—than of the novel. "A Rose for Emily," the first of his stories to be accepted by a national magazine, did not appear in *Forum* until April 1930, after he had published four novels, one of which (*The Sound and the Fury*) he knew to be a masterpiece, and shortly before another novel of the very highest quality (*As I Lay Dying*) was to appear. He had been submitting stories to the mass-circulation magazines for years before "Emily" was finally accepted; as early as 1925 he had apparently accumulated a whole drawer of rejection slips from such magazines as *Collier's* and *The Saturday Evening Post* (*FB* 1:405). Moreover, Faulkner's early correspondence with *Scribner's Magazine*, to which he was submitting fiction at least as early as 1928, could hardly have bolstered his confidence in his abilities as a short-story writer. Alfred Dashiell had some relatively pleasant things to say about his work, but his tone was rather patronizing and condescending. And when he generalized about Faulkner's stories, Dashiell had some fairly harsh things to say. Faulkner could hardly have been pleased, for example, by the advice he received from *Scribner's* in 1928: "The trouble with your writing, it seems to me, is that you get mostly the overtones and seem to avoid the real core of the story. It would seem that in the attempt to avoid the obvious you have manufactured the vague. You are skirting around drama and not writing it" (Meriwether, "Faulkner's Correspondence" 257).

Shortly after he received this letter, Faulkner, in submitting *Miss Zilphia Gant* to *Scribner's*, diffidently expressed his own doubts about his abilities to write effective short stories: " 'Miss Zilphia Gant' may be too diffuse, still; I don't know. I am quite sure that I have no feeling for short stories; that I shall never be able to write them, yet for some strange reason I continue to do so, and to try them on Scribner's with unflagging optimism" ("Faulkner's Correspondence" 258). Dashiell's reply could hardly have been reassuring: "I think perhaps you may be right in that you are like a distance runner trying short sprints" ("Faulkner's Correspondence" 258).

It seems clear, then, that Faulkner had at least some reason to believe that the writing of short fiction was not very congenial to his artistic temperament, in spite of his high regard for the genre. Nevertheless, it is quite easy to exaggerate that regard, to make too much of Faulkner's preference for the tighter and more cohesive literary forms. For he occasionally expressed somewhat contrary sentiments, assessing writers on the "gallantry" of their failure. The fact that he rated Thomas Wolfe higher than Hemingway because Wolfe had more "courage," because Hemingway "never climbed out on a limb" (*LG* 58), perhaps suggests a predilection for the looser and more expansive fictional modes. Faulkner came to regret that statement (which he made at the University of Mississippi in 1947) and qualified it on several occasions. But those qualifications suggest a very real ambivalence. One of the comparisons he made of Wolfe and Hemingway at the University of Virginia in 1957 is quite suggestive:

> I meant only that Hemingway had sense enough to find a method which he could control and didn't need or didn't have to, wasn't driven by his private demon to waste himself in trying to do more than that. So, he has done consistently probably the most solid work of all of us. But it wasn't the splendid magnificent

bust that Wolfe made in trying to put the whole history of the human heart on the head of the pin, you might say. (*FU* 143–44)

It is the ambitiousness of Wolfe's effort, the attempt to "get it all in" that Faulkner finds most admirable. Such a statement may seem rather remote from our central concern here—Faulkner's attitude toward the short story—but surely his emphasis on the importance of gallantry and ambitiousness, on "the splendid magnificent bust," suggests that his apparent preference for the shorter literary modes was more theoretical than pragmatic.

Moreover, there is often a considerable asperity in Faulkner's remarks about his own short stories—an asperity that we almost never find in his remarks about his novels. During a considerable portion of his career—off and on throughout the thirties and the early forties—Faulkner was financially in severe straits and was compelled to write stories simply in order to survive. His correspondence during this period contains many extremely bitter allusions to this need. Early in 1932 he wrote to Hal Smith: "$250.00 will stave me off for the time. Send it on. Sorry to bother you at all right now, when you are cluttered up yourself with overhead instead of revenue. But it's either this, or put the novel aside and go whoring again with short stories" (*SL* 59). In another letter to Smith, written the following year, he equated writing stories with working in Hollywood: "I shall have to peg away at the novel slowly, since I am broke again, with two families to support now, since my father died, and so I shall have to write a short story every so often or go back to Hollywood, which I dont want to do" (*SL* 75). His anger and impatience are clearly very intense in his correspondence with Morton Goldman about the stories he wrote for the *Post*, which in revised form would eventually be incorporated into *The Unvanquished*: "As far as I am concerned, while I have to write trash, I dont care who buys it, as long as they pay the best price I can get; doubtless the Post feels the same way about it; anytime that I sacrifice a high price to a lower one it will not be to refrain from antagonising the Post; it will be to write something better than a pulp series like this" (*SL* 84).

It should be obvious that the negative things Faulkner has to say about his stories in letters such as this do not in any sense constitute a condemnation of the genre as a whole; he is simply expressing his regret about the *kind* of short story he is occasionally compelled to write. Like many writers of his era, Faulkner made very clear-cut distinctions between "commercial" and "serious" fiction. These distinctions are quite clear in a long letter he wrote to Robert Haas in 1940, in which he itemized his financial debits and credits. On the positive side of the ledger he put the following:

5 short stories already written, two others planned, both of which might sell, one of which is a mystery story, original in that the solver is a negro, himself in jail for the murder and is about to be lynched, solves murder in self defense. Of these I can make a more or less continuous narrative, somewhat after THE UNVANQUISHED. 6–12 months.

Four other stories, unwritten, of the first class, but which I now dare not put any time on because first class stories fetch no money in America. (*SL* 128)

Like most clichés, this view of American philistinism is only a kind of half truth—at least in Faulkner's case. For while the "slicks" had rejected many of his very best stories, they had also accepted several of the "first class" ones, notably "Red Leaves" and "Mountain Victory." Faulkner earned as much or more money from them as he had earned from any one of his first five novels.

Another indication of Faulkner's sometimes rather cavalier attitude toward his own short fiction is his willingness to revise some of his stories to meet the objections of the magazine editors—in marked contrast to the scorn he heaped on the editors of his novels when they made similar suggestions. Because of his financial situation, he sometimes did not hesitate to offer to rewrite even rather good stories to meet the specifications of the editors. In a postscript to Morton Goldman in 1935, for example, he wrote: "Had letter from Dashiell at Scribner's. Send 'The Brooch' to me and I will rewrite it. Also send him 'Fool About a Horse' if he has not seen it. Will rewrite that too if necessary" (*SL* 92). Moreover, Faulkner had no compunctions about trying to sell some of his juvenilia (in revised versions) long after he had become an established writer of the first importance. As late as 1933, for instance, he was submitting the dreadful "Love" to *Scribner's* (Meriwether, "Faulkner's Correspondence" 276); all the extant manuscript and typescript versions of this piece suggest that it was never anything more than melodramatic claptrap.

Thus, in assessing Faulkner's attitude toward the short story as an art form, it would seem that any contradictions we may find are not really very basic and can ultimately be traced to the dichotomy between his abstract conception of what a story should be and the pragmatic realities of his career. He had a very genuine respect for the craft of short fiction, which he manifested not only in his theoretical statements but also, of course, in the writing of his very best stories. However, he surely knew from early in his career that his talents were more suited to the novel, and his attitude toward the short story was perhaps a bit soured because of the potboilers he had been compelled to write. But whatever his opinions about the genre may have been, Faulkner did produce a large and significant body of short fiction over a period of nearly 40 years.

# The Periods

It seems valid to assert, as have many critics, that Faulkner's career as a novelist falls into three rather clearly defined stages: the period of apprenticeship, ending with the writing of *Flags in the Dust* in 1927; the middle period of Faulkner's greatest achievement, from the composition of *The Sound and the Fury* in 1928 to the publication of *Go Down, Moses* in 1942; and the later period of decline from 1942 to Faulkner's death in 1962.

Not surprisingly, such a breakdown can also be applied fairly readily to the short stories, but I find a four-period categorization somewhat more useful, although admittedly a bit arbitrary.[2] In the first stage, through about 1927, Faulkner was still struggling to find his proper métier as a writer and experimenting in the shorter fictional modes with a number of techniques and subjects. In the second, from 1928 through 1931, he achieved real mastery of the short story and produced, along with a number of inferior stories, most of his greatest work in the genre: "That Evening Sun," "A Justice," "A Rose for Emily," "Dry September," "Red Leaves," and "Mountain Victory," among others. The third period, from 1932 to 1942, is marked by some decline in quality and quantity, by the increasing "commercialization" of many of the stories, and by the growing tendency to conceive of works of short fiction not as discrete units but as parts of a greater whole—as seen in the composition of the stories which were to become *The Unvanquished*, *Go Down, Moses*, and, to some extent, *Knight's Gambit*.

Actually Faulkner's career as a writer of significant short fiction virtually ends in 1942; he produced very few stories of any importance after this time. Thus his important work in the genre, like that of Hemingway, spans a period of only about fifteen years. But Faulkner did write some scattered works of short fiction in the last two decades of his life. Very few of these works are, in the strictest sense, autonomous short stories; a number are extracts from novels, and others are as much essays as they are stories. The discursive impulse, as opposed to the narrative, became very important in Faulkner's later writing, and we can sense this shift of orientation in the few works of short fiction written after 1942. Nevertheless, in his final twenty years he did enough work in the genre that we can be justified in labeling this a fourth period. We must now examine, in considerable detail, each of these four periods.

## The First Period

Faulkner achieved mastery of his craft when he was able to reconcile and to fuse two dominant impulses of his aesthetic temperament: the poetic and the narrative. There is ample evidence that during his apprentice years he considered himself to be primarily a poet, and it was not until the middle twenties, after he had come under the influence of Sherwood Anderson, had published *Soldiers' Pay*, and was beginning to discover Yoknapatawpha County, that he became convinced that fiction was his proper métier. But, according to evidence that Blotner has gathered, Faulkner was, from a very youthful age, writing both poetry and fiction. While his earliest artistic impulses were satisfied by drawing pictures, he had apparently begun to write poems and stories by the time he was thirteen (*FB* 1: 142). The poetry was to take precedence over the fiction for many years, but the testimony of his family and contemporaries suggests that he wrote many stories when he was in his teens and early twenties.[3] From the beginning of his career as a writer, he was therefore drawn to two very different modes of creative expression. On the one hand, he had a very strong impulse toward the lyrical, the pictorial, the atmospheric, the evocative; toward the timeless, static wholeness of poetry—an inclination intensified by his reading in the early modernist tradition, of the decadents and the symbolists. On the other hand, he was imbued from a very early age with that love of storytelling, of the temporal world of narrative that was a significant aspect of his family heritage and of the Southern cultural tradition. The effete dandy known in Oxford as Count No-Count was also at one time a scoutmaster who delighted his troop by telling them stories after dinner around a campfire (*FB* 1: 348).

The early tension between these two impulses is manifested not only in the fact that Faulkner, at this stage of his career, apparently wrote a great deal of both poetry and fiction but also in the stories and sketches themselves that have survived from this period. Several of these slight though sometimes promising works are essentially static prose poems, but in other pieces the fluidity and dynamism of the narrative impulse are dominant. This dichotomy is strikingly suggested by Faulkner's two earliest published works of prose fiction, both of which appeared in the University of Mississippi student newspaper, *The Mississippian*. The first, "Landing in Luck," published in November 1919, is a 2,500-word account of a flight cadet who on his first solo loses a wheel from his plane but miraculously manages to land unharmed. The story is quite trivial and contains not even the slightest suggestion of the power and complexity of Faulkner's mature fiction, although it does adumbrate some of his obsessive themes, patterns, and images: flight, initiation, motion, height, alienation, etc. The protagonist, Thompson, is a kind of first sketch for the Julian Lowe of *Soldiers' Pay*. But for our purposes now, the most interesting thing about this little piece is the ease and narrative fluency with which it is told. Here the story is everything, and Faulkner tells it cleanly and economically. He betrays very little understanding of modernist theories of fictional technique—his handling of point of view, for instance, seems a bit clumsy—but he does get the job done. Furthermore, there is, with the exception of one or two mildly interesting figures of speech, no "poetry" here at all. There is nothing of the vague lyricism, of the mistily evocative romanticism, the ineffable longings, the melancholy quest for wholeness, significance, or meaning that permeates the poems Faulkner was writing at this time. Trivial as it is, "Landing in Luck" is a clean, simple, unpretentious little piece that already reveals the author's facility as a storyteller.

Contrast this with "The Hill," a sketch published in *The Mississippian* a little more than two years after "Landing in Luck" appeared. This piece, concerned with the experience a laborer, a "tieless casual" (*EPP* 92), has as he mounts a hill on his return home for the evening, is about as different from "Landing in Luck" as a prose sketch by the same author could be; indeed, a casual reader might find it difficult to believe that the same man wrote both of them. For, as Ronald Corwin suggests, this is little more than a "translation" into prose of an impulse that is fundamentally poetic (38). There is in "The Hill" no narrative drive at all; nothing "happens" except the momentary sense the protagonist has that there is something of unutterable significance beyond and above him, that there is, in the scene he sees from the hill, some sort of transcendent meaning that he cannot grasp. The piece is not in any sense a story; it is a rather richly textured prose poem. Moreover, unlike "Landing in Luck," "The Hill" is marked by some unmistakably Faulknerian language. Anyone who has done fairly extensive reading in Faulkner would surely recognize the following as being his work: "His long shadow legs rose perpendicularly and fell, ludicrously, as though without power of progression, as though his body had been mesmerised by a whimsical God to a futile puppet-like activity upon one spot, while time and life terrifically passed him and left him behind" (*EPP* 90).

It is not only the language in this piece that marks it as being Faulkner's but also its thematic matter and its setting. The above quotation, and indeed the entire piece, quite clearly reflect the writer's lifelong obsession, so precisely articulated in the interview with Jean Stein, with the need to arrest motion, to freeze time. The "event" with which the sketch is concerned takes place at twilight—by all odds, the most important time of the day for Faulkner—and on one of the writer's many hills, which overlooks a valley containing a hamlet that might very well be Oxford-Jefferson. The protagonist is also an example of a character type that fascinated Faulkner throughout his career: the unlettered, inarticulate innocent who in the "terrific groping of his mind" (91) suggests the incommensurable gap between thought and experience. But, to repeat, "The Hill" is not a story; it is a poem, and it is far closer in mood, spirit, and language to Faulkner's poetry than to his prose. Indeed, as Skei notes, Poem X of *The Green Bough* is clearly a reworking of "The Hill" (*Short Story Career* 18). Compare the following two passages, the first from the prose piece, the second from the poem:

> Here, in the dusk, nymphs and fauns might riot to a shrilling of thin pipes, to a shivering and hissing of cymbals in a sharp volcanic abasement beneath a tall icy star. (*EPP* 92)

> Nymph and faun in this dusk might riot
> Beyond all oceaned Time's cold greenish bar
> To shrilling pipes, to cymbals' hissing
> Beneath a single icy star (*GB* 30)

Thus these first two published pieces of Faulkner's prose fiction— "Landing in Luck" and "The Hill"—rather effectively suggest by their stark contrast the two poles of Faulkner's creative imagination. Other stories written during the early twenties and unpublished during his lifetime also suggest, although not as obviously, this tension between his poetic and narrative inclinations. The very early typescript version of "Moonlight"[4] is a mood piece about a Saturday night in a town much like Oxford-Jefferson. This very "literary" story is heavily lyrical and atmospheric, but almost nothing happens in the course of its sixteen pages. Two young men, George and his friend Robert Binford, spend some time in a drugstore, where they contemplate "making" a couple of "flusies," then wander through the town and meet George's girl friend, Cecily, whom George later tries, for obvious reasons, to lure into a deserted house.

The intense and frenetic Cecily momentarily comes alive, but the piece contains little sense of character, motivation, or theme; it seems rather static and pointless. Yet its "poetry" is unmistakably Faulkner's. Consider the following: "a world of black and silver and sourceless sounds as dead as the beyond side of the moon, in which invisible mockingbirds reiterant one to another might have been the anonymous and inflectionless chiming of lesser stars" (16–pp. ts. 6: *WFM 25* 19). Here the use of the suffix *-less,* particularly in the word *sourceless,* the imagery of the moon, birds, and the stars, and the general rhythm of the passage are clearly Faulknerian. More- over, the setting, the complex and ambivalent attitude toward sex, and the Freudian imagery anticipate the more mature work.

Much the same can be said about another early story to which Meri- wether gave the title "Frankie and Johnny" when it was published in the *Mississippi Quarterly.*[5] It is concerned with a young woman, Frankie, daughter of a prizefighter (who drowns early in the story) and a prostitute. Frankie falls in love with a boy named Johnny, is made pregnant by him, and, at the end of the story, lies peacefully in bed, calmly accepting her lot. The piece is crude and callow—so much so that it possibly antedates the early version of "Moonlight," a more accomplished and sophisticated work. Frankie's story contains some silly and unintentionally funny writing, especially when it concerns her father. Near the beginning, when he dies trying to save a fat lady from drowning, he thinks of his daughter: " 'Poor kid, she'll have it tough now,' he thought among green bubbles" (*US* 338). In the last scene, as Frankie awaits the birth of her child, "there recurred to her a childish vision of him [her father] triumphant though dead, among green waves" (347).

Nevertheless, silly as such passages are, this extremely sentimental and superficial piece does, like "Moonlight," quite obviously anticipate the later Faulkner—in its use of the imagery of mirrors, windows, birds, and eyes; in its concern with the theme of solipsism; and in its characterization of Frankie as a kind of earth-mother. The final sentence, though clumsy and obvious, looks forward to *As I Lay Dying* and *Light in August*:

> She felt as impersonal as the earth itself: she was a strip of fecund seeded ground lying under the moon and wind and stars of the four seasons, lying beneath grey and sunny weather since before time was measured; and that now was sleeping away a dark winter waiting for her own spring with all the pain and passion of its inescapable ends to a beauty which shall not pass from the earth. (*US* 347)

By contrast, "Love," another story that Faulkner probably began at about this time, seems to be a most peculiar aberration.[6] Here the narrative impulse is far more important than the poetic. "Love" is apparently Faulkner's first attempt to write a commercial piece of fiction. Heavily plotted, extremely melodramatic, and wildly implausible, it is the story of a handsome and suave major; his devoted Oriental servant; a wealthy young flapper; and a fiercely jealous Italian maid who puts a love potion in the major's nightly brandy and eventually decides to poison him when she thinks that he has betrayed her with the flapper. But somehow the servant knows about her machinations and frustrates her plans by drinking the brandy himself.

The story, in all its surviving versions, is astonishingly bad—almost totally without literary merit. Yet it is interesting because it does suggest the range of experimentation of which the young Faulkner was capable and a direction his career might have taken had he been better at writing this kind of melodrama. Furthermore, while it seems at first glance to be a kind of sport, the most atypical piece Faulkner ever wrote, it does contain certain techniques, themes, and preoccupations found in his more characteristic work: the kind of deliberate obscurity that derives from withholding some essential elements of the plot, and his interest in obsessive behavior, in selfless devotion, in a wronged woman striking back.

It is difficult to generalize about these early pieces because they are so different. Generally, they seem less promising than the juvenilia of many other authors. It took far longer for Faulkner to mature as a writer than, say, Hemingway. But Faulkner's apprentice work does reveal from the very beginning a certain verbal facility, an intensity that can sometimes be quite compelling, and an ability to create mood and atmosphere rather effectively—particularly in such pieces as "Moonlight" and "The Hill," works on the poetic end of the literary spectrum to which I have been referring. It is also interesting that, even at this very early stage of his career, the most basic cliché of Faulkner criticism is applicable: he was at his best when his material was close to home, when he was writing about his "own little postage stamp of native soil."

These generalizations about Faulkner's early work can also be applied to the significant body of short fiction he was to produce during one of the most pivotal years of his life: 1925. During the first half of the year he was to take up residence in New Orleans; become friendly with and fall under the influence of Sherwood Anderson (whom he had met in 1924); write *Soldiers' Pay*; and publish those prose pieces in *The Double Dealer* and the *Times-Picayune* that Carvel Collins was later to publish under the title *New Orleans Sketches*.

These latter works are of considerable interest and most assuredly deserve the attention they have already received from a number of critics and scholars. Yet the strongest impression many readers are likely to receive from the sketches is how inferior most of these pieces are. They are generally immature, excessively "literary," obvious, trite, derivative. As Cleanth Brooks has noted, it is difficult to believe that at the same time Faulkner was producing these juvenile exercises, he was writing *Soldiers' Pay*—a book that, for all its faults, deficiencies, and excesses, is well-wrought, subtle and sophisticated, certainly a most promising first novel (*Toward Yoknapatawpha* 100). How can we account for this disparity? Why is so much of the material in the New Orleans sketches almost embarrassingly bad?[7]

I have suggested that it took Faulkner a bit longer to achieve mastery of the short story than of the novel, but such an assessment cannot really begin to account for the vast difference in quality between *Soldiers' Pay* and the sketches. It is likely that the best solution to this problem lies in Brooks's argument that Faulkner simply did not care much about these pieces, was writing them primarily for money, and devoted very little care or attention to them (*Toward Yoknapatawpha* 100).

Brooks's theory about this matter is as good as any we have, but it cannot account totally, I think, for the relatively poor quality of the sketches. For one thing, while Faulkner might very well have considered the pieces he contributed to the *Times-Picayune* to be hack work, he certainly would have had a much higher opinion of *The Double Dealer*, a most distinguished literary publication. He would not have simply dashed off the eleven vignettes he contributed to *The Double Dealer*. But it is likely, as Blotner suggests, that he used material already on hand, which he had written earlier and failed to sell (*FB* 1: 61n). For instance, "Frankie and Johnny," one of the eleven vignettes, is probably derived from the story discussed above to which Meriwether gave the same title,[8] and "The Kid Learns," one of the newspaper sketches, is apparently also derived from it. It is likely that some of the other material in both "New Orleans" and the *Times-Picayune* sketches antedates Faulkner's stay in New Orleans in 1925.[9] Nevertheless, most of the sketches were surely written during 1925, and, for whatever reasons, they are generally of markedly inferior quality. It is astonishing that only three years separate the first publication of these pieces and the composition of *The Sound and the Fury*.

But, in spite of their inferior quality, the sketches are of the greatest importance in tracing Faulkner's development as a writer of short fiction. They have considerable range: in thematic concerns, subject matter, and technique. Some clearly anticipate his more mature fiction. Several are quite derivative, but a few show at least some traces of originality. And collectively they reveal, as well as any of Faulkner's apprentice work, the tension between stasis and dynamism that I have argued is of the greatest importance in understanding Faulkner's growth as a writer.

The *Double Dealer* vignettes and such a piece as "The Cobbler" are prose poems: romantic, lush, sensuous, full of a love of language for its own sake, and a kind of fin de siècle overripeness. They are almost totally static, as are such character sketches as "Mirrors of Chartres Street," "Out of Nazareth," and "Episode." Other pieces have a somewhat stronger narrative impulse but are much too derivative. "Cheest" is a completely unsuccessful reworking of Sherwood Anderson's "I'm a Fool," and "Yo Ho and Two Bottles of Rum," while of greater intrinsic interest than "Cheest," obviously owes too much to Conrad. Other sketches, particularly "The Rosary" and "Chance," are at almost the opposite ends of the spectrum from the very literary "New Orleans"; they are conventional, formulaic, commercial stories, strongly suggestive, as Brooks notes, of the work of O. Henry (*Toward Yoknapatawpha* 106). Somewhat more interesting and even more heavily plotted is "Country Mice," a work reflecting, even at this early stage, Faulkner's interest in the Southwestern tradition of the swindle story, the "biter bit" theme, which was to be so prominent in the Snopes stories and novels. Of even greater interest are those sketches that more directly anticipate Faulkner's later work. Collins and others who have written about the sketches have commented on how the idiot of "The Kingdom of God," with the "ineffable blue eyes" and the "narcissus clenched tightly in his dirty hand" (*NOS* 60), anticipates Benjy in *The Sound and the Fury*; on the motif of the decomposing corpse in "Yo Ho and Two Bottles of Rum"; on the reference to "Little sister Death" in "The Kid Learns," which is to recur in several of Faulkner's other works; and on a number of other interesting relationships and parallels (Collins xxviii–xxx).

In the most successful of the New Orleans pieces the "poetry" is at least somewhat muted, the storytelling impulse is dominant, and Faulkner seems more at home with his materials. But at the same time there is a kind of controlled intensity that, if only vaguely, suggests his mature work. "The Kingdom of God," with its ironic contrasts between the corruption of the bootleggers and the innocence of the idiot, and its emphasis on obsessive family loyalty, generates a surprising amount of power, as does the compassionate but rather obvious "Sunset," the story of an innocent black who has left home in an effort to find "Africa" and is cheated and ultimately killed by white men. The piece in which Faulkner seems most relaxed, most in control of his materials, is perhaps "The Liar," a story of country people laid in a setting suggesting Frenchman's Bend and concerned, like so much of Faulkner's most important fiction, with storytelling itself, with the relationship between life and narrative.

To sum up in this rather cursory fashion some of the most obvious aspects of the New Orleans sketches is not to exhaust their significance. It will be sufficient to note here that almost all those patterns, themes, and technical factors that seem most characteristically Faulknerian can be found, in at least an embryonic state, in these pieces. Faulkner experiments here with a wide variety of points of view, with framed narratives, with rudimentary interior monologues. In the sketches there is ample evidence of Faulkner's interest in the relationship between corruption and innocence; of the motifs of alienation and obsession; of the pattern of the frenzied quest for justice; and of such an archetypal figure as the "holy fool." Collectively, the sketches are by all odds the most important apprentice work Faulkner was to do.

A number of other works probably also date from about this time. Like the sketches they reveal a wide range of subjects and techniques, but most of them do contain one element in common: a relatively explicit concern with sex.

Faulkner's treatment of erotic themes in these works of the mid-twenties seems extremely tepid when compared to the handling of the subject today. But, as Blotner suggests, at least one of these pieces, "Peter," may have been rejected by the *Times-Picayune* because the subject matter was too "gamy" (*FB* 1: 446). It is concerned with a mulatto boy who is the son of a prostitute, and it features some rather racy dialogue. "Don Giovanni," another story of this time, which was probably also intended for the *Times-Picayune*, is concerned with a Prufrock-like would-be Lothario and clearly anticipates Faulkner's treatment of the character of Talliaferro in *Mosquitoes*. A fragment entitled "And Now What's to Do" is concerned with a young man's sexual longings and his wanderings after he gets a girl pregnant, but is of particular interest because it is, as Meriwether notes, the most explicitly autobiographical piece Faulkner ever wrote (*FM* 145). The protagonist's family described in the first paragraph could very well be the author's.

The concern with sex, apparent in all these pieces, is most strikingly evident in "Nympholepsy," a very curious sketch probably written at about this time. "Nympholepsy" is clearly an expansion of "The Hill"; it is again concerned with a laborer who is mounting a hill as he returns home, but here the erotic element is very intense indeed. The protagonist spots a girl, gives chase, almost drowns in a stream in his pursuit, but finally loses her. Like "The Hill," the piece is heavily metaphorical, almost overpoweringly lush, and rife with sexual imagery; it is another prose poem, but it does contain a more forceful narrative element than its predecessor. However, "The Hill" is a more accomplished and unified piece; one has no real sense that Faulkner knows where he is going or what he is trying to achieve in "Nympholepsy." Moreover, the work contains some laughably inept language. We are told that "Before this green cathedral of trees he [the protagonist] stood for a while, empty as a sheep, feeling the dying day draining from the world as a bath-tub drains, or a cracked bowl" (*FM* 151).[10] Later, he thinks: "If I find her, I am safe . . . not knowing whether it was copulation or companionship that he wanted" (*FM* 151). One shudders with embarrassment when reading passages like these. Clearly, this was one more of many false starts.

Another story that Faulkner probably wrote at about this time was, however, much closer to home, anticipating the discovery of Yoknapatawpha. Years later, Faulkner told Meriwether that he had written "Adolescence" early in the twenties ("Short Fiction" 313), but I am inclined to agree with Max Putzel that the story dates from near the middle of the decade ("Two Characters" 61). It concerns Juliet, the adolescent daughter of an improvident bootlegger, Joe Bunden, and his schoolteacher wife. When the mother dies and Joe remarries, Juliet goes to live with her grandmother in a remote hill cabin. There she makes friends with a country boy, Lee Hollowell, but her summer idyll ends when the witchlike grandmother discovers the children lying innocently together in a blanket. After the old woman tells Bunden and he arranges a marriage for his daughter, Juliet apparently betrays him to revenue agents, who kill him. In the final scene, after Lee has left the area, Juliet lies beside the pool where they had swum together, sorrowfully longing for the lost days of her innocence.

Several aspects of this most interesting piece quite obviously suggest some of Faulkner's other works. Such elements as the family name, Bunden, the marriage of the shiftless Joe to a schoolteacher, her death, and his remarriage anticipate *As I Lay Dying*. As Putzel notes, the scene of the children lying together in a blanket can also be found in *Soldiers' Pay* and *Miss Zilphia Gant* ("Two Characters" 61). Faulkner's handling of the fiercely independent Juliet looks forward to his characterization of Caddy Compson, and several of the images of the story remind us of comparable passages in *The Sound and the Fury*.[11] More generally, Faulkner is concerned here with the kind of country and people that he was later to describe so lovingly in the Yoknapatawpha novels and stories. The setting and characterization of "Adolescence," together with its archetypal themes—the lost Eden, the equation of sex and evil, the confrontation between innocence and corruption—were to be found in some of Faulkner's most mature and fully realized achievements. The piece is still clearly apprentice work; it is obvious and sentimental, the portrayal of the grandmother is absurdly grotesque, and the exposition is quite clumsy. But we sense when we read "Adolescence" that Faulkner is more deeply engaged in it than in most of his other early works. His feeling for his characters seems to be genuine, his descriptions of nature are often quite effective, and the language is relatively subdued. "Adolescence" is anything but an accomplished work of art, but it is one of the most significant and attractive of Faulkner's early stories—an indication of the direction he had to take, of the kind of material he had to employ in order to fulfill his potential.

However, the evidence we have suggests that it was to be some time before Faulkner realized what he had to do. Because of the lack of much concrete information about the dating of the short fiction between the European trip Faulkner took in the latter part of 1925 and the beginning of the correspondence with *Scribner's Magazine* in late 1928, it is difficult to get a sense of the direction he was taking in his experiments in the genre at any particular time during this period. Nevertheless, it seems clear that his work was marked by a great amount of uncertainty and of groping, hesitant experimentation. That uncertainty is obvious in the subject matter, themes, and techniques of the next two novels he was to work on after *Soldiers' Pay*: the abortive *Elmer* and *Mosquitoes*. While both works contain some extremely interesting experimental writing, they are generally marred by, among other things, Faulkner's inability to handle satire or to portray aesthetes, intellectuals, and sophisticates convincingly.

For our purposes, one of the most interesting things about *Mosquitoes* is that there is a somewhat tenuous connection between the novel and a most important story—if the word *story* is appropriate—that Faulkner probably wrote at about the time he was working on the novel. There is considerable doubt as to when "Carcassonne" was composed, but the fact that the protagonist's patron is called Mrs. Maurier in an early typescript version of the sketch (7-pp. ts. 4; *WFM 9* 385) suggests, although it is hardly conclusive evidence, that this version may have been written when *Mosquitoes* was still very much on Faulkner's mind.[12]

There is another, far more general reason to link the two works. For if *Mosquitoes* is a farewell to the world of literary conversations, of jejeune romanticism, of the postures and artifices of aestheticism, "Carcassonne" can be seen, in one sense, as another kind of farewell to that world. It is the poetic embodiment of the talk about art that permeates the novel. In its concern with the problems of the poet, with the gap between imagination and reality, between art and life, it constantly echoes the central theme of *Mosquitoes*. It is another prose poem; there is hardly the remotest suggestion of a narrative in it. "Carcassonne" is one of the artiest prose pieces Faulkner ever wrote, and, in that sense, seems to represent anything but progress in his development as a storyteller. Nevertheless, he was always very fond of the work,[13] and its placement as the very last piece in both *These 13* and the *Collected Stories* suggests how important it continued to be to him.

"Carcassonne" can, in turn, be linked to another story, "Black Music," which Faulkner probably wrote at some time in 1926.[14] In this very slight piece, the protagonist—like that of "Carcassonne"—is living in a room owned by a Mrs. Widrington in the Latin-American port of Rincon and sleeping on a bed of tarpaper. The story seems to look backward in its reliance on the pastoral-mythical elements that play so prominent a role in Faulkner's poetry. But, in another sense, it is forward-looking because it pokes fun at those conventions; the protagonist's life is radically altered when he is, for a brief time, turned into a "farn"—his pronunciation of *faun*. However, the satire here, although it is far gentler than that employed in *Elmer* and *Mosquitoes*, again simply does not work. "Black Music" is much too coy—and more than a little silly.

When we assess Faulkner's work from the middle twenties on through the early thirties, we are struck by its range, diversity, and sheer quantity. He clearly had enormous energy at this time, and he must have written

with great speed, verve, and facility. I have already noted the very considerable range of his work in 1925—in the New Orleans sketches, *Soldiers' Pay*,
*Elmer*, and other works from that most productive year. The same thing was
true of 1926. Not only did he write *Mosquitoes* and probably "Black Music,"
but it is likely that he composed a number of other works in that year. At
this time he may have begun a novella or long story called "Once Aboard
the Lugger," a tale of bootleggers.[15] One static but peculiarly atmospheric
portion of this work was published in *Contempo* in 1932; another extremely
violent portion was ultimately published in *Uncollected Stories*. A manuscript
entitled "The Devil Beats His Wife," which consists of a complete scene
and some notes for other scenes, was the genesis of what was much later
to become Faulkner's worst potboiler, "Two Dollar Wife." The manuscript
is of some interest because of its portrayal of a black servant, Della, who
is trying to effect a reconciliation between the husband and wife who employ her. Della is essentially a stereotype, a patronizing caricature, but her
actions and motivations do look forward vaguely to those of Dilsey in *The
Sound and the Fury*.

A completely different piece, at first glance almost totally uncharacteristic of Faulkner, is the strange story, *Mayday*, which he apparently composed early in 1926 and which was probably inspired by his love for Helen
Baird. *Mayday* is an allegorical tale of a quester knight who, like Johnny
in "The Kid Learns," eventually encounters Little sister Death and then,
like Quentin Compson, drowns himself. *Mayday* is another reflection of
the tension between the poetic and narrative impulses that is so basic an
aspect of Faulkner's apprentice work. Remote, romantic, esoteric, "literary," it is another of those pieces of the middle twenties that seem to look
backward to his poetry rather than forward to his mature fiction—in everything except its thematic concerns. But perhaps *Mayday*, like *Mosquitoes*,
had a liberating effect, not only in the personal sense that it helped Faulkner to achieve some distance from his attachment to Helen Baird but also
because composing it helped him to understand that there was another kind
of writing for which he had no talent, which he was simply not equipped
to do. One likes to think that he was clearing the decks—unconsciously, of
course—for Yoknapatawpha County.

Faulkner began writing about Yoknapatawpha (although it was to be
several years before he named his county that) late in 1926 when he began
the "Ur-*Snopes*"—*Father Abraham*— and *Flags in the Dust*. While, as I have
suggested, much of his early fiction was concerned with his native region,
with what could very easily have been northern Mississippi, it was not
until he began his novels about the Snopeses and the Sartorises that Faulkner really took to heart what Sherwood Anderson had told him: "You're a

country boy; all you know is that little patch up there in Mississippi where you started from. But that's all right too. It's America too; pull it out, as little and unknown as it is, and the whole thing will collapse, like when you prize a brick out of a wall" (*ESPL* 8).

One suspects that Faulkner knew very soon after he had begun work on Yoknapatawpha that he was on the right track, for all the evidence suggests that his maturation as an artist, which had been a very slow process up to this point, was now greatly accelerated. It would be another year or so before everything would fall into place with the writing of *The Sound and the Fury*, but there is a kind of fluency and exuberance in the writing of *Father Abraham* and *Flags in the Dust* that Faulkner's work had not had up to this time. Nevertheless, there continued to be problems—false starts, groping, uncertainty. The story of the composition of the Snopes material, in particular, which is too well-known to merit extensive discussion here, is a most tortuous and complex one. But one thing is quite clear, and most important for our purposes: that in composing *Father Abraham* Faulkner was discovering that he did not really have to choose between his poetic and narrative impulses, that it was possible to fuse them in lyrical, evocative, resonant narratives.

One of the most interesting things about Faulkner's early work on the Snopes material is how absolutely central the "spotted horses" story was to him from the beginning. It is the focal point of *Father Abraham* and of almost all the versions and fragments of this material that Faulkner was to write during the twenties. Again and again, until the publication of "Spotted Horses" in *Scribner's* in 1931, he returned to the story, experimenting with any number of different techniques and styles. And it was not until the publication of *The Hamlet* in 1940 that it was to receive its final, definitive form. With the exception of the Cotton-Mink Snopes-Houston story, there is no other comparable portion of Faulkner's work on which he labored over so long a period.

One wonders why. Doubtless, Faulkner sensed not long after he began work on the tale that this was material he could sell (although it took him a remarkably long time to do so). We can also find in the story a theme— the incapacity (or, rather, refusal) of obsessed men to confront objective reality, to acknowledge the injustice underlying life—that spoke to Faulkner's deepest and most abiding concerns. Moreover, he must have realized that here was material that was peculiarly *his own,* that the telling of this story, which was wonderfully rich and comic, yet complex and full of darker overtones, could help to release his latent powers.

But it took him many years to master this material. There was something about *Father Abraham* that at this time proved intractable to Faulkner and caused him to shift his primary attention to the Sartoris material and to *Flags in the Dust*. Perhaps in his delight in discovering Yoknapatawpha he felt the need for a more expansive, comprehensive view of that world than the Snopes material alone could supply. We can certainly sense the joy he must have felt as his awareness grew, while writing *Flags in the Dust*, of how many *stories* there were to tell about the people he was creating—not only about the Sartorises, but also the Snopeses, the McCallums, Horace and Narcissa Benbow, V. K. Suratt, and others. The stories were all there— at least in germinal form.

Indeed, there is evidence that, while *Flags in the Dust* absorbed much of his energy during 1927, Faulkner was also at work at the same time on a collection of stories about his townspeople. He told his publisher, Horace Liveright, that he was doing so in a letter he wrote on February 18, 1927 (*SL* 34). But we have no way of knowing if Faulkner was being truthful with Liveright and, if he was, just what stories he was working on at the time for intended publication in this volume. Still it is most interesting that at this relatively early stage Faulkner was alive to the possibility of writing short fiction about Oxford-Jefferson and that he conceived of publishing a *collection* of these stories.[16]

We are almost certain that Faulkner did compose one piece of very important short fiction in 1927: *The Wishing Tree*. He apparently wrote two rather different versions of the story—one for Victoria Oldham, who was to become his stepdaughter, and the other for the dying Margaret Brown. Most critics have ignored *The Wishing Tree* because it seems to be an occasional piece meriting very little attention, but I believe they err in doing so. It is a very important story because writing it may have suggested to Faulkner certain directions his work could take, certain techniques he could employ to great advantage in his more serious fiction.[17]

*The Wishing Tree* is the story of a little girl, Dulcie in the published version, who on her birthday goes on a quest for a wondrous tree that grants wishes. She is accompanied by a strange guide, a boy named Maurice; two other children; and three adults. In the course of their journey they have many adventures, characterized by the magical but not always pleasant fulfillment of their wishes, until they find the tree and are told by its guardian, the good Saint Francis, how important it is to make generous and selfless wishes. Then, of course, Dulcie wakes up and discovers that it was all a dream.

*The Wishing Tree* is not, according to the standards normally used to evaluate children's fiction, very successful. As Mick Gidley has noted, the plot has too many loose ends (98–99). It contains racial stereotypes, sexual antagonisms, and unnecessary elements of cruelty and violence. On the other hand, many of the adventures that Dulcie and her companions undergo would undoubtedly delight children. They are told with considerable verve, fluency, and imaginative power, and we sense that Faulkner had a good time in writing about them.

We can also sense that the material of *The Wishing Tree* had a peculiar fascination for Faulkner, although it is unlikely that he was fully conscious of the reasons for that fascination. But Faulkner probably knew enough psychoanalytic theory to realize, if he had paused to reflect on it, that *The Wishing Tree* would have pleased Freud. For here we have a kind of textbook example of one of the most significant elements—indeed, a kind of keystone—of Freudian theory: the relationship between wish fulfillment, dreams, and the creative impulse. The story is *quite literally,* at the most immediate level of the narrative, about wish fulfillment; within the framework of Dulcie's dream, desires, aspirations, hopes *do* come true. Faulkner's most mature and important works are centrally concerned with the gap between human desires and their fulfillment, with the frenzied efforts of his solipsistic characters to impose their wills on the world, to make objective "reality" conform to their subjective versions of what life should be. Hence, this strange little fantasy has, at the thematic level, much in common with *Absalom, Absalom!* or *Light in August*—with the significant difference that the dichotomy between the wish and its actualization is not bridged in the great novels, as it is in the children's story.

Even more interesting is the relationship between *The Wishing Tree* and the works dealing with the Compsons, particularly *The Sound and the Fury* and "That Evening Sun." It would be foolish to attempt to draw any very elaborate and precise parallels between these works, but the general situation—a kind of quest involving four children—vaguely suggests the first part of *The Sound and the Fury*. While Dulcie lacks the headstrong, willful qualities of Caddy, she may be a kind of first draft for Faulkner's "heart's darling." Dulcie's selfish and repellent little brother George certainly prefigures Jason. The characterizations of the black servant Alice and of Dilsey are very different, but they are both strong, assertive, outspoken; indeed, the Dilsey of "That Evening Sun" is not dissimilar to Alice.

More generally, the composition of *The Wishing Tree* may have suggested to Faulkner techniques that would greatly enhance the effectiveness of the great early works dealing with the Compsons, as well as some of his other major achievements. He may have discovered from the children's book that telling a story from the viewpoint of a child—as he does in the first part of *The Sound and the Fury* and in most of "That Evening Sun"—would be a most effective means of developing the intense irony and pathos that underlie these works, of underscoring their thematic contrasts between innocence and corruption. The simplicity, clarity, and objectivity of the style of *The Wishing Tree* almost certainly influenced the style of part 1 of *The Sound and the Fury* and of "That Evening Sun." Compare, for example, the following passages, the first from *The Wishing Tree*, and the second from "That Evening Sun":

> "This is the way I used to do at the war," the little old man explained. "Watch me." And he waved his sword and made his pony dash down the road again and then come flying back.
> "I bet you'd be scared as scared," George said.
> "I bet I wouldn't be scared of a hundred enemies," the little old man said. "I bet I'd just ride right into 'em and slice 'em in two with a sword like this."
> "I bet you wouldn't slice a dog in two," George said. "I bet you'd be scared."
> "I bet I wouldn't," the little old man answered. "I bet I'd just—" (*WT* 52)

> "Jesus is gone," I said. Nancy told us how one morning she woke up and Jesus was gone.
> "He quit me," Nancy said. "Done gone to Memphis, I reckon. Dodging them city *po*-lice for a while, I reckon."
> "And a good riddance," father said. "I hope he stays there."
> "Nancy's scaired of the dark," Jason said.
> "So are you," Caddy said.
> "I'm not," Jason said.
> "Scairy cat," Caddy said.
> "I'm not," Jason said. (*CS* 293)

The objectivity and economy of these two passages, their rhythms and their repetitions, and, of course, their subject matter are strikingly similar. There is a clear line of development from *The Wishing Tree* to Faulkner's first masterpieces of narrative art. The composition of this children's book, whatever its intrinsic merits, was a most important event in his career.

Another work of considerable significance in tracing Faulkner's development as a writer of short fiction is *Miss Zilphia Gant*, a version of which was written before the end of 1928, perhaps considerably earlier. Like several of the stories I have already noted, *Miss Zilphia Gant* is concerned with sexual repression, but the focus here is on the frustration of erotic impulses in a *woman,* and hence there is the suggestion that Faulkner was beginning to attain a degree of detachment and distance from his material. However, the work is a failure.

*Miss Zilphia Gant* concerns a woman whose desire for love and fulfillment is thwarted by her mother's hatred of men. When the mother is deserted by her husband for another woman, she kills the lovers and tries to raise her daughter so that she will have nothing to do with the male sex. However, Zilphia falls in love with an itinerant house painter, but her attempt to run away with him is frustrated by Mrs. Gant. After her mother dies, Zilphia, wild with sexual longings, tries to locate her lover. She eventually discovers that he has married another woman, had a child, and been killed in an accident. Zilphia acquires the child, raises it as her own, and becomes as overprotective of little Zilphia as her mother was of her. At the end of the story, Faulkner ironically suggests a kind of "eternal return"; it is probable that Zilphia, who is now very much like her mother, will do to the child what Mrs. Gant did to her.

In all the extant versions, the story is an ugly, obvious, much too intense study of sexual pathology. But the difference between the earliest version and the published one (which may have been written after Faulkner had achieved mastery of the genre with "That Evening Sun" and "A Rose for Emily") is most instructive. In the former version things happen much too fast; it is insufficiently dramatized. To use the standard formula, Faulkner "tells" us; he does not "show" us. The story is grotesquely explicit. When, for example, Mrs. Gant tells Zilphia what her husband did to her, Faulkner writes: "Foul with its repression, with the ceaseless brooding of a woman violent by nature and emotionally inarticulate, it was like a bursting sewer. The language was that of a coarse and brutal man, and beneath it Zilphia shrank and shrank with wide, secret, fearful eyes" (18–pp. ts. 6; *WFM 24* 144). This is uncontrolled, excessive, hyperbolic.

The final version of *Miss Zilphia Gant* is still far inferior to Faulkner's masterpieces in the genre, but it is certainly more objective, controlled, and subtle than the earlier versions. As François Pitavy notes, the difference is strikingly suggested in the printed version of the passage I have quoted above (137): "she told Zilphia what her father had done and what she had done. She sat on the bed while Zilphia cringed swiftly into her clothes, telling her about it in a cold, level voice, in the language of a man while Zilphia's thin body shrank and shrank as though in upon itself, as though at the impact of the words" (*US* 373–74). But there seems to be something in this lurid material that will simply not submit itself to total artistic control. The final version is still much too intense and more than a little silly. However, this story is of great importance, not only because of the technical considerations suggested by the contrasts between the different versions but also because of the manner in which it embodies so many of the most significant themes of Faulkner's later, more mature work. Obviously, there is a direct line from Zilphia to Emily Grierson, Minnie Cooper, and Joanna Burden. During the next few years of his career, Faulkner was often to return to the motif of the revenge, either literal or metaphorical, of the wronged or trapped woman. The characterization of Mrs. Gant suggests the archetype of the "Terrible Mother," which Faulkner was to use again and again, and he also often employed the pattern of a triangle involving a parent or grandparent. Moreover, the theme of the sins of the fathers being visited upon the children and the archetype of the "Search for the Father," which are implicit in *Miss Zilphia Gant*, were to obsess Faulkner during the most productive period of his career.

For all its faults, a story like *Miss Zilphia Gant* certainly suggests what Faulkner's true métier was. But he was never able to confine himself for very long, even after the discovery of Yoknapatawpha, to the "little postage stamp." The European trip inspired several stories—"The Leg," "Mistral," "Ad Astra," and "Victory"—early versions of which were apparently composed before the end of 1928—and several others—"Snow," "Thrift," and "Divorce in Naples"—versions of which were probably written not long after, and perhaps even before, that date.

These stories, in their published forms and in the manuscript and typescript versions that still survive, are among the most elaborate pieces of short fiction Faulkner had produced up to this time. Here his narrative, rather than his poetic, inclinations are in the ascendancy, for all these works, with the exception of the rather slight "Divorce in Naples," are very heavily plotted. Furthermore, they reveal that Faulkner was experimenting fairly successfully with what were to become some of his most characteristic techniques: the deliberate withholding of certain plot elements, the meanings of which are only gradually unveiled; the use of several narrators; a complex treatment of time; and, in general, the employment, to an elaborate extent, of implication and indirection.

However, the most interesting aspect of several of these works is their thematic matter. They are essentially initiation stories concerned with the discovery of evil on the part of the protagonists—an evil generally associated with the encroachments of sexuality. "The Leg," one of several pieces about the supernatural that Faulkner wrote early in his career, is the story of the protagonist's severed leg, lost in battle during the First World War. The leg becomes a kind of doppelgänger, luring a young woman and her father and brother to their deaths. The story is lurid, intense, and overwrought.

Far more interesting are "Mistral" and its companion piece, "Snow."[18] Both of these strikingly similar works are about two young Americans— "Don" and the unnamed narrator—who in the course of their travels in Europe encounter mysterious situations, the significance of which they puzzle over and finally piece together (although we can never be sure that their conclusions are correct). In both stories they make shocking discoveries about the power of sexual passion. And both works employ weather for atmospheric and symbolic effects. "Mistral" is the more accomplished and elaborate of the two. In this story the two young men spend an evening in an Italian village, where they gradually learn about a priest's passion for his young ward and about a murder that has apparently ensued. The experience is a profoundly unsettling one for the two travelers, and we know, as the story ends, that they will never again be the same because they have, for the first time, come face to face with primal evil.

"Mistral" is anything but a totally successful work of art. It is much too long and diffuse, and, in places, maddeningly obscure. The repartee of Don and the narrator is forced and awkwardly handled, almost certainly betraying the influence of Hemingway, who could manage that kind of thing far more skillfully.[19] Nevertheless, "Mistral" is a powerful, complex, and richly atmospheric piece. It generates considerable suspense, and its portrayal of the passion-ridden priest is quite moving. Moreover, the central symbol of the story—the mistral itself, with its suggestion of the power of sexual passion—is well handled.

"Mistral" and "Snow" not only have considerable intrinsic merit but are also interesting because of their connections with some of Faulkner's other works. "Don and I" figure prominently in two other stories: "The Big Shot," which, as we shall see, contains material Faulkner was to use in several of his novels; and "Evangeline," his first relatively elaborate attempt to tell the story of Thomas Sutpen. More generally, the basic narrative strategy of "Mistral" and "Snow"—the attempts by two young men to piece together elaborate and ominous mysteries—clearly fascinated Faulkner and was to receive its most elaborate embodiment in his masterpiece, *Absalom, Absalom!*[20]

The fascination that World War I was always to have for Faulkner was manifested in several of these relatively early stories with European backgrounds: in "Ad Astra," "Victory," and "Thrift." The plotless "Ad Astra," a mood piece devoted to the disillusionment of several veterans on the day the war ends, betrays, like "Mistral," the influence of Hemingway in its apparently static, aimless quality, its clipped dialogue, and the sardonic stoicism of its characters. More characteristic of Faulkner are the other two stories, both of which are about Scotsmen in the British armed forces. The manuscripts of these works suggest that he devoted a considerable amount of effort to them, particularly "Victory," but neither, even in the published forms, has much merit. However, both stories are concerned with the typical Faulknerian theme of monomania, the idée fixe. The protagonist of "Thrift," MacWyrglinchbeath, becomes a successful and daring flyer from one motive only: avarice. Gray, the protagonist of "Victory," cannot adjust to civilian life after the war and, even in a state of total penury, continues to maintain the front of the officer, the gentleman. In their unremitting devotion to their obsessions, in their refusal to adjust to "reality," both figures anticipate many of Faulkner's memorable characters: Quentin Compson, Joe Christmas, Thomas Sutpen, Mink Snopes.

Faulkner's imagination was not confined solely to either European settings or Yoknapatawpha during this period. Two other works, which may have been begun as early as 1927, *Idyll in the Desert* and "Bench for Two," have very different settings: the American southwest in the former, New York City in the latter. Both are also about obsessions, but of a very different kind from those dominating "Thrift" and "Victory"; they are concerned with unremitting devotion in the face of the blackest kind of ingratitude. "Bench for Two" (which in the published version became "Pennsylvania Station") is particularly interesting because the evidence of the manuscripts suggests that Faulkner struggled arduously to master this material, employing some techniques of a highly experimental nature. But the work that was to emerge from all this travail—the story of a small-time hoodlum and his stupidly devoted mother and uncle—is dull and turgid. The material was simply not right for Faulkner.

This is clearly true of many of his experiments in the genre in the middle and late twenties. Nevertheless, the stories begun at this time are, not only in their published forms but also in the manuscript and typescript versions, a vast improvement over the juvenilia and the New Orleans sketches. In writing these works, Faulkner continued to deal with themes that were to obsess him throughout his career, but he also learned how to construct, within the confines of short fiction, complex, oblique narratives. He had come a long way.

## The Second Period

It should now be clear how difficult it is to assign much of Faulkner's short fiction to periods—because of the sometimes tenuous evidence we have about dating and because he often worked on individual stories off and on for several years. Thus most of those works I have referred to that were written after the New Orleans sketches did not receive their final forms until Faulkner was at the height of his powers in what I have labeled his "second period." However, even at this time he could not solve the problems inherent in this largely intractable material. But when the material was right for Faulkner, as was the story of the Compsons, everything ultimately fell into place. He had been struggling for three years, and with only limited success, with the writing of novels, but with the creation of *The Sound and the Fury* in 1928, he was able to solve, with dazzling virtuosity, some extremely difficult technical problems and to achieve real control of the medium.

However, it continued to be more difficult for him to solve comparable problems in his short fiction. If we consider, for example, the evidence about the composition of the story most closely associated with *The Sound and the Fury*, "That Evening Sun," it is obvious that he had a real struggle with this material. (We cannot with certainty date the writing of this story before 1930, but I think it very likely that the earliest manuscript version, "Never Done No Weeping When You Wanted to Laugh," is roughly contemporaneous with *The Sound and the Fury* because of the striking similarities in style, dialogue, and point of view between the piece and the first section of the novel.)[21]

Even the version of "That Evening Sun" published in 1931 as "That Evening Sun Go Down" in *The American Mercury* is substantially different from the definitive version in *These 13* and the *Collected Stories*. While some of the differences can be accounted for by revisions that H. L. Mencken asked Faulkner to make, as Manglavati notes, others are of a much more fundamental nature. Near the end of the magazine version, for example, we read: "Then we had crossed the ditch, walking out of Nancy's life. Then her life was sitting there with the door open and the lamp lit, waiting, and the ditch between us and us going on, the white people going on, dividing the impinged lives of us and Nancy" ("That Evening Sun Go Down," 267). None of this is in the final version—and with good reason, since it is much too explicit and adds nothing to the story that the sensitive reader does not already know. Furthermore, that final phrase, "dividing the impinged lives of us and Nancy," is totally wrong for the narrative voice Faulkner has established for Quentin. This significant change and others Faulkner was to make in the story graphically suggest his struggle—in this case, completely successful—to achieve mastery of the genre.

We can say much the same about two other masterpieces of short fiction, "A Rose for Emily" and "Dry September," on which Faulkner probably worked in 1928 and 1929. Michael Millgate has noted the striking differences between the surviving manuscripts and typescripts of the two stories and their final versions (*Achievement* 262–64). In the case of "Dry September," Faulkner's description of the life of Minnie Cooper, which is now the second section of the story, was originally the first, preceding the scene in the barbershop. By deciding to begin *in medias res* with the latter scene and to eliminate some unnecessarily explicit generalizations about Minnie and about the life of women in Southern towns, Faulkner greatly increased the economy and the dramatic intensity of the story. The contrast between the manuscript and typescript of "A Rose for Emily" and the published version is even more striking. In the early versions there is a rather elaborate scene between Emily and her servant that explicitly calls attention to the upstairs room and the shock the townspeople will experience when they discover what is in it. Such a scene would have virtually destroyed the story because of its explicitness and its egregious violation of point of view.

The evidence seems to suggest that in 1928 and 1929 Faulkner devoted far more time to the novels, *The Sound and the Fury*, *Sanctuary*, and *As I Lay Dying*, than to the short stories, in contrast to 1930 and 1931, when he apparently produced an astonishing number of stories. Nevertheless, during 1928 and 1929 he did at least begin several other works of short fiction aside from those I have already noted. One story, "Selvage," which Faulkner probably wrote in the winter of 1928–29 and later revised and called "Elly,"[22] resembles *Miss Zilphia Gant* in its concern with the revenge of the trapped woman, the romance with an outsider, and the use of the "Terrible Mother" (in this case, a grandmother). Another story, "Through the Window," which was ultimately to become "There Was a Queen," is of considerable interest because it appears to be a very deliberate attempt to add to the Sartoris "saga," an instance of what Olga Vickery calls Faulkner's "adjunctive" or "projective" stories (300). This tale of the death of Aunt Jenny Du Pre looks forward as much as backward because of its portrayal of Narcissa Benbow Sartoris, who is now clearly the Narcissa of *Sanctuary* rather than of *Flags in the Dust*.

The protagonist of "The Big Shot," another story composed at about this time,[23] is Dal Martin, the son of a tenant farmer, who has become a wealthy bootlegger in a big city, presumably Memphis. The crucial event in Martin's life occurred when, as a youngster, he was turned away at the door of a Mississippi mansion; thus he prefigures Sutpen in *Absalom, Absalom!* One of his hoodlums is a man named Popeye, who has many of the same characteristics as the villain of *Sanctuary*. Another character, Gavin Blount, seems, as Millgate notes, to look forward to Hightower in *Light in August* (*Achievement* 161). "The Big Shot" is too diffuse and novelistic, but it is a striking piece because it contains, in rudimentary form, so many character types and situations that Faulkner was to employ later in far more successful works. It seems clear that he was particularly attracted to the character of the eccentric Blount. He gave him a role of greater prominence in a complete revision of "The Big Shot," to which he gave the rather unfortunate title of "Dull Tale," and he also made him the protagonist of another story, "Rose of Lebanon," which he tried to sell in 1930 and 1931. Years later—apparently in 1938—he rewrote the latter piece as "A Return" but was unable to sell the revision.[24]

None of these pieces—"The Big Shot," "Dull Tale," "Rose of Lebanon," or "A Return"—was published during Faulkner's lifetime, but together they make up a rather significant body of Faulkner's short fiction: his "Memphis" or "Gavin Blount stories," virtually unknown until the appearance of the *Uncollected Stories*. Faulkner failed to place these works because he was unable to solve some of the technical problems they posed—problems that were to recur in other contexts and to which I shall return later.

Faulkner's approach to the writing of short stories was somewhat different in 1930 and 1931 from what it was in 1928 and 1929—not primarily because of any basic shift in aesthetic orientation, but because of the significant changes in his life brought on by his marriage in June 1929, the consequent new financial responsibilities he had to assume, and the onset of the Depression in October. It had long since become clear to him that he could not make ends meet through the meager royalties from his novels (unless he were to write something more "commercial," which, he tells us, he tried to do with *Sanctuary*). There were obligations to be met, bills to be taken care of immediately. And the mass-market magazines paid very well for short stories. Hence, Faulkner probably devoted as much time during 1930 and 1931 to short fiction as to novels, until a very different kind of financial opportunity came up. During these two years he apparently worked on more than twenty short stories.[25]

Yet there is little evidence that Faulkner was deliberately tailoring his stories to the mass markets during this period, in marked contrast to what he was to do a few years later. Even the first of his detective stories, the inept "Smoke," probably derived more from Faulkner's fascination with the genre, which was to be manifested in many different ways throughout his career, than from any overt, deliberate impulse to exploit his craft. We can say much the same about a far better commercial piece, "Turn About," another tale of World War I, which, as Blotner tells us, derived from Faulkner's being deeply moved by a story told him by Robert A. Lovett (*FB* 1:732–35). On the other hand, it is possible to exaggerate Faulkner's idealism at this time. One senses, in reading his correspondence with magazines and in studying the "sending schedule," that he simply did not know enough about the requirements of commercial fiction, about what would sell to the mass-market magazines. He was gradually to learn. But he never acquired the facility of being able to crank out a story that he *knew* would sell to the *Post*.

Nevertheless, the quality of the short fiction Faulkner produced during this time is generally high. He not only gave final forms to "Dry September" and "That Evening Sun," but he also wrote two superb Indian stories, the incomparable "Red Leaves," probably his greatest achievement in the genre, and "A Justice," and such other first-rate stories as "Mountain Victory" and "The Hound." He was finally to publish the brilliantly comic "Spotted Horses" (although the magazine story is infinitely inferior to the definitive version in *The Hamlet.*) "Turn About" is an excellent story of its kind. And certainly such works as "Lizards in Jamshyd's Courtyard," "Fox Hunt," "Ad Astra," "Death Drag," "The Brooch," and "Centaur in Brass" have considerable merit. Even such relatively weak stories as "Honor," "Dr. Martino," and "Artist at Home" are of more than passing interest. This two-year period was therefore, both quantitatively and qualitatively, the most remarkable of Faulkner's career as a writer of short fiction.

One is also struck by the range of subject matter in these stories. Faulkner's concern with the alienated, with the eccentrics of Jefferson, was continued in "Centaur in Brass," derived from the Snopes "saga," and in "Hair," the impulse for which probably sprang from Faulkner's interest in the character of Hawkshaw in "Dry September," another example of the fascination that the totally selfless human being always held for him. The Snopes material and Faulkner's interest in country people accounted for such stories as "Spotted Horses," "Lizards in Jamshyd's Courtyard," and "The Hound," all of which were ultimately revised and incorporated in *The Hamlet.*[26] The concern about World War I and the influence of the "Wasteland" school of the twenties was particularly important to Faulkner at this time. All the stories he was to place in "The Wasteland" section of the *Collected Stories*—"Ad Astra," "Victory," "Crevasse," "Turnabout," and "All the Dead Pilots"—were probably completed in 1930 or 1931, as was "Beyond," a tale of the supernatural, followed about a year later by the Gothic "Evangeline," the germ of *Absalom, Absalom!* Faulkner's continuing interest in flying was manifested in "Death Drag" and "Honor," the latter anticipating *Pylon.* Finally, "Honor" can be classified with another kind of story in which Faulkner was particularly interested at this stage of his career: the sophisticated tale of the triangular conflicts of modern love, as exemplified by "Fox Hunt," "The Brooch," "Dr. Martino," and "Artist at Home."

In virtually all these stories, even those that are least successful, we can sense a kind of confidence, a fluency not generally found in the earlier short fiction. Even though he had not completely mastered formula fiction, Faulkner was now a professional—and he knew it. The old dichotomy between the poetic and the narrative impulses was resolved. In the great stories of the period, in the majestic "Red Leaves," for example, the two impulses are perfectly fused in a marvelously subtle and evocative prose. Poem and story are one.

During this period, Faulkner also achieved something else of the very greatest importance for any artist: objectivity, detachment. The sometimes excessive concern with sexual themes in much of the earlier short fiction is still present in the stories of this later period. But the process of objectification that seemed to begin about the time Faulkner started work on *Miss Zilphia Gant* culminates in the detachment of "A Rose for Emily," "Dry September," "That Evening Sun," and "Fox Hunt," and, more generally, in the subtlety of the sexual imagery that pervades many of the other stories. I shall deal with this subject more extensively when I analyze the patterns in Faulkner's short fiction. It is sufficient to say at this point that most of the motifs found in rudimentary form in the early short fiction—the idée fixe, the theme of the wronged woman, the archetype of initiation, the conflict between conceptualization and existence, abstraction and life—receive a kind of definitive embodiment in the great stories of this period, as do a number of other motifs that can be subsumed under Faulkner's overriding concern with the solipsistic quest for justice.

Faulkner's achievement of mastery of his medium soon had, at the practical, public level, tangible results: he began to sell his stories to national magazines. He achieved his first breakthrough with the sale of "A Rose for Emily," published by *Forum* in April 1930, to be followed shortly by the appearance of "Honor" in *The American Mercury*. But neither of these sales was as important as the ones he was to make in the same year to that American institution, *The Saturday Evening Post*, which printed the mediocre "Thrift" in its issue of September 6 and, a few weeks later, on October 25, the brilliant "Red Leaves." The *Post* paid as well as any magazine, and Faulkner was to make many submissions to it in the next decade, publishing more of his stories—by far—in that periodical than in any other. But for every sale he was to make to the *Post* or other magazines, there were three or four rejections.

Nevertheless, every year from 1930 to 1943, with the exception of 1938, at least one and usually several of Faulkner's stories appeared in national magazines. Most of these sales were not to the well-paying mass-circulation periodicals like the *Post*, but to the quality magazines: the *Mercury*, *Harper's*, *Scribner's*. Hence, they did only a little to alleviate the severe financial problems of the Faulkner family. Soon, in spite of these sales and the financial success of *Sanctuary*, Faulkner had to turn to Hollywood in an effort to solve these problems.

But before he did so, he was able to satisfy the desire he had apparently had since at least 1927 to collect his stories. On May 14, 1931, he signed a contract with Cape and Smith for the publication of a book to be called *A Rose for Emily and Other Stories*, published under the title of *These 13* on September 21 (*FB* 1: 692–93, 705).

In a sense, the publication of *These 13* is a kind of climax, a symbolic culmination to this richest period of Faulkner's career as a writer of short fiction. In the second of the three divisions of the volume, the one devoted to the stories of Yoknapatawpha, there is only one work, "Hair," that is not of the very highest quality; the other five—"Red Leaves," "A Rose for Emily," "A Justice," "That Evening Sun," and "Dry September"—are all brilliant examples of the art of short fiction at its very best. The stories in the other two sections, the first of which is concerned with World War I and the third with initiation themes, are by no means up to the quality of those in the second section. But the volume, as a whole, is a most distinguished collection, on a par with *In Our Time* and *Men Without Women*. Like *The Sound and the Fury*, *As I Lay Dying*, and *Light in August*, *These 13* is another instance of consummate artistic integrity and dedication to craft during the most productive period of Faulkner's career.

## The Third Period

At the risk of being accused of an excessive and simplistic concern for artificial categorization, we can, I think, argue that the second period of Faulkner's career as a writer of short fiction ends not long after the publication of *These 13*. The year 1932 does seem to serve as a kind of watershed in Faulkner's life, and, if we wish to be even more arbitrary and precise, the trip to Hollywood in May of that year can be seen as a kind of convenient dividing point. However, we should beware of exaggerating the impact of the time Faulkner was to spend in Hollywood—off and on for the next twenty years—on his work. There is not the slightest indication that his stay in the film capital and his screenwriting for M-G-M, Universal, Fox, and Warner Brothers had any effect whatsoever on the quality of his artistry as a writer of fiction. The bromides about the corrupting influences of Hollywood simply do not apply in his case—if indeed they ever apply in the case of a major artist. Furthermore, during the thirties and forties Faulkner spent far more time at home in Mississippi working on the novels and stories than he did in California.

But it is quite true that he did not have as much time for the fiction after 1932 as he had had before. In the five-year period from 1927 to 1932 he completed five novels; during the next five years he wrote only two. He was to write about as many stories during the rest of the decade as he worked on in 1930 and 1931 alone. In 1932, according to Blotner, he worked on only one new story: the inchoate "With Caution and Dispatch," which was (with good reason) not published during Faulkner's lifetime (*FB* 1: 791). The money Faulkner was to make from his work at the studios can partially account for this decline in his productivity in short fiction; the need for quick money from magazine sales was not quite so compelling.

However, we can sense another reason for this diminution of output; Faulkner may have been simply tired. It is hardly surprising that his energies would flag after that astonishingly fecund period from 1927 through 1931. After producing during that time five novels, at least three of which were masterpieces, and several dozen short stories, including five or six that must be rated among the best in the English language, he probably needed a respite. He had not burned himself out; some marvelous work lay ahead, including his greatest achievement, *Absalom, Absalom!*, and several excellent stories. But it is doubtful that he ever again had quite that pure, fierce, sustained, joyous commitment to his craft that he had when he was discovering his own genius.

Generally, we can note not only a marked decline in the quantity of the short fiction Faulkner wrote from 1932 to 1942 but also in its quality. He did produce some fine pieces during this period—"Wash," "Mule in the Yard," "Barn Burning"—but many of the stories seem obvious, contrived, or slight. These characteristics cannot be attributed simply to a decline in Faulkner's ability to handle the genre. There is another reason of a more pragmatic nature: he was making a far more conscious effort to write commercial fiction, to tailor his stories to the needs and requirements of the mass-circulation magazines.

Faulkner wrote the stories that became *The Unvanquished* with the *Saturday Evening Post* in mind, and he was very bitter about the necessity to write "trash . . . a pulp series like this."[27] Somewhat later he was to produce the trivial racist comedy of "A Point of Law" and "Gold Is Not Always." And while Faulkner did enjoy writing detective fiction, he obviously wrote the later Gavin Stevens stories with the mass markets in mind. Such a story as "A Bear Hunt," which he sold to the *Post*, is little more than a rather elaborate but crude joke. But probably the saddest evidence of this need to write potboilers is "Two Dollar Wife," a story Faulkner sold to *College Life* in 1935, which is without question one of the worst pieces of fiction ever produced by a major American writer.

We must be charitable in evaluating Faulkner's short fiction of this period. Clearly the trips to Hollywood did not completely solve his financial problems, and the quality of many of the short stories produced at this time demonstrates the power of economic factors in his life. It is certainly to Faulkner's credit, and a mark of his peculiar ability to transform the most unpromising material into significant art, that he was able to incorporate a number of these potboilers, in considerably revised form, into his "story-novels," *The Unvanquished* and *Go Down, Moses*.

What Faulkner was to do with these stories suggests another tendency of considerable importance at this stage of his career: his growing inclination to conceive of stories not as discrete units, but in sequences, as parts of greater wholes. Generally speaking, the stories of the earlier periods do seem to be largely autonomous—in the sense that most of them derive from single more or less sharply focused aesthetic impulses and are whole, self-contained, complete in themselves. Insofar as Faulkner wrote "sequence fiction"—and he certainly did so after the discovery of Yoknapatawpha—he was to employ many of the same settings and characters from work to work. However, in spite of this Balzacian tendency and Faulkner's increasing fascination with the aesthetic potential of the "little postage stamp," he certainly conceived of most of these stories as discrete works of art. Moreover, there is little in the organization of Faulkner's second collection of stories, *Doctor Martino and Other Stories* (1934), which suggests the tendency to envisage these pieces, most of which were written in the second period, as anything but discrete.[28]

However, many of the stories Faulkner wrote from 1932 through 1942 were originally conceived as parts of a sequence or were eventually incorporated into longer works. The evidence suggests that the stories of Bayard and Ringo, which Faulkner wrote in 1934 and 1935, were, from the start, planned as a sequence to be published in the *Post*. The use of Gavin Stevens as a detective, which had begun with "Smoke" in 1930, was revived with "Monk" in 1937, "Hand Upon the Waters" in 1939, and with a flurry of stories in the early forties: "Tomorrow," "An Error in Chemistry," and the original versions of "Knight's Gambit." "Barn Burning" was apparently originally conceived as the first chapter of *The Hamlet*. There are also the stories of the Grier family—"Two Soldiers," "Shall Not Perish," and "Shingles for the Lord"—which were written in 1942, the last year Faulkner did a significant amount of work in the genre.

In this regard the pieces Faulkner wrote in 1939 and 1940 about Lucas Beauchamp—"A Point of Law," "Gold Is Not Always," and "The Fire on the Hearth"—are most important. In a letter he wrote to Robert Haas in May, 1940, he suggested he might be able to make a book out of these stories (*SL* 124). Here we have the genesis of *Go Down, Moses*, which, from the tone of the letter to Haas, clearly began with a relatively trivial conception but was finally to become one—perhaps the last—of Faulkner's major achievements. Certainly not all the stories finally incorporated in the book, most of which Faulkner initially sold, or tried to sell, as autonomous works, were originally conceived as parts of a sequence. Apparently the Beauchamp stories were, but "Lion," which was probably written in 1935 and was incorporated, in greatly modified form in "The Bear," was not.

Furthermore, it is quite unlikely that Faulkner had any conscious awareness when he originally wrote "The Old People" or "Pantaloon in Black" that these pieces could be anything but completely discrete works. But it is also evident that he was interested in a rather sharply focused and relatively narrow range of subject matter and themes at this time; hence, these stories would readily lend themselves to sequential treatment. Thus, the genetic history of *Go Down, Moses* is another, and certainly the most important, demonstration of his tendency toward agglutination of material at this stage of his career.

Thematically, *Go Down, Moses* epitomizes Faulkner's concerns at this time. By all odds the most important archetype in the works from 1932 to 1942 is initiation. This motif becomes almost obsessive during this period and can be found, in more or less overt form, in most of the stories: in, for example, "Uncle Willy," "Lion," "Barn Burning," "Two Soldiers," and in a number of the "chapters" that constitute *The Unvanquished* and *Go Down, Moses*. In the latter work in particular, Faulkner seems to be handling the theme with a more sophisticated awareness of its origins in myth and ritual—so sophisticated that critics with an archetypal orientation have written, almost endlessly it would seem, about "The Old People" and, particularly, "The Bear."

Faulkner's use of the initiation theme is related to an even larger thematic concern: the conflict between primitive, intuitional spontaneity and the corruptions of mechanization and civilization—a motif found in the gradual corruption of Granny Millard in the Bayard-Ringo stories, the triumph of Lucas Beauchamp over city slickers, the contrast between the McCallums and the government man in "The Tall Men," etc.

This emphasis on the Fall, on the conflict between the Edenic and the postlapsarian suggests, in turn, another quality of Faulkner's short fiction of this period: a kind of overriding nostalgia, evident in many of the works I have mentioned but most obvious in such stories as "Was" and "A Courtship." In another sense, this quality is suggested by Faulkner's tendency in some of the pieces he wrote at this time to echo early influences or his own works of a prior period. "Uncle Willy" very obviously betrays the influence of Sherwood Anderson. "That Will Be Fine" suggests *The Sound and the Fury* in a number of ways: in its handling of point of view and characterization and in its use of Christian symbolism as a kind of ironic backdrop. Perhaps there is also at least a touch of nostalgia in Faulkner's use, in some of the stories of 1941 or 1942, of characters he had not employed, at least extensively, for a long time: the McCallums in "The Tall Men" or the Indians in "A Courtship."

Nostalgia and sentimentality seem to go hand in hand, and certainly the latter quality also becomes increasingly evident in the years from 1932 through 1942. We can expect sentimentality in works such as the Bayard-Ringo pieces and the stories of 1942, which were specifically tailored for the mass-circulation magazines. But there is almost nothing in the earlier fiction to prepare us for the saccharine inanities of "Two Soldiers" and "Shall Not Perish." Even when we consider one of the best of the 1942 stories, the delightful "A Courtship," it is instructive to compare the golden glow pervading this work with the complex ambiguities and wry ironies of the earlier Indian stories, "Red Leaves" and "A Justice."

Joseph Gold's argument that Faulkner moved in the latter stages of his career from "metaphor" to "discourse" is borne out in much of the short fiction he wrote in 1941 and 1942. "The Tall Men," the short version of "The Bear" which he sold to *The Saturday Evening Post* in 1942, "Two Soldiers," and "Shall Not Perish" are didactic and sententious. Several of these pieces—particularly the Grier stories (with the exception of "Shingles for the Lord")—are also marred by an altogether offensive jingoism. The author of *Soldiers' Pay*, "Ad Astra," and "Turnabout" had apparently forgotten a great deal. The evidence of Blotner's biography and of the letters indicates that the chauvinistic sentiments Faulkner expressed in these works were quite sincere and were not simply worked up for commercial purposes. We must, I suppose, bear in mind the mood of the times. Those of us who are old enough to remember the early forties can vividly recall the great waves of nationalistic and militaristic fervor that swept over the country in the wake of Pearl Harbor. But one would think that an artist of Faulkner's stature might have been able to see, and condemn, this hysteria for what it was. Unfortunately, like most other Americans of the time—even many of the most distinguished—he failed to do so.

Thus the history of this third period of Faulkner's career as a writer of short fiction seems to be a somewhat melancholy one. But we must not exaggerate the decline of his powers at this time. There is not much evidence of decline in the longer fictional modes; the man who wrote *Absalom, Absalom!*, *The Hamlet*, and *Go Down, Moses* was still an artist of the first rank. Furthermore, uneven as the short stories are, they are generally technically quite accomplished. There is little experimentation, but Faulkner seems quite adept in his handling of point of view. When he becomes fully absorbed in his subject, as he obviously is when he sets out to tell the story of Sarty Snopes in "Barn Burning," his virtuosity is altogether dazzling. The stories of 1942 may be superficial, obvious, and sentimental, but, for the most part, they show real mastery of the medium. "Two Soldiers" is certainly saccharine, but Faulkner knows what he is doing in that story, as he does in the brilliantly controlled "A Courtship."

Nevertheless, when one compares the total body of short fiction Faulkner produced in the early forties with what he had done a decade earlier, there is no question that there is a marked decline of quality. Aside from the reasons I have already suggested for this decline, there may be one other factor of importance here: Faulkner's loss of interest in the short story as an art form. His greater commitment to the longer fictional modes grew more obvious as his career proceeded. There is little in this third period of his career as a writer of short fiction to match in quality *Absalom, Absalom!* or *The Hamlet*. And in the final two decades of his life he produced virtually no completely autonomous short stories.

## The Fourth Period

The decline of interest, of quality and output in the short story in the later stages of his career is not peculiar to Faulkner's work alone. Something like it has happened to several significant American writers: Hemingway, for example, or Steinbeck, both of whom produced very little short fiction during the last two or three decades of their lives. There seems to be a tendency among a number of important American writers, once they have attained a degree of success and recognition, to desert the short story— perhaps because of some sense of obligation to their reading publics to work in a mode generally considered to be more serious, more significant.

Like his contemporaries, Faulkner wrote so few genuine short stories during the last years of his life that there is some doubt, as I have suggested, as to whether this time span should be called a "period" in his career as a writer of short fiction. Still, there are some interesting developments in these last two decades, which merit discussion.

Most obviously, Faulkner's "public" career, the external events of his life, had a far greater influence on his writing than ever before. I have noted the effect his Hollywood employment had on his work in the thirties. But this quantitative reduction in his serious writing was to be even more marked for several years after he began working for Warner Brothers in 1942. In the period from 1939 through 1942, largely because of his severe economic straits, he had written about twenty stories; there is no evidence that he wrote *any* during the next four or five years (with the possible exception of an early version of *A Fable*, which he may have originally conceived as a short story [*FB* 2: 1152–53]). Moreover, there is a comparable hiatus in his work on novels. Between the publication of *Go Down, Moses* in 1942 and the writing of *Intruder in the Dust* in 1948, he did a considerable amount of preliminary work on *A Fable*, but nothing else. From 1926 through 1942, there was never a period of more than two years between the publication of his books; however, there was a gap of six years between the publication of *Go Down, Moses* and that of *Intruder in the Dust*. Obviously this relative degree of inactivity in the writing of serious fiction can be blamed in part on the protracted periods he spent at Warner Brothers from 1942 through 1945.

Other factors in Faulkner's life were to have a greater long-range effect on his writing. The publication of *The Portable Faulkner* in 1946, his receipt of the Nobel Prize in 1950, and the extraordinary revival of interest in his work during the last fifteen years of his life made Faulkner world-famous. This shy, reclusive, intensely private man became a public figure who gave speeches, addressed college classes, took public stands on controversial issues, and traveled extensively as a kind of cultural ambassador for the United States government. When we consider how involved he was in these activities during the last decade and a half of his life, it is surprising that he was able to do as much writing as he did. But this work was largely in the novel.

Faulkner's achievement of world fame may indeed have caused him to believe—perhaps largely unconsciously—that novels, because of their greater prestige and ambitiousness, were more worthy of his creative efforts than short stories. Closely related to this factor is the sense of mission that was to color Faulkner's work in his final years, especially after he had received the Nobel Prize: his belief that the writer must celebrate the primal virtues, must "help man endure by lifting his heart, by reminding him of the courage and honor and hope and pride and compassion and pity and sacrifice which have been the glory of his past" (*ESPL* 120). I have noted the sententious quality in some of Faulkner's fiction of the early forties. But it is far more apparent in the work he was to do after the reception of the prize. It seems likely that he sensed that short fiction simply did not afford him the scope he had to have in order to "impart the problems of the human heart in conflict with itself" (*ESPL* 119).

While Faulkner did write a few short stories during this period, his most important work—by far—in this area was one of consolidation, collection, compilation. He worked with Malcolm Cowley on *The Portable Faulkner* and published *Knight's Gambit* in 1949, the *Collected Stories* in 1950, and *Big Woods* in 1955. In his correspondence with Cowley about the *Portable*, he took a retrospective look at his career and formulated, as clearly as he was ever to do, the most basic principles of his aesthetic credo. Cowley's idea that Faulkner had been engaging, more or less consciously, throughout his mature career in the construction of a saga may have influenced his later writing and contributed to his growing lack of regard for the autonomy of his short stories, his tendency to see them as parts of a greater whole. It is certainly clear that Faulkner was far more aware during and after his work on the *Portable* of the unity and coherence of his total achievement. He made a number of conscious efforts to fill in the gaps, most strikingly perhaps in the Appendix to *The Sound and the Fury* but also in the narrative portions of *Requiem for a Nun* and in the last two volumes of the Snopes trilogy.

One other outcome of the correspondence with Cowley was the suggestion made by the critic that Faulkner collect his stories, which was to lead five years later to the publication of the *Collected Stories*. Faulkner was enthusiastic about the project from the start and went to work on it seriously in 1948 after completing *Intruder in the Dust*. But perhaps because *Intruder* was still fresh in his mind and he continued to be intrigued by the genre of the detective story and by the character of Gavin Stevens, another, far less important project intervened. *Knight's Gambit*, which appeared the following year, probably has less merit than any other volume of fiction Faulkner ever published, including *Mosquitoes* and *Pylon*. The best of the stories, "Tomorrow," is a rather moving piece, but the other works have little to recommend them, even if they are considered only as representative of the mystery genre.

A year after the publication of *Knight's Gambit*, the infinitely more important *Collected Stories* appeared—to be greeted by greater *immediate* critical acclaim than any other book Faulkner ever published. The *Collected Stories* did as much as any volume produced during the last twenty years of his life, with the exception of *The Portable Faulkner*, to enhance his fame and to solidify his position as one of the foremost American writers of fiction. Whatever the unevenness and deficiencies of the volume, it is surely as distinguished a collection of short fiction as any produced by an American in this century. Moreover, as Millgate has so well demonstrated, the structure of the volume, the arrangement of the stories again suggests an altogether scrupulous attention to form (*Achievement* 270–75). I shall have more to say about this matter when I consider, in greater detail, the relationship of Faulkner's stories to his books.

The publication of the *Collected Stories*, important as it was, did not complete Faulkner's task of the collection and compilation of his short fiction. He incorporated several of his stories—"Centaur in Brass," "Mule in the Yard," "By the People," and "Hog Pawn"—in the final two volumes of the Snopes trilogy. He also did some work on *The Faulkner Reader*, contributing a foreword and approving the material to be included (*FB* 2: 1472, 1474); the result is certainly the best one-volume collection of Faulkner's works (including an excellent selection of short stories). On the other hand, he gave Random House carte blanche on the choice of stories for the Modern Library *Selected Short Stories of William Faulkner* (*SL* 456), and the result in this case was anything but felicitous. While the volume includes most of the best-known stories—"A Rose for Emily," "Dry September," "That Evening Sun," "Red Leaves," etc.—it also contains a number of inferior works: "Honor," "Beyond," "Two Soldiers," "Lo!"

Of considerably greater importance than these latter two volumes is *Big Woods*, a collection of four hunting stories—"The Bear," "The Old People," "A Bear Hunt," and "Race at Morning"—on which Faulkner expended a considerable amount of care and attention. He supplied transitional material, what he called "interrupted catalysts," between the stories by drawing from and revising portions of other works, including several short stories (*FB* 2: 1522). His most controversial editorial decision was the omission of the fourth part of "The Bear," which he always insisted was written only for inclusion in *Go Down, Moses* and should therefore be excluded when "The Bear" was separately printed in anthologies. The result of this work was an intriguing and attractive volume. *Big Woods* is certainly minor Faulkner, but its genetic history reveals again his devotion to his craft.

We need not devote a great amount of space to the few stories Faulkner produced during his last two decades. The longest and most ambitious of these—the final version of "Knight's Gambit" and "Notes on a Horsethief"—are, in a sense, novellas, which can be analyzed as discrete works, but they are not totally autonomous. The published version of "Knight's Gambit" was written to round out the volume that bears its name, and "Notes on a Horsethief" was extracted from *A Fable*. The latter piece has something of Faulkner's old power and intensity, but is marred by its sententiousness and its lack of narrative drive, characteristics that are only too obvious in most of the stories of the last period. "A Name for the City" contains some gorgeously high-flown rhetoric reminiscent of *Absalom, Absalom!*, but it too is only a modified extract from a longer work, *Requiem for a Nun*.

There was, however, a brief period of about two years, during 1953 and 1954, when, for some obscure reason, Faulkner's interest in the short story per se revived. Early in 1953 he apparently wrote "Weekend Revisited," later retitled "Mr. Acarius" and posthumously published in *The Saturday Evening Post*. This little-known and curiously uncharacteristic piece is about a perverse idealist who gets himself committed to an alcoholic ward. Obviously deriving from Faulkner's own bouts with alcoholism, it has some psychological and biographical interest, but it is unpleasantly frenetic and uncontrolled, certainly one of the strangest stories he ever wrote.

Far more characteristic are three stories he probably wrote the following year: "Race at Morning," "By the People," and "Hog Pawn." The first, one of the hunting stories incorporated into *Big Woods*, contains some beautifully evocative writing but gets bogged down in details and is marred by its platitudinous ending. The other two pieces were apparently written before Faulkner resumed work on the trilogy but obviously owe their inception to his continuing interest in the Snopes material. Both are mildly amusing but are certainly far below the quality of Faulkner's best comic stories; they are crude and rather dull.

I have used that sad word *dull* on more than one occasion in the last few pages to characterize some of Faulkner's final short stories. This dullness seems to derive, as much as anything, from Faulkner's declining interest in storytelling. When he was able to resolve the dichotomy between his poetic and narrative impulses in the fiction of his greatest period, he achieved real mastery of his medium. One senses even in such a relatively static atmospheric work as "That Evening Sun," where the poetic impulse seems dominant, the underlying fascination of *story*—a fascination far more obvious in "A Justice" or "Red Leaves" or "Spotted Horses." In all these works the sensitive reader is aware of at least an implicit strong narrative drive, of Faulkner's delight in the yarn, the tale. He never completely lost that delight; it is apparent, in muted form, in such stories of the final period as "By the People" and "Hog Pawn." But in the closing years of his career it seems to be largely superseded by the obligation he now felt to *teach,* to impart the "old universal truths," to be "one of the props, the pillars to help [man] endure and prevail" (*ESPL* 120). Hence, the clumsy moralism of such stories as "Race at Morning" or "Mr. Acarius."

This didacticism is apparent not only in the fiction of the period but also in the increasing amount of work Faulkner did in his final years in the discursive modes. Particularly in the last ten years of his life, Faulkner felt an obligation as a public man, a world-renowned artist, a Nobel laureate to speak out in his own voice on matters of public interest. A glance at the table of contents of the volume James Meriwether edited, *Essays, Speeches & Public Letters*, reveals that the great majority of these pieces were done after 1950. Faulkner seriously considered doing an entire book of nonfiction, *The American Dream*, and indeed completed two of the essays that he planned to include in that volume (*FB* 2: 1518–19). But of greater interest for our purposes is another idea he had some years before he conceived *The American Dream*. In a letter that cannot be precisely dated he wrote the following to Robert Haas:

> I am thinking about writing my memoirs. That is, it will be a book in the shape of a biography but actually about half fiction, chapters resembling essays about dogs and horses and family niggers and kin, chapters based on actual happenings but "improved" where fiction would help, which will probably be short stories.

I would like to use some photographs. Maybe some of my own drawings. It would probably run about novel length, it will ramble some but will mostly be confined between Rowan Oak, my home in town here, and the farm, Greenfield. (*SL* 320–21)

This letter is an intriguing indication of the kind of writing Faulkner might have done had he lived longer, and of a trend that we can sense, although only very vaguely, in two of the last pieces of "short fiction" he was to compose.

I have enclosed the term "short fiction" in quotation marks for a valid reason. In his bibliography of Faulkner's works in the genre, Meriwether has included both "Mississippi" and "Sepulture South: Gaslight" because they contain fictional elements ("Short Fiction" 304, 307–08). However, neither piece is really a short story. "Mississippi," an essay on his native state that Faulkner did for *Holiday*, contains a number of allusions to Yoknapatawpha County—to the Sartorises, Compsons and De Spains, even to Old Ben—and incorporates other material from his fiction. "Sepulture South: Gaslight" is more difficult to classify than "Mississippi." Occasioned by a photograph Anthony West showed Faulkner of some marble effigies in a cemetery (*FB* 2: 1516–18) and published in *Harper's Bazaar*, it is a kind of autobiographical reminiscence of his experience of funerals as a child, but it contains a number of modifications of the facts of his life—and again seems to draw on his own fiction.

The pieces are quite different. "Mississippi" is far more ambitious; it has a considerably greater scope, and the purely discursive element is more important. "Sepulture South: Gaslight" has a greater immediacy, a stronger emphasis on the personal elements of experience rather than the public and the social, and more of the texture and feeling of a story. But both works suggest that the idea Faulkner outlined in his letter to Haas about a mixture of the fictional and nonfictional modes was quite valid. For these are certainly among the finest pieces of writing he did in his final years. "Mississippi" covers an extraordinary amount of ground in about 10,000 words and gives us a memorable picture of Faulkner's native land; it is fluent, relaxed, genial, confident. And "Sepulture South" conveys with warm nostalgia but without sentimentality the atmosphere and tonality of the distant past, of a childhood in the Deep South.

The latter work may be, with the exception of a few pieces extracted from novels and sold to magazines, the last piece of short fiction Faulkner ever wrote. If it is, it seems peculiarly appropriate. For this gentle, quiet, rather slight work moves us not only because of its intrinsic qualities but also because of the manner in which it recalls some of Faulkner's greatest achievements. The narrator has a sister, Maggie, whom the children are told to mind on the day of the funeral of a grandparent. His Uncle Rodney stands at the sideboard and chews cloves to hide the smell of whiskey on his breath. Half concealed in shrubbery, the children catch a glimpse of a hearse. The protagonist refuses to comprehend or to accept the reality of death. And there are other reminiscences—not only of *The Sound and the Fury* but also of *Flags in the Dust*, *As I Lay Dying*, "An Odor of Verbena," and "That Will Be Fine." Here that tendency toward nostalgia, which seems so cloying in many of the later works, is deeply affecting.

Again, the narrative element in "Sepulture South" is slight; in no sense does it have a plot. We can classify it as a personal essay or, as I have suggested, as a kind of semifictional autobiographical reminiscence. But perhaps it would be just as appropriate to use a touch of critical license and call this static, lyrical, evocative piece a poem. I have stressed that one means of analyzing Faulkner's achievement is to examine the tension in his work between his poetic and narrative impulses. When he was able to fuse those impulses, he created his most memorable stories. Surely one of the most regrettable aspects of his late fiction is its loss of narrative drive. But there is something very moving in the "poetry" of "Sepulture South: Gaslight"; for in this piece we have come, in a sense, full circle. After all, the greatest writer of fiction this country has produced always considered himself a "failed poet."

# CHAPTER 2

# *Patterns*

## The Theme of Solipsism

One of Faulkner's favorite themes is the dichotomy between life and language, the concrete and the abstract, the existential and the conceptual.[1] But ironically that dichotomy is also the central problem of literary criticism. Every critic must contend with the disparity between the experience of the work of art, in all its complex, vital immediacy, and the obligation to formulate that experience, to systematize it, to find the necessarily crude and inadequate equivalents for it in the framework of language. Unfortunately, too many critics lose sight of this problem and succumb to the temptation of reductionism. They discover a theory, a formula, a key that "explains" the work of art with which they are dealing or, indeed, the entire achievement of a significant artist. Almost inevitably such an approach is misguided. No theory can explain a first-rate work of art. In a very real sense, no theory is worthy of such a work.

Nevertheless, criticism *is* conceptualization. We must theorize. We must abstract. We must formulate. If we avoid reductionism, if we understand the limitations of the critical process—particularly in dealing with an artist of Faulkner's stature—we can devise formulas that can give us useful and valid insights. It is possible, I think, to develop such a rubric under which what we might call "Faulknerian archetypes," the obsessive patterns and motifs permeating not only his short fiction but also his entire work, can be subsumed. I will argue that that rubric is *solipsism.*[2]

Numerous critics have called attention to Faulkner's interest in narcissism,[3] as evidenced by his use of mirror imagery, shadows, and doubles, and by his fascination with incest. This interest is manifested in his employment of the narcissus itself in the famous final scene of *The Sound and the Fury* and the early sketch, "The Kingdom of God," on which he drew for that scene, and by his use of the name Narcissa for one of the most important of his early female characters. Most readers will surely agree that the inability to love, springing from an excessive concern with the self, underlies the problems of the Compsons, the Bundrens, the Sutpens and the Snopeses, of Temple Drake and Joe Christmas and Horace Benbow. But the term *narcissism,* with its psychiatric and sexual connotations, seems somehat too limiting and confining to employ here. I prefer *solipsism*—not in the technical philosophical sense of the word, but in the most general and figurative sense. Faulkner's characters, with some notable exceptions, are solipsistic in their refusal to acknowledge the importance of what is external to them, to come to terms with the other, with all that is "not I." They refuse to accommodate themselves to the universe, insisting that it must accommodate itself to them, that the external world must somehow conform to their desires and expectations. They refuse to acknowledge their own contingency, their limited, creaturely status.[4]

This theme is almost never explicitly stated in Faulkner's best and most mature short fiction, but it is quite clearly developed in the very early "Frankie and Johnny." Near the end of this juvenile and inept piece, the pregnant Frankie lies in bed

> thinking of all the other girls throughout the world, lying with babies in the dark. Like the center of the world, she thought; wondering how many centers the world had; whether the world was a round thing with peoples' lives like fly-specks on it, or whether each person's life was the center of a world and you couldn't see anybody's world except yours. How funny it must look to whoever made it! Unless he, too, was the center of a world and couldn't see any other world except his. Or if he was a fly-speck on somebody else's world. (*US* 346)

Callow as this passage is, with its ugly and embarrassing allusions to fly-specks, it sums up as clearly as anything in Faulkner's work his concern with solipsism. The motivating impulses and the tensions in his world can ultimately be traced to Faulkner's conviction that "each person's life was the center of a world and you couldn't see anybody's world except yours."

We can find a somewhat different perspective on this theme in another very weak story, the inchoate "A Dangerous Man," which concerns the peculiar marriage of a feisty train agent, Mr. Bowman. In the opening paragraphs of this piece, Faulkner engages in another of his tiresome generalizations about the differences between the sexes, but what he says about men here can be applied to many of his women as well: "Perhaps . . . a man has everything, what he believes is right and what he believes is wrong and what he believes ought to happen and must happen and what he believes ought not to happen and cant happen, all neatly ticketed and catalogued and fitted into a pattern" (*US* 575). Underlying much of Faulkner's work is his characters' conviction that what "ought to happen . . . must happen" because of their belief that the world was created for them.

It would be nonsensical to argue that this theme of solipsism can be discerned, in one form or other, in everything Faulkner ever wrote. But if we bear in mind that he was obsessively concerned with the problem throughout most of his career, we will find it much easier to understand his short fiction. For the theme is certainly manifested in a number of basic patterns found in Faulkner's work—patterns that should help us to understand not only the short stories but also his entire achievement because they are revealed in a simpler, more elemental form in the stories than in the novels. Of course, we cannot dispose of any story by applying one neat and precise label to it. The system of classification I am suggesting here is anything but rigid; some of Faulkner's stories are so rich that several of the patterns I shall discuss in these pages can be applied to them. In any case, what follows is simply one admittedly rather arbitrary means of attempting to assess the thematic basis of Faulkner's short fiction.

## The Prelapsarian

In the first place, the need to transcend solipsism and to acknowledge otherness is implicit in Faulkner's stories of initiation—an archetypal pattern that has been peculiarly attractive to major American writers and one that Faulkner employed throughout his career. But when I apply this archetype to Faulkner's work, I am using the term in a very broad sense to refer to any story in which there is at least the potential for an initiatory experience or that is predicated on the contrast between a prelapsarian and postlapsarian world, any story in which an innocent has at least the opportunity to come to terms with the reality of otherness, to discover that the world is not made for him or her.

It should be clear that many of the potentially initiatory experiences with which Faulkner deals do not fully "take." While the would-be initiate may be thrust into life and may in some measure learn and grow, he or she will not necessarily be able to understand the limitations of the self and the need for love. Nevertheless, implicit in such experiences is the *ideal* of that kind of initiation that enables the character to transcend the destructive effects of solipsism.

Before I discuss the short fiction that is most obviously initiatory, it will be necessary to deal with those stories concerned with conditions anterior to initiation: with essentially prelapsarian worlds and with children (or childlike characters). In a few of these works—but only a few—the focus is *primarily* Edenic, on a kind of Garden before the Fall. The qualification is important. Since there can be no fiction without conflict, tension, opposition, some sense of the reality of moral choice, no story can be purely Edenic. The Garden presupposes the Fall; Adam and Eve have no story until the Serpent appears. Hence, none of Faulkner's pieces is completely idyllic. But several are largely concerned with remote worlds of purity and innocence. Virtually all of these stories were composed relatively late in Faulkner's career when he found it only too easy to succumb to the temptations of nostalgia and sentimentality. Perhaps the most purely Edenic of the earlier pieces is "Out of Nazareth," one of the New Orleans sketches, which is concerned with David, a charming and innocent young wanderer with literary aspirations, who will probably remain totally guileless until the day he dies. But the focus here is not on Eden, not on an untarnished world, but on an Adam who is incapable of even being tempted. Even in *The Wishing Tree* the children seem only *relatively* innocent, and they must contend with several corrupt adults. The relationship between the maid Alice and her long-lost soldier husband is anything but idyllic. However, Saint Francis's little sermon to the children in the climactic passage of the story reveals Faulkner's concern with solipsism:

> "Didn't you each pick a leaf from a tree back there in the forest?" . . .
> "Well, that was the Wishing Tree. But suppose there had been a thousand leaves on it, and a thousand boys and girls had each taken one, when the next one came along, there wouldn't be any leaf for him, would there?" . . .
> "So a wish you make that way is a selfish wish, isn't it?" (*WT* 76–77)

*The Wishing Tree* is about the need to transcend selfhood, to find one's place in the universe through one's relationship to others, through love.

It was not until Faulkner began to write the stories that were eventually to be incorporated into *Go Down, Moses* that he devoted much attention to the myth of the Garden itself (as opposed to the Fall, which concerned him throughout his career). Such hunting pieces as "The Old People" and the version of "The Bear" that appeared in *The Saturday Evening Post* are certainly initiation stories, but the protagonist (who was to become Ike McCaslin in *Go Down, Moses*) does not "fall." We have a strong sense of his closeness to the natural world. There seems to be no real dichotomy between the "I" and the "other," even when the former must destroy the latter, as the boy does when he shoots the deer. In the much later "Race at Morning," another largely Edenic piece closely resembling the earlier hunting stories, Mister Ernest removes the ammunition from the rifle, and the animal survives. The worlds portrayed in all three of these stories seem whole, serene, pure. Moreover, they are almost totally masculine worlds. Eve has yet to make her appearance, or, in the case of "Race at Morning," it is her defection that has created the paradise, as the young narrator makes clear: "So I come home with him [Mr. Ernest] and it was all right, it was jest fine—his wife had died about three years ago—without no women to worry us or take off in the middle of the night [as the boy's mother had done] with a durn Vicksburg roadhouse jake without even waiting to cook breakfast" (*US* 308). Like Hemingway, Faulkner cannot portray an idyll involving women.

The closest thing in his work to such an idyll is "Was," the first "chapter" of *Go Down, Moses*, early versions of which Faulkner attempted to sell to the *Post* and other magazines (*FB* 2: 1050–51, 1054–55). Here women—notably Miss Sophonsiba and the slave Tennie—are very much in evidence, and they do pose a threat, but we're never convinced that it's a very serious one. The atmosphere of the story is fresh and lighthearted. We are aware, from the context of the rest of *Go Down, Moses*, that Sophonsiba does ultimately succeed in ensnaring Uncle Buck and that Isaac McCaslin himself is the product of that union. But there is nothing apart from that context in any of the versions of the story itself that suggests the inevitability of her victory, of her intrusion into the masculine world of Uncle Buck, Uncle Buddy, and Cass. Nevertheless, her very presence, in Faulkner's terms, taints that world, suggests a corrupting force—as does also the reality of slavery. The attempt, at the beginning of the story, to head off Tomey's Turl before he can reach his sweetheart Tennie at the Beauchamp place and thus bring Buck into the presence of Sophonsiba again is, in one sense, a delightfully funny game. But the fact remains that Buck and Cass are hunting a human being as if he were an animal.

Because of the effects of the relationship between the white man and the black man, together with a sense of mortality and the passing of time, there is also a kind of shadow over the Edenic worlds portrayed in "The Old People" and the shorter version of "The Bear." Of course, that shadow is even more obvious in the definitive versions of the stories in *Go Down, Moses*. But it is certainly present in the magazine versions, as it is in even many of the most lighthearted of Faulkner's stories. We know that the Expulsion from the Garden can never be avoided for very long. Indeed, in "Race at Morning," the other Edenic story to which I have referred, the Expulsion is announced in unmistakable terms. After Mister Ernest ends the comic chase of a great buck by refusing to kill him, much to the chagrin of the protagonist (whom Ernest has unofficially adopted), he tells the boy that it's time for him to go to school: "And that used to be enough—just to do right. But not now. You got to know why it's right and why it's wrong, and be able to tell the folks that never had no chance to learn it; teach them how to do what's right, not just because they know it's right, but because they know now why it's right because you just showed them, told them, taught them why. So you're going to school" (*US* 310). This is almost painfully sententious, but it does make very clear the need to confront the moral complexity of the postlapsarian world.

There are two other relatively late stories concerned with essentially prelapsarian worlds. The first, "The Tall Men," written in 1941, is even more didactic than the later "Race at Morning," but the focus here is economic and political, on Faulkner's anger at the New Deal. The story is concerned with the contrast between the individualism of the McCallum family and big government. In *Flags in the Dust* the McCallums, whom the despairing Bayard Sartoris visits immediately after he has been responsible for the death of his grandfather, give him a temporary refuge of peace, wholeness, and serenity, suggesting what life could be if people were able to free themselves from artificial abstractions and live attuned to the rhythms of nature. The McCallums continue to serve essentially that kind of function in "The Tall Men," but Faulkner's aims here are far more narrowly social than they were in *Flags in the Dust*. When a state draft inspector goes to the McCallum farm to arrest two of the boys because they have failed to register for the draft, he learns some lessons about human priorities and the values of stoic individualism. The inspector seems impressed, but the story implies that such an Eden cannot endure for very long. The forces of modernism, of "progress" will ultimately overwhelm it.

Again the world of "The Tall Men," like those of "The Old People" and "Race at Morning," is a totally masculine one. That of "A Courtship" is not. The basic conflict, the rivalry between Ikkemotubbe and David Hogganbeck, is caused by their infatuation for Herman Basket's sister (although we shall later question the intensity of their commitment to the woman). That rivalry, consisting of incredible eating and drinking contests and a climactic marathon race, takes place, as Faulkner tells us in the first and last lines of the story, "in the old days" (*CS* 361, 380), in a kind of Homeric age when men were far more capable, far stronger, far more dignified and loving than they are now. In its celebration of the glories of the past, of a primal legendary wilderness, "A Courtship" is perhaps the most Edenic of Faulkner's stories, even though its mode is primarily comic, and we cannot take the nostalgia expressed by the narrator very seriously. However, the heroic feats of Ikkemotubbe and David Hogganbeck are counterpointed, on several occasions, against what is eventually to happen to Ikkemotubbe. Faulkner's point is made most forcefully in a passage near the end of the story:

> Presently Ikkemotubbe was gone completely away, to be gone a long time before he came back named Doom, with his new white friend whom no man wished to love either and the eight more slaves which we had no use for either because at times someone would have to get up and walk somewhere to find something for the ones we already owned to do, and the fine gold-trimmed clothes and the little gold box of salt which caused the other four puppies to become dead too one after another, and then anything else which happened to stand between Doom and what he wanted. (*CS* 379)

How different Doom is from the loving and selfless Ikkemotubbe of "the old days"! Clearly this Adam falls too—and brings down his world with him.

The locus of all the stories in this category is the prelapsarian. In another kind of piece, Faulkner shifted the locus to the postlapsarian but very strongly emphasized the longing for a lost Eden. This nostalgia is quite apparent in several of Faulkner's longer works, in portions of *Go Down, Moses*, *The Unvanquished*, *The Reivers*, and, most memorably, in the first section of *The Sound and the Fury*. But it is nowhere more evident than in the New Orleans sketches because Faulkner concentrates in several of these pieces so intensely on the contrast between the corruption of the present world and the harmony and serenity of the past. In "New Orleans," the brief, impressionistic sketches published in *The Double Dealer*, that contrast is apparent in the Cobbler's dreams of Tuscany and his lost bride, in the Cop's sorrowful recollections of childhood, in "Magdalen's" memories of the days of gold. The theme is also of importance in several of the *Times-Picayune* sketches. In "Home" the lost paradise is described very explicitly, as it is also in the expanded version of "The Cobbler":

> When I was young I lived much in the sun, tending goats. The people of my village labored among the vineyards sprawled upon the slopes drinking up the sun; as I followed my flocks I could see them, the bright colors, and hear the faint, sweet singing like the broken flight of golden birds. I munched my bread and cheese at noon, and drowsed among the sun-swelled rocks until the air and heat and silence sent me to swim in warm slumber. And always at sunset an ancient father of goats roused me with his cold nose. (*NOS* 66)

As I have noted before, one of the most interesting things about the New Orleans sketches, when they are considered collectively, is the tension they reveal between Faulkner's poetic and narrative impulses. In the self-indulgent and sentimental pieces just cited, the poetic impulses are largely dominant. In order to make the most of his concern with the contrast between the prelapsarian and the postlapsarian, Faulkner had to learn to dramatize it, to transcend the urge for stasis, to capture and epitomize the dynamism of this conflict. For the static and the solipsistic go hand in hand. Only in the world of time and tension can we learn to acknowledge and understand otherness.

## Children

The relationship between stasis and solipsism is sometimes strikingly dramatized in a most characteristic Faulknerian pattern: in those stories in which children or childlike characters, in spite of their confrontations with the world of evil, ugliness, and corruption, continue to maintain their fundamental innocence—because they are not yet ready to understand that world, because they can never understand it, or because they simply refuse to do so.[5] A major source of whatever density and complexity these stories possess is the irony implicit in such a situation.

If we are to believe what Faulkner had to say about the genesis of *The Sound and the Fury*, that great novel began with the impulse to write just such a story, one that would focus on the failure of the Compson children to understand that their grandmother has died.[6] A comparable irony underlies "That Evening Sun," in which the innocence of two of the Compson children, Caddy and Jason, is counterpointed against the anguish and terror of the black prostitute, Nancy. However, those who argue that Quentin also fails to understand the plight of Nancy misread the story. The increasing silence of the boy in the final scenes and his unforgettable culminating question, "Who will do our washing now, Father?" (*CS* 309), suggest that Quentin *does* understand that Jesus will murder Nancy. For Quentin, the situation in "That Evening Sun" serves as a kind of terrible initiation, as does also the sequence of the death of Damuddy in *The Sound and the Fury*.[7]

Faulkner uses the Compson children in another story, "A Justice," which counterpoints innocence and corruption. But there is a significant difference here: the children appear only in the frame. Quentin is again the narrator, as he is in "That Evening Sun," but the substance of the story is what Sam Fathers tells him about the old Indian days, a strange, grotesque, dark, but wickedly funny tale of sexual rivalry and murder. However, when we return to the frame, Quentin tells us that he did not understand Sam's story but that he knew he would someday. Here the contrast between innocence and corruption is more muted than it is in "That Evening Sun" because it is suggested only in the frame, but the irony is perhaps even stronger because of Quentin's failure to comprehend what Sam tells him.

Faulkner's most successful use of this pattern is in those works which involve the Compson children. But several years before he created the Compsons he revealed his interest in the pattern in some of the sketches he published or intended to publish in the *Times-Picayune*. The motif is revealed in its purest, starkest form in the very slight sketch, "Peter." The protagonist, a small mulatto boy, is the son of a prostitute, and the obvious ironies of the piece derive from his lack of comprehension of the kind of "business" his mother is engaged in upstairs. A far better use of the pattern—no doubt because the story engaged Faulkner's sympathies more deeply—is "Sunset," which is not concerned with a literal child but with a childlike black who, in the process of trying to go to Africa, "whar de preacher say us come fum" (*NOS* 78), is hunted down as an insane desperado and killed.

The idiot in another of the New Orleans sketches, "The Kingdom of God," is the first of many mental defectives in Faulkner's work. It seems obvious, as he tells us explicitly in his comments about the use of Benjy in *The Sound and the Fury*,[8] that Faulkner employed so many characters of this type because of the opportunities their usage afforded for the kind of irony I have been discussing. While the focus of "The Kingdom of God" is on the obsessive concern of the bootlegger for his idiot brother (who is clearly the prototype for Benjy), the innocence of the idiot is effectively counterpointed against the corruption of his brother's world. In a much later story, "Monk," which Faulkner apparently wrote in the mid-thirties and eventually incorporated into *Knight's Gambit*, a moron is sent to prison for a crime he did not commit and then bamboozled by another convict into murdering the warden. The story following this one in *Knight's Gambit*, "Hand Upon the Waters," involves *two* idiots: the first is murdered for his insurance money, but the second, in a rather obvious and unconvincing irony, avenges him.

Faulkner wrote such pieces as these with his left hand; they are clumsy and dull. However, he did write some far better stories involving certain variations on this pattern of childlike characters maintaining their innocence. In "Turnabout" the incredibly brave British torpedo boatmen, Hope and Ronnie, are, because of their apparent naïveté and insouciance, portrayed as very childlike indeed. But the story would really not have much point if these boys were as innocent as they seem to be. For bravery, by definition, involves some awareness of the risks one undergoes. Hope's state of drunkenness in the opening scene of the story suggests that he is only too aware of the horror of what he must do.

There are other variations—or apparent variations—on the pattern in two most interesting stories Faulkner wrote in 1935, "That Will Be Fine" and "Uncle Willy." In the former story, the child-narrator is very naive; he is unknowingly—but for a price!—helping his profligate Uncle Rodney carry on his sexual affairs. But in spite of his ignorance of sex, the little boy is, in other respects, utterly corrupt, one of the most loathsome children in all of fiction. A monster of greed, he is obsessively concerned with the acquisition of money and hence totally selfish, involuted, solipsistic. If any one of Faulkner's works suggests the figurative reality of Original Sin, it is this one.

The other story, "Uncle Willy," also involves a young narrator who *seems* to be unaware of the full implications of what he is telling us. He is apparently blindly loyal to his much older friend, the title character, a dope addict and alcoholic druggist who uses the boy shamelessly. The narrator loses his illusions about the community that ruthlessly destroys Uncle Willy, and in that respect he does undergo a kind of initiation. Joseph Reed suggests that he also becomes aware of the corruption of his friend (40–41). However, such an interpretation seems rather tenuous. Unless the narrator knows the truth but is trying throughout the story to convince himself of his love for Uncle Willy, he seems to maintain his loyalty to his friend to the end.

If we use the word *children* in a more figurative sense than the way I have been employing it, we can find other instances of basically the same pattern—a character maintaining his or her innocence—in Faulkner's short fiction. The would-be seducer in "Don Giovanni" is childlike in his inability to understand the futility of his schemes. So, too, in spite of many potentially initiatory experiences, is the naive protagonist of "Portrait of Elmer," who seems to learn nothing at all in the course of that incoherent story. And if we remember that, in spite of the evil he perpetrates, Thomas Sutpen's most basic problem in *Absalom, Absalom!* is, in the words of Quentin Compson, his "innocence" (*AA* 274), perhaps we can apply the same term to his prototype, Dal Martin. The protagonist of "The Big Shot" and "Dull Tale" is obviously, because of his ties to the Memphis underworld, his use of bribery, his ruthless drive for power, one of the most corrupt of Faulkner's characters. Yet there is no indication in these stories that he has any understanding at all of what he is doing to people, particularly to Gavin Blount, whom he bribes and drives to suicide in order to get an entrée for his daughter to a prestigious ball that Blount chairs. Like Sutpen, like so many of Faulkner's other characters, Martin cannot acknowledge the reality of other people. He too is a solipsist.

It is interesting that the best stories involving the use of this pattern were written during Faulkner's greatest period and that the pattern ceased to attract him after the middle thirties—perhaps because its basic mode is ironic, and in his later years his tendency toward sentimentality largely overcame his interest in irony, at least in its subtler forms. We can find evidence of this change when we turn to a kind of variation on the pattern I have been discussing. In this kind of story an innocent (or often only an apparent innocent) confronts the world of corruption head-on and achieves a kind of victory over it, a kind of triumph. It should be obvious that this pattern is almost inherently sentimental, and it is not therefore surprising that it was somewhat more attractive to Faulkner in the middle and later stages of his career. The best stories involving its use are generally comic.

We can again find prototypical instances of the pattern in at least two of the New Orleans sketches: "Country Mice" and "Yo Ho and Two Bottles of Rum." In "Country Mice" some ostensibly sophisticated bootleggers are outwitted by "hicks," who succeed in hijacking their liquor. In the other piece, an ugly and crudely derivative Conradian tale, the Chinese crewmen of a British ship manage, in spite of their British officers, to bury one of their compatriots, who has been callously murdered by the first mate. The racial element is of great importance here, as it is in most of Faulkner's stories that employ this pattern. Members of a supposedly primitive—hence, more innocent—race are able to triumph over their corrupt white antagonists.

However, race is not predominant in all of Faulkner's stories of this type. In perhaps the best of the stories in which we can discern the pattern, the deliriously funny "Mule in the Yard" (1934), a black, the delightful Old Het, does play a role, but the plot turns on the success of a white woman, Mrs. Hait—in effect, another hick—in outwitting the nefarious I. O. Snopes. Another instance of the pattern that does not involve race is in "Hand Upon the Waters," in which the deaf-mute "feeb" avenges the murder of the man who has raised him. In a very late story, "By the People," written in 1954, two white children, set on by the indefatigable Ratliff, destroy the political career of another Snopes, Clarence, by rubbing some switches from a "dog thicket" on his pants at a political rally, causing him to be pursued by several dogs and thereby destroying his usefulness in the eyes of his patron, Will (Uncle Billy) Varner.

Nevertheless, the pattern is more clearly evidenced in stories like "Yo Ho and Two Bottles of Rum" in which members of a supposedly inferior race triumph over whites. It can even be found in one of the Indian stories, "Lo!," published in 1934. In this piece some red men, who are anything but noble savages, come to Washington to ask the president (who is not named but is clearly Andrew Jackson) to resolve a little legal problem involving the murder of a white man by an Indian. Led by the redoubtable Francis Weddel, their half-French, half-Chickasaw chief, they are able to attain their ends by blackmailing the entire United States government by their very presence in the capital. In spite of appearances to the contrary, they are clearly wiser, craftier, wilier than the white men to whom they ostensibly owe their allegiance.

So too are many of the black men in Faulkner's short stories. Even Flem Snopes comes a cropper in "Centaur in Brass" when his efforts to steal brass from the Jefferson power plant are frustrated by two blacks, Tom Tom and Turl, whom he has been using in his schemes. In the very slight "A Bear Hunt," another black, Ash, gets revenge on a white man, Luke Provine, for a practical joke Luke had perpetrated on him years before. There are obvious instances of the pattern in the stories involving Lucas Beauchamp that were eventually incorporated into *Go Down, Moses*. His manipulation of the city slicker by means of the gold-hunting machine in "Gold Is Not Always" is a case in point. Finally, there is the role played by Ringo in several of *The Unvanquished* stories. It is Ringo, not the curiously passive Bayard, who helps Granny Millard bilk the Federal Army out of several hundred mules.

## Initiation: Sexual and Otherwise

We must now turn to those stories of Faulkner that are initiatory in the more limited and precise meaning of the term, to those works in which a child or childlike character starts to attain maturity by confronting the corruption and injustice of the real world, by acknowledging otherness and his or her own contingency. We can, although somewhat arbitrarily, further subdivide the manner in which Faulkner handles this more precisely initiatory pattern. There are those stories in which the initiation clearly involves a confrontation with the reality of sex. On the other hand, there are stories in which the erotic element is not obviously present or is at least muted.

We can find these latter stories of initiation, in which the emphasis does not seem to be on the erotic, at every stage of Faulkner's career. One can make a case that his very first published story, "Landing in Luck," is initiatory. The theme of the first solo flight, with which the piece is concerned, certainly suggests initiation. But it is not clear that the obtuse Cadet Thompson really learns anything from his experience; the characterization is not sufficiently developed in this very slight work.

The initiation pattern is more obvious in the second of the two early pieces entitled "Once Aboard the Lugger." There is the implication in this grisly story of bootlegging and murder that the narrator learns a great deal from the sudden intrusion of irrationality, of raw evil into the world of the mundane. In a more mature story of the thirties, the title character of "Wash," even though he is a grandfather, undergoes a terrible loss of innocence when he has to confront the corruption of Thomas Sutpen. Several years later Faulkner uses the archetype in the lovely "Barn Burning," in which Sarty Snopes learns a great deal about the agony of moral commitment. The pattern is also suggested in a very late story: in the discovery by the title character of "Mr. Acarius," after his experience in an alcoholic ward, of the futility of his idealism.

As I have already noted, the initiation theme is also often manifested in Faulkner's stories of hunting—or, in a broader sense, in most of those works involving the archetype of the quest or search. In none of these pieces is Faulkner's understanding of the mythical, ritualistic implications of the hunt more obvious than in the stories of Ike McCaslin, which were to become part of *Go Down, Moses*—as so many critics with a Jungian orientation have noted. One thinks, for example, of the marking of Ike's forehead with blood by Sam Fathers after he has killed his first buck. Less obviously, the initiation of Bayard Sartoris in *The Unvanquished* stories involves several quests—for his father, for the family's lost silver, and for the murderer of his grandmother. In the maudlin "Two Soldiers" (1942), the eight-year-old narrator clearly learns a great deal from his search for his brother Pete after the older boy has been drafted. In one case at least, we might argue that the process can be reversed and that it is the hunted rather than the hunter who achieves a kind of initiation. I am thinking of that unforgettable moment in "Red Leaves" when the black slave who is being hunted down by his Indian masters allows the moccasin to strike him:

> "Olé, grandfather," the Negro said. He touched its head and watched it slash him again across his arm, and again, with thick, raking, awkward blows. "It's that I do not wish to die," he said. Then he said it again—"It's that I do not wish to die"—in a quiet tone of slow and low amaze, as though it were something that, until the words had said themselves, he found that he had not known or had not known the depth and extent of his desire. (*CS* 335)

In this great scene the slave confronts his own mortality, the mystery of his own contingency. And how mythically appropriate it is that the initiation involve a snake!

In dealing with those stories of initiation in which the sexual element is of importance, we are considering a very controversial aspect of Faulkner's art. But whatever our opinions may be about his attitude toward the erotic and toward women, surely no reader of Faulkner can deny that his fiction is permeated by a very basic uneasiness about sex, an intense and sometimes unhealthy dualism, which he never completely overcame. He certainly did his best work when he was able to achieve some distance from that concern.

There is no distance at all in the intense sexual longing and dualism that are all too evident in the early "poetic" sketches: in "Nympholepsy" and "And Now What's to Do," for example. In the latter fragment, the dualism is quite explicit:

> and on the drug store corner where the girls passed in soft troops, touching one another with their hands and with their arms you could not tell him from a lawyer's or a merchant's or a doctor's son. The girls didn't, with their ripening thighs and their mouths that keep you awake at night with unnameable things—shame of lost integrity, manhood's pride, desire like a drug. The body is tarnished, soiled in its pride, now. But what is it for, anyway? (*FM* 146–47)

That dualism is just as apparent in the sexual frustration expressed in "The Priest," another of the 1925 pieces that Faulkner originally intended to publish in the *Times-Picayune*:

> "Is it youth I want? Is it youth in me crying out to youth in others which troubles me? Then why does not exercise satisfy me—physical strife with other young men? Or is it Woman, the nameless feminine? Is my entire philosophy to be overthrown here? If one be born in this world to suffer such compulsions, where is my church, where that mystical union which has been promised me? And which is right: to obey these impulses and sin, or refrain and be forever tortured with the fear that I have somehow thrown away my life through abnegation?" (*US* 351)

In "Carcassonne," on the other hand, which Faulkner probably wrote a year or two later, the sexual theme is muted because it is only one aspect of a very complex—indeed, obscure—prose poem, but the dialogue between the poet and his skeleton, expressing the desire to gallop *"up the hill and right off into the high heaven of the world"* (*CS* 899), is intensely dualistic.

In any case, this uneasiness about the erotic is quite apparent in many of Faulkner's pieces employing the archetype of initiation and dealing with the intrusion of sex into a clean and pure world of children or childlike adults. This pattern is present almost from the start of Faulkner's career as a writer of short fiction. It is vaguely adumbrated in the two versions of "Moonlight," but in these stories of abortive seduction the initiation does not take place. On the other hand, it most certainly does occur in the manner I have already noted in "Frankie and Johnny," in Frankie's discovery of her contingency through her love for Johnny and through her pregnancy.

The archetype is also quite explicit in "Adolescence." What Juliet Bunden does when her Eden is destroyed is another interesting aspect of Faulkner's handling of the pattern: the tendency to associate a sexual initiation (whether it be literal or figurative, as it is in the case of Juliet) with death. For after her grandmother and her father disrupt her friendship with Lee Hollowell, Juliet betrays Bunden to the revenuers, who kill him. She seems to feel little regret for the loss of her father, but when she discovers that Lee has left the area, she becomes bitterly unhappy. In her musings Faulkner makes the initiatory pattern and the association of sex and death quite clear: "Joe Bunden she hated no longer, but Lee, Lee was different, his leaving was more tangible than the death of a hundred men: it was like dying herself. So she sat in the dark, watching her childhood leaving her" (*US* 471).

Sex and death are very closely linked in two other interestingly related stories of initiation that Faulkner wrote in the mid twenties. "The Kid Learns," a reworking of material from "Frankie and Johnny" (with a title in which the initiatory theme could hardly be more explicit), is the story of how a young hoodlum falls in love when he rescues a girl from a potential rival, the "Wop." But it is clear, from the concluding passage of the piece, that when Johnny thinks he sees his love again, the Wop gets his revenge:

> Why, say, here she was again beside him, with her young body all shining and her hair that wasn't brown and wasn't gold and her eyes the color of sleep; but she was somehow different at the same time.
> "Mary?" said Johnny, tentatively.
> "Little sister Death," corrected the shining one, taking his hand. (*NOS* 91)

Faulkner's fascination with this image, an allusion to Saint Francis, is also revealed at the end of *Mayday*, which he wrote not long after "The Kid Learns." After a series of completely disillusioning experiences with women, young Sir Galwyn of Arthgyl is offered a way out of his misery by drowning himself in a stream beside a wondrous tree:

> And the tree covered with leaves of a thousand different colours spoke, and all the leaves whirled up into the air and spun about it; and the tree was an old man with a shining white beard like a silver cuirass, and the leaves were birds.
> What sayest thou, good Saint Francis?
> "Little sister Death," said the good Saint Francis.
> Thus it was in the old days. (*MAY* 87)

These almost obsessive images of the tree, the stream, and Saint Francis recur (without the allusions to death) at the end of *The Wishing Tree*. But, of course, much of this significant complex can be found in definitive form in the second section of *The Sound and the Fury*, where another quester knight, Quentin Compson, chooses to drown himself because of what sex has done to *his* Eden.

The relationship between sex and death is also evident in "Mistral" and "Snow," in which the two innocent young Americans learn at first hand about the corruption of the old world as they piece together the fragments of two mysteries involving sexual triangles, jealousy, death, and, at least in the case of "Mistral," murder. While the two young men are not directly involved and only learn about these horrors at second hand, it is clear that they are thoroughly shaken by their experiences, that they now know some profoundly unsettling things about the power of sex and the nature of evil. Furthermore, the imagery of the two stories contains some revealing indications of a kind of revulsion against female sexuality. On a single page in "Mistral" we find the following: "It was like being at the bottom of a dead volcano. . . . The presbytery was of stone too, bleak in a rank garden. . . . The hall behind her was dark; a stale, chill smell came out of it (*CS* 860; ellipses mine).

Near the end of "Snow" there is another most suggestive passage, redolent with sexual implications:

> when we looked back from the station, the village was once more beneath us; we looked down into the true valley from what we had merely taken for the valley, standing again in snow, between the crumpled ramparts of snow which the plows had hurled up into a gutter funneling not only the shining rails but the living light and sun too into the black orifice of the tunnel until soon the tunnel too would overflow and the mountain it pierced dissolve in fierce light. (*US* 675)

This latter passage is of particular interest because it suggests a basic dichotomy in Faulkner's imagery, one that he employs again and again: the opposition between mountains and valleys or, more generally speaking, between high and low places. For Faulkner heights almost always have very positive connotations; they suggest wholeness, cleanness, purity, transcendence, the domain of the masculine principle, as manifested in his constant use of hills, balloons (a symbol for Freud of erection), and flying. On the other hand, low places in Faulkner's works often suggest chaos, corruption, death—and female sexuality. These connotations are quite evident in a passage from "Crevasse," a curious piece about some World War I soldiers who fall into a cavern containing the skeletons of some troops who have been gassed:

> Then a crack springs like a sword slash beneath them all; the earth breaks under their feet and tilts like jagged squares of pale fudge, framing a black yawn out of which, like a silent explosion, bursts the unmistakable smell of rotted flesh. While they scramble and leap (in silence now; there has been no sound since the

first man screamed) from one cake to another, the cakes tilt and slide until the whole floor of the valley rushes slowly under them and plunges them downward into darkness. A grave rumbling rises into the sunlight on a blast of decay and of faint dust which hangs and drifts in the faint air about the black orifice. (*CS* 471)

There is nothing really surprising about Faulkner's employment of this imagery of high and low places; it is apparent in some of the most basic of the world's myth patterns—the opposition, for example, between the male god of the sky and the goddess of the earth. Indeed, it is implicit in the very idea of the *Fall*. In any case, in both "Mistral" and "Snow," Don and the narrator descend from a pure, clean world of masculine companionship in the mountains into valleys, where they must be initiated into what is for them the corrupt, often mortally destructive effects of female sexuality.

"Divorce in Naples," another story deriving from Faulkner's European trip, is about the most overtly homosexual relationship in his fiction—between two seamen, George, and his young friend, Carl. The relationship is disrupted when Carl loses his virginity to a Naples prostitute, but he is finally forgiven by the older sailor. A conversation between the two near the end of the story about Carl's initiation contains one of the ugliest of Faulkner's allusions to female sexuality. In recounting the conversation, George says: "So I knew what the trouble was, what had been worrying him. I remember the first time it come as a surprise to me. 'Oh,' I says, 'the smell. It don't mean nothing,' I says; you don't want to let that worry you. It ain't that they smell bad,' I says, 'that's just the Italian national air'" (*CS* 892). In this passage, as well as others in these initiation stories to which I have referred, the olfactory imagery, unpleasant in the highest degree, suggests one of the chief stumbling blocks for Faulkner's men as they attempt to come to terms with the opposite sex. Fortunately, as the writer matured, as his handling of the initiation pattern became more sophisticated, he was able to use considerably more subtle sexual imagery.

In two other stories probably begun in the late twenties, Faulkner tried to achieve some distance from this aversion to female sexuality through the use of the double. While he was not as fascinated by such symbolism as, say, Conrad or Dostoevsky, Faulkner's employment of mirrors, shadows, and twins, the repetition in his novels of names from generation to generation, and, more specifically, the handling of the Charles Bon-Henry Sutpen-Quentin-Shreve relationship in *Absalom, Absalom!* suggests a long-standing interest in this device.[9] In "The Leg" he employs a most curious double.[10] The story concerns two Oxford undergraduates, Davy (the narrator) and George, who is jokingly courting a fair young maiden, Everbe Corinthia. The war intervenes, George is killed, and Davy loses a leg.[11]

When the ghost of George visits Davy in the hospital, the latter pleads with his friend to make sure the severed limb is "dead." Later, Davy dreams about it:

> Suddenly I knew that I was about to come upon it. I could feel in the darkness the dark walls of the corridor and the invisible corner, and I knew that it was just around the corner. I could smell a rank, animal odor. It was an odor which I had never smelled before, but I knew it at once, blown suddenly down the corridor from the old fetid caves where experience began. I felt dread and disgust and determination, as when you sense suddenly a snake beside a garden path. (*CS* 833)

Here the Freudian symbolism is certainly obvious. Moreover, the Serpent is—almost literally—intruding into Eden.

These sexual implications are borne out by what occurs in the dénouement of the story. The leg (suggestive of a kind of disembodied phallus) takes on Davy's bodily form, seduces Corinthia, and drives her to her death. After her brother attempts to kill Davy and is condemned to die, a priest finds among his effects what caused the brother to attempt the murder: a vicious, leering photograph of Davy's double containing an unprintable inscription to Corinthia.

This grotesque, ugly, and rather silly story is clearly a highly experimental attempt to handle the initiation theme in a novel manner. However, the effort to achieve some distance is not really very successful. The obvious, lurid symbolism makes this piece quite unpalatable.

"Black Music," another early story that also employs, in a somewhat more figurative sense, a kind of doppelgänger motif, is not much more effective than "The Leg," but it is certainly more genial. It is the tale of a mousy little architect's draftsman, Wilfred Midgleston, who gets drunk and becomes for one day what he calls a "farn"—a faun, or, more precisely, a satyr. His discovery of this Dionysian side of himself constitutes his initiation. When he recovers his senses the next morning after causing all kinds of trouble, he realizes that he cannot go back to his old life and leaves for South America. In effect, the original Wilfred Midgleston dies.

Here, because of the comic mode, Faulkner does achieve some distance from his sexual preoccupations. But "Black Music" is quite slight and not very funny, another unsuccessful effort to suggest an initiation into the world of sex.

A relatively successful treatment of this initiatory pattern occurs in a complex story of the early thirties, "Fox Hunt." The work, which is concerned with a sexual triangle, contains a number of strands, but one of the most important involves an unnamed country boy whom Faulkner calls "the youth." Like Quentin in "That Evening Sun," he does not play an active role in the narrative; he is an observer-auditor who learns some ugly truths about life in the course of the narrative. Near the end of the story he watches the vicious Harrison Blair take out his sexual enmity on the fox he has hunted down. As the youth's companion explains:

> "Only the fox was still in the briers, and while he [Blair] was going through the air he looked down and seen the fox and he clumb off the horse while it was jumping and dropped feet first into the briers like the fox done. Maybe it dodged some then; I don't know. He says it just swirled and jumped at his face and he knocked it down with his fist and trompled it dead with his boot-heels. The dogs hadn't got there then. But it so happened he never needed them." (*CS* 606)

The companion tells this to Gawtrey, the man who has pursued and apparently just succeeded in seducing the source of Blair's hatred, his wife. As the youth leaves Gawtrey and the woman, the young man is

> projecting, trying to project, himself, after the way of the young, toward that remote and inaccessible she, trying to encompass the vain and inarticulate instant of division and despair which, being young, was very like rage: rage at the lost woman, despair of the man in whose shape there walked the tragic and inescapable earth her ruin. "She was crying," he said, then he began to curse, savagely, without point or subject. (*CS* 607)

Thus sex and death are linked in another of Faulkner's initiatory stories—this time one of his more successful.

Faulkner was not drawn so much to stories of initiation involving the overt use of sexual themes after he had attained mastery of his medium. But he was interested in the more general pattern throughout his career. There are initiatory elements in many other stories that I have not discussed here. Faulkner's handling of no other archetype can tell us more about his art and thought—because this one is so centrally concerned with the need for a breakthrough to an awareness of one's creaturely limitations.

What conclusions can we draw about Faulkner's handling of the archetype at different stages of his career, particularly the tendency to concentrate on sexual themes in the earlier initiation stories and the increasing interest in the ritualistic and symbolic potentialities of the hunt in the later works? There is, I think, a complex of reasons for this development. As I have already indicated, it suggests Faulkner's increasing ability, as he mastered technique and as his art became more complex and subtle, to achieve some kind of objectivity, a degree of distance from his own preoccupations and obsessions. We need not subscribe slavishly to the dogmas of Freud to insist that sexual themes and images are nearly always present, at least in covert form, in Faulkner's works. But in the later initiation stories they are not so obtrusive, so obvious, so oppressive because they are incorporated in and subsumed under other aspects of his art.

On the other hand, we can take a somewhat more negative view of this change in orientation. We can argue that, after Faulkner achieved the balance and maturity that are characteristic of the works of the greatest period of his career—the time from about 1928 to 1932 when his art achieved that marvelous tension and beautifully controlled irony that are present in the very best fiction—a kind of fatigue set in, and Faulkner chose to handle the initiation pattern in an easier, less demanding manner. He had always been interested in the hunt, and he was enough of a mythicist to understand something of its archetypal significance, that it could be a most effective means of dramatizing the theme of the coming of age. Both in their magazine versions and the final forms in which they are incorporated into *Go Down, Moses,* "The Old People" and "The Bear" are, for the most part, impressive works of art, but they also contain tendencies that were to mar Faulkner's later works: moralism, didacticism, and more than a touch of sentimentality. One can sense that "The Old People" contains in embryo the turgid, flabby qualities of "Race at Morning."

## Love Relationships: Triangles and Wronged Women

Faulkner's concern with solipsism is admirably revealed in his handling of love relationships, which, by their very nature, must, if they are to be successful, entail an acute and often painful sense of human contingency. But generally those who are involved in such relationships in Faulkner's fiction do *not* have that sense, and the consequence is usually pain, anxiety, torment—and often catastrophe.

There is a curious lack of equality and reciprocity in Faulkner's handling of his lovers. Almost never do we find in his work a genuinely healthy one-to-one heterosexual relationship—partly because, I think, this imbalance gives Faulkner a means of dramatizing his characters' solipsism. This lack of parity is often apparent in Faulkner's handling of love triangles and is most strikingly revealed in the numerous triangles, or quadrangles, involving a parent or parental figure.[12]

The oedipal implications of this pattern, found in many of Faulkner's stories of the twenties and thirties, are obvious. They are apparent in "Jealousy," the New Orleans sketch that is the story of an older man, his wife, and the handsome young waiter he employs. They can also be found in

"The Kid Learns," in the struggle between Frankie and the "Wop" for Mary, which leads to the apparent murder of the younger man by the father surrogate. Both these parental figures are portrayed in very negative terms, but we can say the same about Faulkner's handling of this kind of personage in many of the stories; the characterizations are often extremely unflattering.

There is a kind of cliché of Faulkner criticism that he is very fond of old ladies, as evidenced by his largely positive portrayals of such characters as Jenny Du Pre, Granny Millard, and Miss Habersham. However, his handling of the older women in his short fiction implies, at best, a most ambivalent attitude toward this kind of character. His work in this genre contains a whole gallery of extremely ugly and hostile characterizations of "Terrible Mothers," witches, old bitches.[13] And such personages are often involved, in a figurative sense, in sexual triangles or quadrangles.[14]

Such a pattern can be found in some of Faulkner's very earliest stories. This kind of characterization is anticipated in the portrayal in "Frankie and Johnny" of Frankie's querulous, complaining mother, apparently a prostitute, with her "white flaccid hands, . . . dyed hair" (*US* 342), and "petulant puffy face" (*US* 343). The type is more fully developed in the characterization of the grandmother in "Adolescence," who destroys the Edenic comradeship of Juliet and Lee by insisting on the sexual basis of their friendship. An even more appalling portrait is that of Zilphia Gant's mother, with her pathological hatred of men and of sex. In the more mature fiction of the thirties, there is the vicious, domineering Mrs. Boyd of "The Brooch," who ruins her son's marriage and causes his suicide because his wife does not measure up to her standards. There is the cold and implacable grandmother of "Elly," who somehow knows that Elly's friend Paul de Montigny has Negro blood. There is the interfering mother of "Dr. Martino," who succeeds in destroying the doctor's influence on her daughter and indirectly causes his death by tricking her into eloping with the priggish Hubert Jarrod. Finally, at a more comic level, there is Aunt Louisa in "Skirmish at Sartoris," who forces the marriage of John Sartoris and Drusilla.

The father figures in such relationships are not generally as well portrayed or as memorable as the mother figures. There is one other significant difference: the primary function of the maternal characters is to interfere with, to thwart the love affairs; they are not themselves, of course, romantically involved. On the other hand, the older men in Faulkner's fiction are sometimes so involved. They play such roles in "Jealousy" and "The Kid Learns." Consider also (although triangles are only vaguely suggested in some of these stories) the love of Hawkshaw for Susan in "Hair," the liaison between Sutpen and Milly in "Wash," the mountain girl's attraction to Weddel in "Mountain Victory," and even the curious bond between Dr. Martino and Louise King. In the extremely tangled web of relationships in "Knight's Gambit"—perhaps the appropriate geometrical metaphor would be a hexagon—Gavin Stevens clearly qualifies in his courtship of Melisandre Harriss as both a father figure and a lover (as he does also in his fruitless pursuit of Linda Snopes in *The Town* and *The Mansion*). However, older men do sometimes play their more conventional paternal roles in a few of Faulkner's triangles. This is the function of the title character in "Wash" and of the thoroughly unpleasant Mr. Meadowfill in "Hog Pawn," whose efforts to prevent the marriage of his daughter are finally frustrated.

It is tempting to try to find reasons in Faulkner's life for his handling of these patterns and character types. Knowing what we do now about his biography, we can assume that his interest in the relationships between older men and younger women can be traced in part to his own love life. However, we can find this pattern in stories throughout his career, including some very early work, long before his affairs with Meta Carpenter and Joan Williams. A more substantial reason for Faulkner's interest in such relationships is probably his conviction that it is extraordinarily difficult to attain genuine equity and reciprocity in matters of love, sex, romance.

Again, one can find a reason in Faulkner's life for the more effective characterizations of strong maternal figures in these triangles and in all of his fiction: it is clear that his mother was a far more forceful person than his relatively weak and inadequate father. Yet a great deal more is involved here than simple biographical information or generalizations about Faulkner's attitudes toward women, whatever their ages. Any knowledgeable reader knows that an archetype of peculiar importance in the twentieth century is the Search for the Father. In this respect, one thinks of the works of Joyce, Lawrence, Hemingway, Wolfe, Proust—and, of course, Faulkner. There are remarkably few positive characterizations of paternal figures in the entire corpus of Faulkner's work. His fathers are inept or cynical or lazy or preoccupied—or, simply, absent. The dogmatic Freudian can find very obvious, and certainly partially valid, reasons for this tendency, but it surely also suggests, as it does in the works of Faulkner's great contemporaries, a most fundamental spiritual malaise, the loss of that sense of stability and coherence that gave life meaning in previous epochs. In other words, the Search for the Father cannot be dissociated in our age—and in the works of Faulkner—from the search for God.[15]

But, to return to Faulkner's handling of triangles, we must, in justice, note that the parental figures in such situations are not always handled unsympathetically. We have considerable sympathy for such older men as Wash or even that dreadful bore Gavin Stevens. In the triangle in "An Odor of Verbena" involving Drusilla, Bayard, and John Sartoris, Faulkner generates considerable sympathy for both Drusilla and John. And his treatment of Roger and Anne Howes in "Artist at Home," as they attempt to come to terms with the calf love of the young poet John Blair, is gentle and kindly. But this kind of approach to triangular situations is relatively rare in Faulkner's short fiction.

Of course, not all his triangles involve parental figures. In several of those that do not, there is a very curious shift in the rivalries we would normally expect between two men over a woman. In such stories as "Divorce in Naples," "Honor," and "A Courtship," the real bond of affection is between the two men, and the rivalry for the woman ultimately seems to be little more than an excuse for demonstrating that affection. This homosexual element is so obvious in "Divorce in Naples" that it requires no further comment here. It is not quite so obvious in the triangle in "Honor," which involves the narrator, Monaghan, a "wing walker"; Rogers, his pilot; and Rogers's wife, Mildred.[16] In the scene that occurs after Rogers has learned about the affair between Monaghan and Mildred, when she declares her love for Monaghan, there is a most revealing passage:

> He was looking at me, and she running her hands over my face and making a little moaning sound against my neck, and me like a stone or something. Do you know what I was thinking? I wasn't thinking about her at all. I was thinking that he and I were upstairs and me out on top and I had just found that he had thrown the stick away and was flying her on the rudder alone and that he knew that I knew the stick was gone and so it was all right now, whatever happened. So it was like a piece of wood with another piece of wood leaning against it, and she held back and looked at my face. . . .
>
> I wanted to be out of there. I wanted to run. I wasn't scared. It was because it was all kind of hot and dirty. I wanted to be away from her a little while, for Rogers and me to be out where it was cold and hard and quiet, to settle things. (*CS* 557–58)

This is one of the clearest statements in Faulkner's short fiction of his equation of heights and masculine sexuality and of the opposition, in his terms, between the clean, cold, simple world of men and the "hot and dirty" world of women.[17] It seems clear, throughout this rather weak and unconvincing story, that it is the intrusion of women into the pure and honorable world of men that causes all the trouble, that Rogers is far more important to Monaghan than Rogers's wife.

We can say much the same about the triangle in "A Courtship." The "love" which Ikkemotubbe and David Hogganbeck have for Herman Basket's sister is simply an excuse for the two men to prove their prowess and to demonstrate their affection for each other.[18] The woman herself is lazy and bovine—much like the Eula Varner of the early portions of *The Hamlet.*

But the rivals for her hand are truly men of Homeric stature, of infinitely greater worth than the object of their love. Again, as in "Honor," the climax of the story involves a rescue that proves, more clearly than anything else, the selfless feelings the men have for each other. But in this case both men, in a kind of Alphonse-and-Gaston act, save each other—from the consequences of firing a gun in a perilous cave! The Freudian imagery in this passage is, to say the least, striking.

Perhaps enough has been said here to indicate how peculiar Faulkner's handling of triangles is. We can suggest several reasons for this anomaly. Most obviously, Faulkner was simply not interested in conventional triangles, the stuff of slick fiction and second-rate films. Truth for him was to be found in the bizarre, in the outré. And he knew enough about depth psychology to sense that the very concept of "normality" in sexual relationships is virtually meaningless. However, we can also argue, as so many critics have done and as much of the evidence of this chapter suggests, that Faulkner *was* profoundly uneasy about female sexuality and hence could handle it only in a peculiarly oblique manner. There seems little reason to doubt that there is at least something of Quentin Compson and Joe Christmas in their creator.[19]

But there is still another explanation for Faulkner's idiosyncratic handling of triangles, one that does more justice to the complexity and profundity of his art. The lack of parity, the inequity in these triangles again suggests his concern with solipsism. For it is in sexual relationships that our need to come to terms with otherness is most pronounced, that our involuted, narcissistic concern with selfhood is most damaging. We are drawn to the opposite sex because of the mystery of sexual difference, but that very difference can be an almost insuperable barrier between men and women, dramatizing more painfully than anything else human isolation and loneliness—*unless* we are willing to acknowledge our ineluctable separateness, our creaturely limitations, our radical contingency. Hence, the peculiarities in Faulkner's treatment of triangles, most notably their obviously oedipal or homosexual implications, suggest, at least metaphorically, that there can be no genuine love without a fully developed, equitable, balanced sense of otherness.

One of the measures of Faulkner's achievement as an artist is that, in spite of the very real problems he had in confronting that otherness, particularly as it was manifested in female sexuality, he *was* able, at his best, to treat it with sympathy, compassion, and understanding. Whatever we may say about the relative paucity of fully three-dimensional portraits of female characters in Faulkner's works, about those often tiresome and superficial generalizations concerning women which can be found in many of the short stories and novels, about the traces of misogynism that do occasionally appear, we must also concede that one of the most striking aspects of his art—particularly of his short fiction—is his many sympathetic portrayals of wronged or trapped women.[20]

As I have noted on several occasions, a sign of Faulkner's maturation as an artist was his increasing ability to handle the problems of the female sex with some degree of objectivity. But throughout his career we can find compassionate characterizations of women in difficult or impossible situations: in such early pieces as "Frankie and Johnny" and "Adolescence"; at a somewhat later stage in "The Leg" and "Mistral"; and during Faulkner's greatest period in "That Evening Sun," "Mountain Victory," "Dr. Martino," and many other stories.

One of the most obvious patterns in the short fiction—a pattern that would be recognizable to even a relatively casual reader of Faulkner—is that of the wronged woman striking back, seeking vengeance, trying to redress the balance. In this respect, one thinks of Emily Grierson's murder of Homer Barron in "A Rose for Emily"; of Mrs. Gant's pathological hatred of the male sex in *Miss Zilphia Gant*, culminating in her refusal to acknowledge Zilphia's marriage; of Minnie Cooper's attempts in "Dry September" to call attention to herself by falsely accusing Will Mayes of attacking her; and in "Elly" of the title character's vengeance on her grandmother. Then too there is the purely verbal but memorable "putdown" of Ike McCaslin by the woman of "Delta Autumn": "Old man . . . have you lived so long that you have forgotten all you ever knew or felt or even heard about love" (*US* 279)?

## The Quest for Justice

Faulkner's handling of wronged women is an example of one of the most basic of his concerns: the quest for justice. Again we can argue that his very strong emphasis on this subject can be traced back to his concern with solipsism. I have stressed the problems his characters have in coming to terms with the separate existence of other human beings. A closely related problem is the solipsist's insistence that the universe has been created for him or her alone; and that there must consequently be a kind of balance in the very nature of things, a cosmic quid pro quo that will insure that he or she will achieve justice. Faulkner's characters are often so obsessed, so dominated by various idées fixes because they cannot understand why

they have not received their just deserts. In "Death Drag" we have one of
the most explicit statements in the short fiction of this theme after Ginsfarb
learns that he has not been paid what he demanded for his death-defying
aerial feat and therefore jumps off the death-drag ladder while the plane is
going over a barn. Captain Warren explains why:

> "Yes. He jumped. He wasn't thinking about being killed, or even hurt. That's
> why he wasn't hurt. He was too mad, too in a hurry to receive justice. He
> couldn't wait to fly back down. Providence knew that he was too busy and that
> he deserved justice, so Providence put that barn there with the rotting roof. He
> wasn't even thinking about hitting the barn; if he'd tried to, let go of his belief
> in a cosmic balance to bother about landing, he would have missed the barn and
> killed himself." (*CS* 202)

Grotesque and extreme as his characterization is, Ginsfarb is like many of
Faulkner's people in his refusal to "let go of his belief in a cosmic balance."
In almost all of Faulkner's stories, we can find at least traces of this theme,
of his concern with the meaning of justice, the gap between the desires and
aspirations of the individual and the larger realities of human existence.

Ginsfarb, in at least this one instance, is able to satisfy his insistence
on the quid pro quo because Captain Warren gives him the extra money.
Generally, in Faulkner's greatest fiction this kind of justice is not achieved.
But in some rather slight stories it is. In several of his comic pieces and in
the more sentimental works he produced toward the end of his career there
are instances of the purest kind of wish fulfillment, in which everything
comes out all right. We can find this pattern in one of his early attempts
at formula fiction—"Cheest" in the *New Orleans Sketches*. This very slight
piece is quite unsatisfying because it suggests that Faulkner deliberately set
out to do something in the mode of Sherwood Anderson—but from a more
positive perspective—and hence produced a weak and silly story about a
jockey who meets an attractive "jane," wears her garter on his arm, and
wins a big race. On the other hand, there is considerably more justification
for wish fulfillment, at the most literal level, in *The Wishing Tree*. Nor is
there any reason to object to the happy endings of such comic pieces as
"Centaur in Brass" or "A Bear Hunt," in both of which black men attain a
full measure of vengeance against whites who have mistreated them. Perhaps the most completely satisfactory treatment of the motif of triumphant
justice is Mrs. Hait's wonderful victory over Snopes in "Mule in the Yard,"
culminating in her shooting of the mule.

However, the handling of this theme of vengeance is more than a little
dubious in two of *The Unvanquished* stories. In "Vendée" the revenge of
Bayard and Ringo on Grumby for the murder of Granny Millard seems ex-

cessively grisly, and the motivations in the story are unconvincing. In the mawkish "Skirmish at Sartoris," "justice" is achieved through the murder of carpetbaggers and the denial of the vote to black men. I find it difficult to believe that Faulkner intended any irony in the cheers of the townspeople before the wedding of John Sartoris and Drusilla: " 'Yaaaaay, Drusilla!' . . . 'Yaaaaaay, John Sartoris! Yaaaaaaay!' " (*US* 73). There is no justification in the story for assuming that this is, in Faulkner's terms, anything but a happy ending.

This kind of sentimentality is even more apparent in his later treatment of similar themes. In "My Grandmother Millard" the sentimentality is bearable because the work, in spite of its flaws, *is* funny. However, the triumph of the "good guys" and the defeat of the Snopeses through various machinations in "By the People" and "Hog Pawn" seem unconvincing because the stories are turgid, listless, dull—and unfunny. Faulkner's optimism in such pieces, as is so often true of the works of his final decades, seems hollow and forced.

There are other stories in which a kind of quid pro quo is achieved but of a somewhat more qualified, muted, ironic nature. The outcomes of two early formula pieces, "Chance" and "The Big Shot," suggest a kind of poetic justice. In the former a bum finds a penny, is mistakenly given a five-dollar gold piece with which he wins two thousand dollars on a horse race, buys a car but promptly wrecks it, is fined ten dollars for speeding, and discovers that he has one cent left. The irony is a bit more complex in the ending of "The Big Shot," where the daughter of Dal Martin, the corrupt millionaire, is run over and killed by an early but recognizable version of the Popeye of *Sanctuary*, a hoodlum Martin has been protecting and whom he succeeds in getting out of town before he knows who the victim is. O. Henry would have approved!

But Faulkner rarely indulges in such cheap tricks. In some far more characteristic—and far better—stories, justice is again achieved in spite of obsessive efforts to thwart it, but our feelings about these outcomes are more complex. In "The Hound," Cotton (who was to become Mink Snopes in the Snopes trilogy) is eventually apprehended for the murder of Houston, but the anguish and terror the protagonist has gone through have been so intense that our reactions at the end of the story are not those of relief or triumph but of exhaustion—and of compassion for Cotton. (Our reaction to the most marked instance in the novels of this pattern—the murder of Flem by Mink in *The Mansion*—is even more ambiguous.) Similarly, we are, if anything, shocked by the dénouement of "That Will Be Fine": the killing of Uncle Rodney by the angry men of Mottstown. Rodney certainly was a rogue, but perhaps a less extreme punishment might have been devised, even for cuckolding so many husbands. Our laughter at the young narrator's unknowing allusion to the body of his uncle as "a side of beef" (*CS* 286) is hardly the laughter of delight; this is clearly an instance of very black comedy. Moreover, the central ironies of the story derive from the appallingly mercenary and self-centered character of the narrator. Hence, our reactions to this underrated piece are very complex indeed.

Within this category—the kind of work in which justice wins out in spite of desperate efforts to circumvent it—we can also place most of Faulkner's detective stories. He was interested in the genre throughout most of his career. There are at least elements of the mystery story in as early a work as "Love," in "Mistral," "Snow," and "Evangeline," and, of course, in the *Knight's Gambit* pieces, on which Faulkner worked, off and on, for nearly two decades. It is not difficult to understand why he was attracted to the detective story. Interested as he was in complex plotting, in the mysteries of human motivation, in working from effect to cause, in the technique of partial, inconclusive disclosures, in the careful erection of various barriers to comprehension that the reader must patiently overcome, it was only natural that he would be drawn to the genre. But surely another important factor here is the concern of detective fiction—often in a most elemental way but sometimes in a far more complex form—with justice.

In spite of the weakness of the pieces in *Knight's Gambit*, Faulkner's handling of the theme of justice in most of these stories *is* relatively complex. The earliest piece, "Smoke," is the most conventional and is of little interest, and "An Error in Chemistry," while somewhat ingenious and perhaps the most competent as a detective story, is quite superficial. However, all the works, including the title story, raise pertinent questions about the nature of justice: about the inequity rooted in the very nature of things, inequity that creates the pathetic title character in "Monk," and Lonnie Grinnup and the deaf-mute orphan in "Hand Upon the Waters." They raise questions about that most virulent form of solipsism that causes people to murder, or try to murder, other human beings; and about the often very great disparity between legality and justice, as manifested in the venal parole-board hearing in "Monk" and in the pathetic story of Jackson Fentry in "Tomorrow," who loses the adopted child he loves to the boy's kinsmen but years later is at least able to hang the jury that is expected to acquit the young man's killer.

Justice is also a central concern of Faulkner's swindle stories, those tales of the biter bit, the bilker bilked, which clearly owe a great deal to the traditions of Southwestern humor.[21] But because of the very nature of such pieces (to many of which I have already referred under other rubrics), the handling of the subject of justice in them is again somewhat complex. For the antagonists in such works are never guiltless; in a sense they should all be punished because they all lie, cheat, deceive. Yet there must always be winners and losers in these stories. Someone always gets away with something, always achieves a victory he or she doesn't really deserve. Of course, the reader's sympathies are usually very clearly aligned with one of the parties, and often the good guys—tainted though they are—win. The city slickers are outwitted by the country bumpkins in "Country Mice," Mannie Hait triumphs over a Snopes in "Mule in the Yard," and blacks are able to win significant victories over devious and mendacious whites in "Centaur in Brass," "A Bear Hunt," and "Gold Is Not Always." Our attitudes toward the issues in other stories of this type are more ambivalent. We want Pap to triumph in "Fool About a Horse," but we are so delighted by the wondrous trickery involved in the horse trading that we don't really care very much that he does not win. We know that the treasure hunters—Suratt and Tull and Armstid—in "Lizards in Jamshyd's Courtyard" deserve to be bilked by Flem and his gold-salting scheme, but the tonality of that story is very dark indeed because of our compassion for the insane Armstid. Even darker is the mood of "The Unvanquished,"[22] since the story ends with the murder of Granny Millard, who is destroyed because she has allowed herself, from the best of motives, to become corrupted. In an effort to help the war-ravaged people of her country and to restore the fortunes of her family, Granny has engaged in the worst kind of financial chicanery in her handling of the sale of mules to the Yankees. But when she tries to make one last deal, she is lured into ambush and killed. Here something very like tragedy derives from the conflict between two "rights" or two "wrongs." The moral issues are quite complex.

In three of his finest stories Faulkner deals with essentially the same theme, a kind of Aeschylean conflict between two different forms of justice. The tremendous tensions in "An Odor of Verbena," "Barn Burning," and "Mountain Victory" derive from the necessity for important characters to choose between two different sets of moral imperatives: the ties of blood and kinship, on the one hand, and, on the other, a kind of intuitive sense of simple decency and compassion and of the integrity of others. Bayard Sartoris, Sarty Snopes, and the boy in "Mountain Victory" choose the latter imperative and in the process learn much about the irreducible complexity of moral choice.

In a sense, Faulkner's greatest stories always deal, in one way or another, with this fundamental human truth. In virtually all of them justice is achieved *from someone's perspective*. In "Dry September" McLendon and his companions believe that the lynching of Will Mayes has restored Miss Minnie's honor and that of the white race. The presumed murder of Nancy by her husband, Jesus, will fulfill his need for the quid pro quo in "That Evening Sun." In "Red Leaves" the Indians are able to carry on the age-old traditions of their society by capturing and executing the runaway slave so that he can be buried with his master. But in experiencing these stories the reader is always achingly aware that some terrible wrongs have been— or will be—perpetrated. He or she knows that, in the last analysis, justice is *not* being done because of the failure on the part of these characters to understand the dignity and integrity of those whom they destroy. Again, a kind of solipsistic refusal to acknowledge otherness is ultimately to blame.

## The Idée Fixe

It is also solipsism that largely accounts for one of the most characteristic of Faulkner's themes: monomania, the idée fixe. The peculiarly obsessive quality of so many of his characters' motivations derives, I think, from their failure to acknowledge their own contingency, their inability to understand that the universe has not been created for them.

However, in a few of Faulkner's stories obsession does triumph; a character, through a total devotion to his or her idée fixe, is able to surmount great obstacles and come out on top. Such works are, more often than not, essentially comic or sentimental. I have already referred to the idée fixe in "Thrift," the story of a stereotyped parsimonious Scotsman who manages to survive as a flier in World War I and returns home a considerably wealthier man because of his obsessive devotion to money. In "My Grandmother Millard" the youthful Confederate officer, Philip St-Just Backhouse, falls overwhelmingly in love with Cousin Melisandre of the Sartoris family, is spurned by her because his surname reminds her of a traumatic experience she had involving some Yankees and an outhouse, and takes out his frustrations by performing foolhardy deeds of valor in the war. Finally, through the machinations of his commanding officer, General Forrest, and Granny Millard, he manages to get rid of his unfortunate name and wins the girl.

Such stories of the virtually total triumph of an obsessed character are quite rare in Faulkner. Sometimes a kind of triumph is achieved, but it is muted or qualified. In "Two Soldiers" the little Grier boy does succeed in getting to Memphis and finding his brother Pete before he is shipped out to fight in World War II, but, of course, the eight-year-old child is not allowed to join the army and must return home. In "Go Down, Moses" Mollie Beauchamp is able to find her lost grandson, but it is too late to help him; Samuel Worsham Beauchamp comes home a corpse after he has been executed for murder. Dal Martin, the protagonist of "Dull Tale," does manage, after considerable effort, to get his daughter invited to the Nonconnah Guards' Ball, but he can do so only by driving Gavin Blount, the chairman of the ball, to suicide.

More often, the idée fixe leads not to a qualified victory but to defeat, even to destruction. The protagonist of "Jealousy" will probably be executed or imprisoned for life for the murder of the man he presumes to be his wife's lover. In "Spotted Horses" Armstid's irrational fascination with the pony the Texan is auctioning leads to a broken leg and destitution for his family. Rider's inability in "Pantaloon in Black" to overcome his grief for the dead Mannie causes him, in effect, to commit suicide by killing a white man who has been cheating in a dice game. In this category too we might place many of those stories of wronged women to which I have already referred in another context. One thinks of the destruction wrought by the solipsistic title character of "Elly" and of the wasted lives of Emily Grierson, Zilphia Gant, and Minnie Cooper.

## Self-Abnegation

Not everyone in Faulkner's world is solipsistic. In a few of his stories there are personages who, through their selfless devotion, their commitment to others, their sense of the integrity of their fellow human beings, stand out in marked contrast to Faulkner's more typical characters. I have already referred to the selflessness, in "Honor," of Rogers, who agrees to permit his wife to leave him for Monaghan, then saves the latter's life when the wing-walker almost falls off the plane piloted by Rogers. There is a somewhat comparable situation in "Artist at Home," in which the affronted husband, Howes, looks out for the interests of the foolish but talented poet, John Blair, in spite of Blair's infatuation for Howes's wife. In "Hair" Hawkshaw falls in love with Susan because she reminds him of his dead fiancée. He finally marries her, but only after he has spent many years doggedly paying off the mortgage on the house that belonged to the dead girl's family. In "Snow" the mountain climbing guide, Brix, saves the lives of his bride and of the other members of the climbing party by cutting the rope that ties him to the others and thereby plunging to his death. And in *Idyll in the Desert*, a selfless woman gives up her husband and children to minister to her tubercular lover; the lover recovers and leaves her, but she acquires the illness and eventually dies.

It is interesting that the examples I have cited here of decent, self-abnegating characters are all drawn from stories presumably written (at least in their earliest forms) by 1931—long before Faulkner had begun to make the hollow affirmations that were so often present in his later work.[23] Such characterizations suggest that it is easy to exaggerate Faulkner's pessimism during his greatest period. On the other hand, the contrasts between the lives, the actions, the motivations of such personages and those of the other characters in these pieces are so striking that the general effects of the stories are, more often than not, bitterly ironic. Faulkner seems to be saying here: "This is what people *could* be. But they rarely are."

## Abstractions

There is an obvious danger in placing too much stress on the theme of solipsism in Faulkner's fiction. A consideration of its significance does surely throw a considerable amount of light on his achievement, but many other approaches can be fruitful.

One of the best of these approaches is to emphasize, as a kind of key to Faulkner's thematic concerns, his awareness of the dangers of abstraction.[24] The tensions in his work often derive from the attempt to impose artificial and arbitrary formulas, axioms, conceptualizations on the complexities of human experience. Faulkner was not an existentialist—at least in the narrow sense of the term—but it can certainly be argued that a kind of Sartrean conflict between essence and existence underlies his work. In many of his short stories (and, of course, also in the novels) the adherence to abstraction has a destructive effect. Consider the consequences of such an abstraction as race in "Dry September," "Pantaloon in Black," and all the other stories eventually incorporated into *Go Down, Moses*; of the abstraction of social class in "Victory," "Mountain Victory," "A Rose for Emily," and "Wash"; of the abstraction of legality in "By the People," "Point of Law," "The Tall Men," and "Lo!" Consider the gap between language and life in such stories as "My Grandmother Millard" and "A Name for the City"; and the consequences of one of the most abused of all abstractions—honor—in many of the stories: "Honor," "There Was a Queen," "Death Drag," "An Odor of Verbena," "Wash," etc. Finally, consider how the concept of community, in spite of its often very positive values, can become destructive when it is pitted against the integrity of the individual, as it is in "Uncle Willy," "The Tall Men," "Dry September," and "Red Leaves."

But it might seem that an emphasis on the destructive effects of abstractions would virtually contradict the stress I have placed on the negative consequences of solipsism. How much stock can solipsists place in such abstractions as race, class, and community? If they believe that they are the center of the universe, that the world was made for them, can they also believe in the ontological validity, the "reality" of such conceptualizations?

I think they can. For I have been using the term *solipsism* here in a figurative sense to mean the refusal to acknowledge one's contingency, to accept the separate existence of other human beings. Faulkner's solipsistic characters impose such abstractions as race, class, and community on others because they can use these concepts to deny the messy contingency of all that is external to them. A belief in the primacy of pattern is a repudiation of particularity and individuality. Whether our starting point in categorizing Faulkner's short fiction is solipsism or abstraction, we inevitably become aware of the supreme importance in his work of the denial of otherness, of the failure to love.

The very fact that such themes bulk so large in Faulkner's world should make the critic even more aware of his or her own very special obligation in assessing that world. The critic must avoid pitfalls similar to those confronting so many of Faulkner's characters. Just as those characters should— although they rarely do—acknowledge the mysterious contingency and opacity of other people, so too must the critic acknowledge the integrity and individuality of every story Faulkner wrote and the limitations of any system employed in assessing those works. I have not, therefore, attempted to apply the system of classification I have devised to every piece of Faulkner's short fiction. His range was so great that it would be a disservice to his art to do so.

However, at least elements of some of the patterns I have noted can be discerned in virtually every one of Faulkner's stories. "Ad Astra," for example, seems, at first glance, to be very different from anything else that Faulkner ever wrote and, hence, does not apparently lend itself to the kind of categorization I have been suggesting. But this story about a few hours in the lives of several soldiers in France who are celebrating the Armistice is really concerned with the cosmic injustice that the carnage of World War I seemed to reveal and with the consequent disillusionment and anguished attempts to adjust to that new view of life. Most of the characters are lost and lonely, unable to communicate, and ultimately solipsistic in their obsessive concerns with their own little centers of consciousness.

Their solipsism is manifested in their idées fixes: in Comyn's concern with sex, in Bland's make-believe wife, in Sartoris's guilty feelings about the death of his brother, in the class consciousness of Monaghan. On the other hand, two characters, the Indian subadar and a German prisoner of war, are sane, serene, and whole. Both of these men argue (quite sententiously) that the answer to the problems besetting all of them is brotherhood—in other words, the transcendence of the solipsistic barriers separating one human being from another.

It would seem therefore that there are at least some elements in "Ad Astra" that suggest the patterns with which I have been concerned. A study of this piece, the many stories discussed in this chapter, and others as well surely suggests a continuity of pattern, of motif, of archetype in Faulkner's short fiction.

# CHAPTER 3

# *Point of View*

One of the most impressive things about Faulkner's short fiction is its extraordinary range. When we compare his work in the genre to that of some of his more distinguished contemporaries—Hemingway, Fitzgerald, Porter, Steinbeck, Flannery O'Connor—we are struck by how much richer Faulkner's achievement seems because of its diversity and variety, even though it is more uneven in quality. Yet as I have tried to demonstrate in the preceding chapter, that richness cannot be accounted for by a wide range of themes; from the beginning to the end of his career as a writer of short fiction, Faulkner employed a relatively narrow spectrum of patterns and motifs. He did embody those preoccupations in a great range of subject matter: in tales of the supernatural and in detective fiction, in stories of Indians and aristocrats, of blacks and poor whites, of bootleggers and priests, adolescents and ninety-year old women, children and vagrants, fliers and hunters and seamen, of the Civil War and World War I, of the wilderness, the village, and the metropolis. There is truly a profusion, an abundance here.

But the sense of variety that Faulkner's short fiction conveys cannot be accounted for solely by the diversity of its subject matter. There is another factor of the very greatest importance here: the range of techniques employed in these works. How different is the writer's craft in such excellent stories as "Barn Burning," "That Evening Sun," "Dry September," and "Red Leaves." And it is difficult to believe, even discounting the differences in subject matter, that the man who wrote "Fool About a Horse" also wrote "Carcassonne," that the author of "Ad Astra" also composed "A Return." Because of this great variety, it will be impossible in a study of this kind to do any kind of justice to Faulkner's technical achievement in his short fiction.[1] Nevertheless, it should be useful to focus in some detail on what is surely the most important single aspect of that achievement: his management of point of view.[2] It is easier to generalize about, say, Hemingway's or O'Connor's handling of point of view than it is to reach valid conclusions about Faulkner's approach to that problem because he probably employed a greater number of different vantage points from which to tell his stories than has any other significant American writer. Still, it is possible to acquire some insights not only into Faulkner's craft but also into the ideas underlying his art by examining certain patterns in his management of point of view.

As Henry James and his followers discovered, the vantage point from which a story is told will have a determining influence on the kind of effect it achieves. And because of the modernist influence on the importance of objectivity, immediacy, and intensity, our writers and theoreticians have stressed the superiority of a *limited* point of view, that is, of telling the tale from the perspective of one of the characters in the work, who will experience the story for us at first hand as it impinges on his or her consciousness and will thus impart a kind of drama to it that it would not have if the consciousness of an omniscient narrator were to intervene. James believed that the most effective way to achieve this drama is to tell the story in the third person because doing so gives us the sense that it is happening *now;* the use of the first person, on the other hand, sets up a kind of distance that inevitably reduces the drama because the narrator is reporting to us on what has already happened.

One can hardly exaggerate the significance of this concern. But I think there is another, more far-reaching reason for this emphasis on the limited point of view. It springs, in part, from the modernist consciousness of our inability to *know* in any categorical sense, to bridge the gap between the self and the external world. It derives from our awareness of the inevitable subjectivity of human experience. In such an intellectual milieu it is hardly surprising that the omniscient point of view seems pretentious, unrealistic, artificial. Such ideas relate to what I have argued is the central theme in Faulkner's fiction: solipsism. In his many different approaches to a limited point of view, he dramatizes or at least reflects on a technical level his awareness of what was for him the most significant of human problems. But Faulkner was a working artist contending on a daily basis with the problems of his craft. I know of no evidence from his correspondence or his public pronouncements that he was ever much concerned *on a theoretical basis* with point of view. We can be grateful that he wasn't. For in his concern with telling his stories in the most effective possible ways, he never rigidly adhered to the dogmas of modern criticism. He occasionally violated the doctrines of James, Lubbock, and Beach with impunity—and sometimes with dazzling success.

One reason for what may seem to be Faulkner's cavalier treatment of point of view derives from a difference of emphasis between his work and that of some of the greatest of modernists. In the latter, narration often seems largely a means to an end: to the suggestion of theme, the revelation of character, the creation of atmosphere. Of course, Faulkner was aware that stories can and should do these things, but he also took a visceral pleasure in the *process* of telling. Hence the emphasis in many of his works is virtually as much on the telling as it is on what is told. In the fiction of most of the great modernists—Conrad is an obvious exception—an attempt is made to hide or at least obscure the mechanism of narration, so that what is narrated may be fully dramatized. But Faulkner often wants to dramatize the storytelling itself—occasionally at the expense of the vividness and immediacy of what is told. (In this respect his work anticipates postmodernist fiction.)

This interest in dramatizing the process of narration is suggested by the unusually large numbers of stories in which Faulkner uses a first-person narrator—either an "I" or sometimes a "we." It is impossible to make any sort of valid count of the proportion of first-person to third-person narrators in Faulkner's short fiction because of the difficulties we have in agreeing on what constitutes a piece of short fiction or on what is the dominant voice in some of Faulkner's more complex experiments in narration. Nevertheless, it seems clear that more than half of his short stories are in the first person. Furthermore, several of the stories in the third person contain characters who serve as narrators and who impart, in the first person, vital information to the reader. There are surely many reasons why Faulkner employed the first person so often, some of which I shall attempt to develop later in this chapter, but one of the most significant, I think, is that the first person more clearly and vividly calls attention to the act of narration itself than does the third person.

## Selective Omniscience

In spite of his greater interest in the first person, Faulkner did use the third in a wide variety of short stories, including some of his very best. Although he was well aware of the value of a limited point of view in certain kinds of stories, he sometimes employed what might be called, in a highly qualified sense, "omniscience." While such a technique often seems clumsy and obvious, it can, in some kinds of fiction, be very effective indeed. Norman Friedman has suggested that omniscience is quite appropriate for a writer like Aldous Huxley whose intent is to capture the ambiance of a particular social milieu by entering the consciousness of a number of different characters ("Point of View" 1181). The most memorable uses of omniscience were, of course, in the great novels of the nineteenth century—in *War and Peace* and *The Brothers Karamazov* (although there is a most peculiar use of an "I" in the latter) and the work of the Victorians. No narrative technique gives a greater sense of scope and sweep and range, of epic grandeur.

But, obviously, epic grandeur is hardly an appropriate characteristic for short fiction, for a genre in which compression and concentration are imperatives. Nevertheless, Faulkner's struggles with the genre did teach him that certain kinds of effects in certain stories can be most efficiently achieved if the point of view is *not* rigidly limited to a single consciousness.

Not surprisingly, the point of view in much of Faulkner's apprentice fiction is essentially omniscient, for in his earliest work he was probably not yet sufficiently aware of the options available to him. And the most obvious way to tell a story is without imposing any kinds of limitations on the narrator. Thus, all of "Landing in Luck," his first published piece, could have been told from the perspective of its not very bright protagonist, Cadet Thompson, as he attempts his first solo flight. But about halfway through the piece Faulkner suddenly—and quite awkwardly—shifts from the consciousness of Thompson, after he discovers that his plane is missing a wheel, to a scene on the airfield involving those who have discovered his plight. In "The Hill" and its expanded version, "Nympholepsy," his first efforts to deal with an inarticulate protagonist, he does not hesitate to editorialize about the character, to tell us things about him that the "tieless casual" (*EPP* 92) does not and cannot know himself. In the earlier piece Faulkner tells us: "for a moment he had almost grasped something alien to him, but it eluded him; and being unaware that there was anything which had tried to break down the barriers of his mind and communicate with him, he was unaware that he had been eluded" (*EPP* 91–92).

In another early piece, the version of "Frankie and Johnny" in *Uncollected Stories*, we are inside the minds of several characters, those of Frankie's parents and her boyfriend Johnny, before the story becomes focused on the perspective of Frankie herself. Faulkner employs essentially the same technique in "Adolescence," in which he gives us a considerable amount of background information about Juliet's family before we enter the consciousness of the protagonist. In most of the New Orleans sketches the point of view is limited, but "The Rosary" shifts back and forth between the perspectives of the two enemies, Juan Venturia and Mr. Harris, and in "Yo Ho and Two Bottles of Rum" Faulkner editorializes about the "scum" on the ship before concentrating on the problem caused by Mr. Ayers.

Some of the examples of narrative strategy I have cited are very clumsy, and it would be easy to dismiss them as abortive fumblings of no great consequence. Yet I think it is possible to discern a kind of pattern here that prefigures Faulkner's more mature use of an essentially omniscient point of view in some of his best stories. In most of these early works the focus is *primarily* on one consciousness, that of the protagonist. What we have is largely a limited third-person point of view. In several of the pieces cited— most obviously "The Hill" and "Nympholepsy"—the only consciousness that we enter, aside from the narrator's, is that of the protagonist. When Faulkner shifts away from the point of view of Thompson in "Landing in Luck" to the scene on the field, that scene is presented dramatically, as if it were an episode in a play, through dialogue and description, and not from the perspective of any of the characters. In the panoramic description of Juliet Bunden's background in "Adolescence," the narrator does briefly tell us something of the illusions and sorrows of her mother, but we are so far removed from the mother that we can hardly have entered her consciousness. And after the narrator has set the stage for us in "Yo Ho and Two Bottles of Rum," the point of view is almost exclusively that of Ayers. Thus even in these early works Faulkner seems to be groping toward a sense of the greater immediacy and compression that can be attained by focusing on a single consciousness. Perhaps he was also learning that a limited point of view is a means of dramatizing a concern with the limitations of mind, with solipsism. For the protagonists of these stories and sketches are generally as lonely and involuted as are the more convincingly developed characters in Faulkner's mature works.

In spite of his awkwardness in handling point of view, we can often sense a kind of rationale for what the young author was trying to do. Because he did not yet know how to dramatize the consciousness of an inarticulate protagonist (something he was to learn to do brilliantly a few years later), he felt the need for authorial comment in "The Hill" and "Nympholepsy." If he had confined himself exclusively to the consciousness of Juliet Bunden in "Adolescence," it would have been very difficult to establish the necessary setting for her coming of age. He had essentially the same problem in "Frankie and Johnny" and "Yo Ho and Two Bottles of Rum": the need to fill the reader in as concisely as possible on important background information for these somewhat too ambitious stories. The solutions he devised for these technical problems were hardly satisfactory, but they do reveal at least a commendable awareness of the demands of his craft.

In most of Faulkner's mature short stories, the point of view is limited in one way or another, but in several works in which he had to solve basically the same problems he had confronted in the early fiction, he did not confine himself totally to the mind of one character. I hesitate to apply the word *omniscience* to these stories because it is really too sweeping and too reminiscent of the very different techniques employed by the Victorian novelists. Perhaps I can qualify the word by using, as Norman Friedman does in his cataloging of kinds of points of view, the term *selective omniscience* ("Point of View" 1177–78). But when Friedman employs the term, he uses it in a more precise sense than I intend; he means the third-person limited, i.e., the strict confining of the narrative perspective to the mind of only one of the characters in the story. I use the phrase loosely to suggest that Faulkner had a more sophisticated sense of the value of a limited point of view than did the Victorians, together with an awareness of the greater flexibility that can be attained by not confining oneself totally to the mind of only one character. What I mean can be clarified by briefly considering a few stories in which Faulkner employed "selective omniscience" in the sense in which I am using the term.

He experimented with this kind of point of view in several stories that were largely unsuccessful because of their novelistic tendencies. The central consciousness of *Miss Zilphia Gant* is primarily that of the title character, but in the first few pages of the story we must enter the consciousness of her mother and those of some townspeople to establish the necessary background for the pathos of Zilphia's life. In this respect, the story is similar to "Adolescence" and "Frankie and Johnny." However, there is nothing in those earlier stories like the final section of *Miss Zilphia Gant*, where Faulkner closes off the consciousness of Zilphia and returns to the largely detached and objective perspective of the town, thereby compelling readers to draw their own conclusions about the ironies of her pathetic existence. In "Lizards in Jamshyd's Courtyard," the central consciousness is Suratt's, but it is necessary for an omniscient narrator to give us considerable background information, and several episodes, including the scenes of treasure hunting in the climactic portions, are presented dramatically and objectively, without benefit of an intervening consciousness. The result is a story that generates much power.

On the other hand, Faulkner's handling of point of view could not resolve the problems generated by the diffuse material of "There Was a Queen." The story shifts awkwardly from the mind of the servant Elnora to that of Miss Jenny, then to the dramatic perspective of the climactic scenes in which Narcissa tells the old lady of her affair with the Yankee who has been blackmailing her and Elnora discovers that Miss Jenny has died from the shock. The general effect of the narrative strategy here makes the reader uneasy. It seems halting, uncertain, inconsistent, lacking in focus.

An even clumsier handling of third-person narration can be found in "Dr. Martino," an incoherent story of the triangular relationship between the elderly title character, his protégée, Louise King, and her fiancé, Hubert Jarrod. For two-thirds of "Dr. Martino" we are rigidly confined to the mind of that most unpleasant young man, Hubert. We gradually acquire an ironic sense of the limitations of Jarrod's character, particularly of his insensitivity in his handling of the relationship with Louise. We have every reason to anticipate that the entire story of the triangle will be told from the perspective of Louise's fiancé. But suddenly, without warning, as the work nears its climax in a tense colloquy between Jarrod and Louise's mother, Faulkner clumsily shifts the point of view: "But Jarrod was already moving away. 'You go on to Louise,' he said. 'I'll attend to this.' . . . Mrs. King watched him go on down the path. Then she turned herself and flung the stained tumbler into an oleander bush and went to the hotel, walking fast, and mounted the stairs" (*CS* 579). There follows a scene between Mrs. King and Louise, in which the point of view is purely dramatic. When Hubert returns to tell Mrs. King about his conversation with Martino, Faulkner has closed off Hubert's consciousness, and the scene is, like the preceding one, reported objectively through dialogue and description. But later, when Louise has deserted Martino through the machinations of Mrs. King, and Hubert drives off with Louise, the point of view is again shifted to that of Hubert, who now realizes that he has been shamelessly manipulated by his future mother-in-law. In the final scene, the discovery of the death of Martino by Lily, the proprietor of the hotel, the point of view is again objective. Faulkner puts us at a great distance from everything in that scene, including the consciousness of Lily:

> [The hotel guests] were still sitting forward, hushed, when [Lily] reappeared; they watched her come through the dusk and mount the porch, with on her face also a look of having seen something which she knew to be true but which she was not quite yet ready to believe. Perhaps that was why her voice was quite quiet when she addressed one of the guests by name, calling her "honey":
> "Doctor Martino has just died. Will you telephone to town for me?" (*CS* 585)

This last scene is masterful—the best in the story—in its quiet intensity, its distance and detachment. Here the handling of point of view could hardly be improved. But what of the rest of "Dr. Martino"? Even granting that the material was wrong for Faulkner, surely he could have written a much better work—more ironic, more economical, more tightly paced— if he had confined himself throughout the story, with the exception of the final scene, to the consciousness of Jarrod. In the course of the story Hubert learns everything that the reader needs to know. The shifts in narrative perspective up to that last episode are confusing and unnecessary. However, when Hubert and Louise have left, *their* story is over; we don't need the perspective of the young man any longer. But we do need the irony and distance afforded by the purely objective point of view in the final scene. As we shall see later, such a technique is fairly common in other stories in which Faulkner uses a primarily limited point of view.

Fortunately, in several other pieces of short fiction Faulkner handled selective omniscience far more successfully than in "Dr. Martino." He used this technique with virtually total mastery in two of his best stories: "Red Leaves" and "Dry September." Perhaps the brilliance of his manipulation of point of view in the former piece is as good an indication of what can be done with omniscience as we have in modern American short fiction. Moreover, it seems to demonstrate that there are some stories that can be told in no other way. Considering the scope of the work and the complexity of the ironic contrasts and parallels it develops, the point of view could not have been limited. Obviously, a considerable portion of the story of the ritualistic chase has to be told from the perspective of the black slave in order to emphasize his terror and anguish. On the other hand, the information we must have about the Indians' acquisition of slaves and about Doom, Issetibbeha, and Moketubbe can be supplied only by an omniscient narrator. But if we are to work as hard as Faulkner expected his readers to do, if we are to appreciate the multiple ironies and the black comedy of the narrative, we sometimes need distance—and that can best be achieved through the use of a dramatic point of view, which is indeed employed in the scenes that begin and end the story.

In the initial scene, involving that marvelously droll dialogue between the two Indians, Three Basket and Louis Berry, we are introduced to a set of circumstances rather unlike anything in our experience. We are probably puzzled, disoriented, confused for a few pages. And the narrator does not help us much. He reports the dialogue, tells us the name of Three Basket, and describes the two men and the setting. But everything is seen from the outside; the minds of the characters are blocked off from us. Nevertheless, we gradually acquire some sense of what is occurring. We learn that the Indians possess slaves and that they are trying to find one of them who has escaped. We also deduce that they have a new leader, Moketubbe, who has attained power under decidedly dubious circumstances involving, of all things, a pair of red shoes. The first section of the story ends with a wonderfully suggestive piece of Hemingwayesque dialogue:

". . . And then Issetibbeha became dead, who was not old, and the shoes are Moketubbe's, since he is the Man now. What do you think of that?"

"I don't think about it," Basket said. "Do you?"

"No," the second said.

"Good," Basket said. "You are wise." (*CS* 317)

In the second section, there is an elaborate, largely panoramic flashback that generally clarifies the mysteries of the first part by filling us in on the recent history of the Indian leadership, the story of how the tribe acquired the slaves, and finally the conflict over the shoes and the death of Issetibbeha. Here for the first time the narrator enters the consciousness of one of the characters—but only in a highly qualified, partial sense—as he describes from the perspective of Issetibbeha the birth and early years of his son. We are told, for example, that "He [Isetibbeha] laughed at Moketubbe and the shoes for several years, because Moketubbe did not give up trying to put them on until he was sixteen. Then he quit. Or Issetibbeha *thought* he had" (*CS* 321; emphasis mine). Or again: "Isetibbeha looked at him. He could never tell if Moketubbe saw anything, looked at anything" (*CS* 321). Somewhat earlier, on the same page, we have a characteristically Faulknerian speculation on the part of the presumably omniscient narrator as he describes Issetibbeha's first view of the woman who was to become Moketubbe's mother: "He was on his way to the creek to fish that day, but he didn't go any farther; *perhaps* while he stood there watching the unaware girl he may have remembered his own mother, the city woman, the fugitive with her fans and laces and her Negro blood, and all the tawdry shabbiness of that sorry affair" (*CS* 321; emphasis mine). A little later we are told that Issetibbeha "looked at his son, then his gaze went blank in turn, unseeing, and he mused for an instant. *You could not tell what he was thinking,* save that he said half aloud: "Yao. But Doom's uncle had no shoes with red heels" (*CS* 322; emphasis mine).

Faulkner reminds us in these passages, as he does through this kind of speculation in many of his works, that storytelling should reflect the limitations of the human consciousness, even when the narrative perspective is not limited to a single mind. The entire passage recounting the story of Issetibbeha's relationship with his son is a fine example of an extraordinarily subtle use of point of view. We are allowed to enter the mind of Issetibbeha just enough to enhance our sense of the peculiar combination of alarm, helplessness, and stoicism in his attitude toward Moketubbe, but not enough to militate against the black comedy of the episode or to destroy the great sense of distance between these characters and the reader.

In the third section of the story we return to the dramatic point of view and to the present (except for a brief anecdote about Issetibbeha's bed) as

Three Basket and Louis Berry go to the house of "the Man" to report that the slave is missing and that Moketubbe must lead the chase. By the time this section ends, we see that Faulkner has completed his basic portrait of this bizarre, cruel, effete culture and its degenerate leader. Because of the detachment he has created in us, the story seems to be a kind of dark, wry comedy. But suddenly in the fourth section when the point of view becomes that of the runaway slave, the distance is collapsed, and we experience at first hand the full horror of the situation as the black (who is never named) runs for his life, knowing full well that he is doomed. We are with the slave all the time, *inside* him, identifying intensely with him until at the end of the section, when the moccasin strikes him and he hails the beast, "Olé Grandfather" (*CS* 335), we acknowledge with him our kinship with all of life, our sense of mortality, and our fierce desire to *live*.[3]

At this point Faulkner closes off the consciousness of the slave, and we never return to it directly. Again distance is established through a largely dramatic point of view, our perspective switches back to the black's pursuers, and the story moves quickly in the final two sections toward its grim conclusion. But because of these changes in narrative distance, these manipulations of point of view, and particularly our identification with the slave in the fourth section, our attitude toward the story and the world portrayed in it is now extraordinarily complex. We can say of "Red Leaves," as we can of much of the greatest literature, that it is at the same time detached and engaged, tragic and comic, grim and funny, remotely sardonic and intensely moving.

Faulkner's handling of omniscience in "Dry September" is somewhat different and certainly less complex than it is in "Red Leaves." Some might argue that the point of view in this story of lynching is basically dramatic, not omniscient. Here there is no protracted passage, like the fourth section of "Red Leaves," reflected through the mind of a character. However, there are things in "Dry September" that can only be told by briefly opening up the consciousness of one of the characters: that of Miss Minnie Cooper. In the second section, in the description of Minnie's loss of social status, we learn that: "She was the last to realize that she was losing ground. . . . One evening at a party she heard a boy and two girls, all schoolmates, talking. She never accepted another invitation" (*CS* 174). In the fourth section, in the episode after the lynching, when her friends have taken her to a movie, "Her lips began to tingle. In the dark, when the picture began, it would be all right; she could hold back the laughing so it would not waste away so fast and so soon" (*CS* 181). But even Minnie is seen largely from the outside—as are all the other characters and events in "Dry September." In the first and third sections we are always *with* the barber, and everything that he sees, we see. But we never get inside his mind. And the same thing applies to McLendon in the brief concluding section of the story. For Faulkner would have achieved nothing, would have indeed vitiated the power of the story by disclosing the thoughts of these characters. All that we need to know is revealed by what they say and do. To have entered their minds would have pushed this work, which is, in its present state, almost too intense, over the edge into melodrama.

"Dry September" reveals about as well as any of Faulkner's short stories what can be achieved by letting dialogue and objective description carry the burden of the narrative. This kind of technique is right for a work of a relatively limited temporal and spatial scope. But it can cause real problems for a narrative of greater range. In "Victory," the story of the Scotsman whose life is ruined because of his experiences in World War I, the point of view is again largely dramatic. Our view of Gray is almost totally external. Occasionally we have very brief insights into his perceptions—"in the corpse glare Gray sees the sergeant-major methodically tossing grenades into the next traverse" (*CS* 445)—or his thoughts—"He was already planning to ask for leave, when one day the manager broached the subject himself" (*CS* 456). But such passages are exceptions; almost everything we learn about Gray is derived from what he says and does and from the views others have of him. However, in a work of such range, which is, in effect, a kind of biography of the protagonist, covering many years of his life and taking place in many different settings, such a device becomes tiresome. The distance Faulkner establishes between Gray and the reader is too great. Hence we find it difficult to care about him, to sympathize with him; to many he will seem stupid and repellent. Moreover, because of the objective point of view, because we see Gray largely from the outside, we have trouble understanding his motivations. We can understand that his assignment to a penal battalion because he has failed to shave would embitter him, but that punishment does not adequately explain Gray's murder of the sergeant-major or his subsequent courage in battle. We cannot bridge the gap between the naive innocent whom we see portrayed in the early flashbacks and the dour, sterile, empty shell of a man at the end. Here the dramatic point of view seems too *pure;* in spite of the length of the story, we don't really know enough about the character.

These experiments with what I have called "selective omniscience" (which sometimes become almost totally dramatic point of view, as in "Dry September" and "Victory") were largely confined to Faulkner's early career: to his first two periods. In spite of his success with stories like "Red

Leaves" and "Dry September," he seemed more comfortable after the early
thirties with points of view more strictly limited to single consciousnesses.
But there were a few exceptions. The point of view in the wonderfully
funny "Mule in the Yard," for example, is largely dramatic, but the background information we are afforded and the comic imagery used to describe
the attempt to recapture the mule suggest a kind of omniscient narrator.
However, the most interesting handling of narrative strategy in Faulkner's
relatively late short fiction occurs in "Barn Burning," perhaps the last of his
truly great short stories.

Here the point of view is largely limited to the consciousness of Sarty
Snopes, but in spite of his sensitivity and his intuitive sense of right and
wrong, the little boy is far too young to understand his father and the
complexities of the moral choice he must make. To enhance the pathos of
his situation and the drama of Sarty's initiation into life, Faulkner felt the
need for the occasional intrusion of an authorial voice giving the reader
insights far beyond the capabilities of the youthful protagonist. A passage,
for example, about the fires Abner Snopes builds affords us a sense of the
rationale for the man's actions, of his strangely perverse integrity, which
could not be supplied to us by the consciousness of his son:

> The nights were still cool and they had a fire against it, of a rail lifted from a
> nearby fence and cut into lengths—a small fire, neat, niggard almost, a shrewd
> fire; such fires were his father's habit and custom always, even in freezing
> weather. Older, the boy might have remarked this and wondered why not a big
> one; why should not a man who had not only seen the waste and extravagance
> of war, but who had in his blood an inherent voracious prodigality with material
> not his own, have burned everything in sight? Then he might have gone a step
> farther and thought that that was the reason: that niggard blaze was the living
> fruit of nights passed during those four years in the woods hiding from all men,
> blue or gray, with his strings of horses (captured horses, he called them). And
> older still, he might have divined the true reason: that the element of fire spoke
> to some deep mainspring of his father's being, as the element of steel or of pow-
> der spoke to other men, as the one weapon for the preservation of integrity, else
> breath were not worth the breathing, and hence to be regarded with respect and
> used with discretion. (*CS* 7–8)

Again, near the end of the story, after Sarty has betrayed his father, there
is another brief shift away from the consciousness of the protagonist:

> "He was brave!" he cried suddenly, aloud but not loud, no more than a whisper:
> "He was! He was in the war! He was in Colonel Sartoris' cav'ry!" not knowing
> that his father had gone to that war a private in the fine old European sense,
> wearing no uniform, admitting the authority of and giving fidelity to no man

or army or flag, going to war as Malbrouck himself did: for booty—it meant nothing and less than nothing to him if it were enemy booty or his own. (*CS* 24–25)[4]

"Barn Burning" is incomparably richer than it would have been without such additions not only because they supply us with ironies otherwise unavailable to us but also because these manipulations of point of view dramatize *on the level of technique* the thematic matter of the story. The tensions between the awareness of the boy and the information supplied us by the authorial voice undergird and emphasize the conflicts between youth and age, innocence and sophistication, intuition and abstraction, decency and corruption, all of which lie at the core of the work. Some purists might cavil about such manipulations, but they are absolutely right for *this* story.

## The Third-Person Limited

Faulkner's handling of the point of view more strictly confined to the consciousness of one character—the third-person limited—is not as interesting as his management of selective omniscience.[5] For he generally employs it in his short fiction in relatively conventional ways. While it takes great skill to handle it well, the third-person limited now seems, if anything, somewhat safer and easier than other techniques—perhaps because so much critical attention has been devoted to it.

As I have noted, any confinement of point of view to a single sensibility, as opposed to omniscience, has the effect of dramatizing the reality of solipsism. I have also noted that the third-person limited has the great advantage over first-person narration of presenting the events of the story *as* they impinge on the consciousness of the viewpoint character directly; hence, they can be experienced more dramatically and intensely by the reader. Another considerable advantage of third-person narration is that the author can employ his own language even though he chooses to focus his story within the sensibility of one character; he can use all the stylistic resources available to him rather than having to confine himself to what would generally be the far more limited resources of the character. Friedman suggests that the third-person limited is the ideal medium if the author's basic purpose is to portray a consciousness in the process of making a discovery or discoveries ("Point of View" 1181–82). For this kind of point of view, with its focus on the immediacy of the reaction of a single sensibility to environmental stimuli, can greatly intensify the drama inherent in the act of discovery.

Faulkner's handling of the third-person limited suggests his awareness of these factors. He is likely to use it in stories in which the themes of alienation or of discovery, or both, are significant. Generally he employs the third person rather than the first *when he is not concerned with dramatizing the process of narration itself* and the ironies and temporal dislocations accompanying that process. In this sense, then, his stories in the third-person limited are often not as complex as those in the first person.

Faulkner used the former technique from almost the beginning of his career, as early as the first version of the callow "Moonlight," but it seems clear that he learned a great deal about its advantages and limitations in the pieces he wrote for the New Orleans *Times-Picayune*. At this time he was particularly interested in dramatizing, in the brief compass he had because of the limitations of newspaper space, the eccentricity and isolation of some of the human types he had encountered in New Orleans and elsewhere. While he used a wide variety of different kinds of points of view for these works, he discovered that if his primary focus was to be on the alienation of a single character, he could achieve some success by confining himself to that character's consciousness and using the third person. He did so in such sketches as "Home," "Chance," "Sunset," and "The Priest." The sense of alienation the protagonists have is clearly primary in all these pieces. But both "Home" and "Sunset" are also significantly concerned with momentous discoveries made by their protagonists. These sketches are fundamentally initiatory, as is another piece in the third-person limited, "The Kid Learns."

In writing these sketches, crude as they are, Faulkner probably learned more than a little about the flexibility of the third-person limited. He learned that by employing it he could present in highly compressed form the pathos of human loneliness. He also discovered that he could achieve a variety of very different effects through manipulation of the authorial voice. He could achieve a kind of rudimentary irony if the language employed, even in the third person, was essentially that of the viewpoint figure, if the distance between the authorial voice and that of the character was relatively slight. In "Chance" the language allows us to enter rather directly into the consciousness of the protagonist: "A copper cent. What in the world could you buy with a copper cent? Why, chewing gum, provided he could find one of those gum vending machines; or he could get weighed for a cent; or he could buy a box of matches for it. So he picked himself up, wiping the mud from his clothes. Alas! he no longer looked as if he might have a roll on him" (*NOS* 72). Only the word *alas* suggests any sort of authorial intrusion; we get a direct look here into the sensibility of the foolish protagonist. The same thing is largely true of the language of "The Kid Learns":

> Competition is everywhere: competition makes the world go round. Not love, as some say. Who would want a woman nobody else wanted? Not me. And not you. And not Johnny. Same way about money. If nobody wanted the stuff, it wouldn't be worth fighting for. But more than this is being good in your own line, whether it is selling aluminum or ladies' underwear or running whiskey, or what. Be good, or die. (*NOS* 86)

In essence, these viewpoint figures tell their own stories, but the limitations of the language suggest, like comparable first-person narration, the moral and intellectual inadequacies of the characters. In this way Faulkner achieves some rather crude ironies.

But such a manipulation of authorial voice is obviously not appropriate if the sensibility of the viewpoint figure is considerably more refined, as it is in the case of the protagonist of "Home." On the other hand, if the sensibility is far more primitive or childlike, as in such a piece as "Sunset," any attempt to approximate the language of the protagonist in the third person would be simply grotesque. Hence, the styles of both stories are much richer than they are in "Chance" or "The Kid Learns." For example, Faulkner dramatizes the sensitivity of Jean-Baptiste in "Home" by means of some rather cloyingly "poetic" language. Hearing the song, "Jean-Baptiste paused, stricken, and about him rose the land he called his; the wooded hills, and valleys, willow and tall chestnuts in the meadows where quiet cattle grazed or stood knee-deep in the water; of young love and nightingales among the chestnut trees after the sun had gone out of heaven and the intimate stars swam in a velvet sky" (*NOS* 33).

This apprentice work is hardly characterized by the subtlety of a Henry James in the handling of point of view! Nevertheless, the principles Faulkner discovered in writing these sketches and other early works served him in good stead in his use of the third-person limited in his mature short fiction. He employed it in a number of stories in which the theme of alienation is basic: in "The Brooch," his portrayal of the pathetic Howard Boyd and his unhappy marriage; in "Elly," the study of a young woman in revolt against the constraints of her family and her small-town environment; and in "The Hound," a tale of murder and its effects on the criminal. The protagonists of these stories cannot adjust to the realities of other human beings, and Faulkner's use of the constraints imposed by the third-person limited dramatizes their solipsism.

In these and other stories it also effectively dramatizes a consciousness in the process of discovery. The conflict between Dal Martin and Gavin Blount in "Dull Tale" eventually compels the latter to kill himself when he recognizes his own corruption, the compromise he has made with his principles by permitting Martin to build the Blount Memorial Art Gallery. In "Beyond" the old judge discovers through his quest in the afterlife that one's existence attains meaning only through the acknowledgment of loss, of death, of the reality of time. "Wash" focuses on the disillusionment of the title character when he discovers the callous insensitivity of the man he has idealized—a disillusionment so intense that it leads him to murder his granddaughter and her child and then to kill himself.

The disparity between the authorial voice and the viewpoint character's language in Faulkner's more mature use of the third-person limited is often even greater than it is in such New Orleans sketches as "Sunset" or "Home." Because of the limitations of Wash's mind or of the youthful protagonist's in the *Post* version of "The Bear" or of Rider's in "Pantaloon in Black," the distance between author and viewpoint character is great indeed. Focused as we are in the latter story on the consciousness of the protagonist, we are always thoroughly aware that it is filtered through the intermediary of a distinctive authorial voice:

> after a while he began to believe he had forgot about breathing since now he could not hear it himself above the steady thunder of the rolling logs; whereupon as soon as he found himself believing he had forgotten it, he knew that he had not, so that, instead of tipping the final log on to the skidway, he stood up and cast his cant hook away as if it were a burnt match, and in the dying reverberation of the last log's rumbling descent he vaulted down between the two slanted tracks of the skid, facing the log which still lay on the truck. (*US* 245)

Here and throughout the story (with the exception of the final scene involving the deputy) we have the best of both worlds: the kind of controlled intensity that derives from limiting the perspective to a single consciousness and the suggestion of a rich range of experience clearly beyond that of the protagonist, through the use of the language, the rhythms, the metaphors of the controlling authorial voice.

On the other hand, there are instances in some of Faulkner's more mature short fiction of a relative degree of similarity between the voice of the author and that of the viewpoint character. Several of the protagonists of stories in the third-person limited are sensitive, intelligent, articulate men: the Judge in "Beyond," Gavin Blount in "Dull Tale," Gavin Stevens in "Hand Upon the Waters" and "Go Down, Moses," old Ike in "Delta Autumn." There is not, therefore, the kind of disparity between their minds and that suggested by the authorial voice as there is in stories like "Sunset" or "Pantaloon in Black." Obviously, however, there is considerable *moral* distance between many of these characters and Faulkner himself. As numerous critics have argued, the Ike of "Delta Autumn" or the Stevens of "Go

Down, Moses" must be viewed ironically and as anything but spokesmen for Faulkner.

Thus far, all the viewpoint characters to whom I have referred in my discussion of the third-person limited have been the protagonists of the stories in which they appear. This is hardly surprising considering what has been said about the effectiveness of this narrative perspective in emphasizing the themes of solipsism and the process of discovery by a single human mind. In stories in which one or both of these purposes are dominant, they can generally be most intensely dramatized by opening up the consciousnesses of the protagonists. However, there are in Faulkner's short fiction at least qualified exceptions to these principles. In "The Tall Men" the investigator is an important agent in the development of the action; he has come with the old deputy to the McCallum farm to arrest Buddy's boys, Anse and Lucius, for failing to register for the draft. But "The Tall Men" is not really his story; the core of the work is the family itself and the values it epitomizes. The investigator remains on the periphery, observing the McCallums and listening to the sententious old marshall. He is a necessary but somewhat obvious narrative *device* for the development of the platitudinous thematic material of the story.

Faulkner uses basically the same technique but more effectively in "Turnabout." In the plot, Bogard, the viewpoint character, is an agent of the greatest importance; it is his offer to take the English boy, Hope, along on a flying mission that initiates the action. But again, as significant a character as Bogard is, his primary function in the story is that of an observer; through his eyes we learn about the courage of Hope and his comrade Ronnie, when he accompanies them on one of *their* missions on a torpedo boat. "Turnabout" is essentially their story, but Bogard reminds us a bit of a Jamesian "reflector," of one of those fine and subtle intelligences like, say, Strether in *The Ambassadors*, through whose perspective we view the emotional, moral, and intellectual drama of one of James's works. "Turnabout" is popular, commercial fiction—infinitely less complex than one of James's exquisitely modulated works—and Bogard hardly has the sensibility of a Strether. But he is sensitive, quiet, controlled, *aware;* his refusal to pass judgment on Hope as readily as his companions do suggests his decency and intelligence. In spite of the limitations of the story, its relative lack of depth, its somewhat sentimental view of the gallantry of young men like Hope and Ronnie, the use of Bogard as the viewpoint character gives the work the kind of solidity that most commercial fiction lacks.

It is interesting to speculate on why Faulkner, in the process of composing several of his stories, changed their points of view from the first person to the third. A rather special case, which I shall discuss later, involves three stories whose points of view were altered largely for the sake of uniformity when they were incorporated into *Go Down, Moses.* "The Big Shot," Faulkner's first attempt to deal with the conflict between Dal Martin and Gavin Blount about Martin's desire to get his daughter into Memphis society, employs a first-person narrator, who is, in turn, told the story by the reporter Don Reeves. But this clumsy device raises questions about how Reeves could have acquired the information he imparts. When Faulkner reworked the material in "Dull Tale," he therefore shifted to the third-person point of view of Blount, and by focusing on his perspective turned the work into a very characteristic study of an obsessed, solipsistic consciousness in the process of discovering some unpleasant truths about itself.

Faulkner also experimented with different points of view in writing the title story of *Knight's Gambit.* The evidence of one of the typescripts suggests that at one time he considered having Chick Mallison tell the story in the first person but that he ultimately settled on the third-person limited.[6] It is curious that he made this change, because three of the other stories in the volume—"Monk," "Tomorrow," and "An Error in Chemistry"—are told in the first person by Chick. Moreover, it would seem, as Friedman notes, that the natural mode for detective fiction, where the piecemeal revelation of a situation is of primary importance, is a first-person witness narrator, like, say, Dr. Watson in the Sherlock Holmes stories ("Point of View" 1181). But in this case Faulkner probably decided to use the third person because of the need for a relatively complex style in developing the elaborate background material about the Harriss family—a style inappropriate for the youthful Chick. Everything that occurs in the novella is reflected through the consciousness of Chick, but the kind of scope and breadth Faulkner wanted for the work could be conveyed only through the use of the authorial voice. However, that voice almost seems to crowd Chick out of the story. One of the many problems of the work is that Chick, even more than the investigator in "The Tall Men," seems to be not so much a character as a device. In his discovery of McCallum's sale of the horse to the Harriss boy, Chick does serve a useful function in the plot, and his dreams about military glory vaguely relate to the thematic concerns about obsession and abstraction that underlie "Knight's Gambit." But generally Chick is simply *there,* serving as a sounding board for his Uncle Gavin, asking the necessary questions and reacting appropriately to what he sees and hears. We do not have here, as in Faulkner's very best use of the third-person limited, the sense of a developing consciousness discovering and grappling with issues of fundamental importance.

It is impossible to categorize in any sort of final, authoritative way Faulkner's use of third-person narration. The point of view employed in a short story that we might call "omniscient" cannot always be easily differentiated from the point of view employed in another that we might somewhat arbitrarily call the "third-person limited"; they tend to shade into one another. The disparity in "Knight's Gambit" and in several of Faulkner's other stories between the authorial voice and the sensibility of the viewpoint character produces effects similar to those caused by the selective omniscience of works like "Red Leaves" and "Dry September." Faulkner's flexibility in handling third-person narration is also suggested by his using what are essentially "prologues" or "epilogues" employing another point of view in several stories in which the perspective is basically the third-person limited. The viewpoint character of both "Hand Upon the Waters" and "Go Down, Moses" is Gavin Stevens, but there are introductory scenes in these works—the discovery of the body of Lonnie Grinnup in the former, and in the latter the interview by the census taker of Samuel Worsham Beauchamp before he is executed—which lay the foundations for the plots before the appearance of Stevens. On the other hand, Faulkner shifts away from the viewpoint characters in the final scenes of "Dull Tale," "Golden Land," and "Pantaloon in Black" in order to give us some extremely different perspectives on the protagonists of these pieces and thus bring the stories to appropriately ironic conclusions.

## The First Person

Elsewhere in this study I have stressed Faulkner's pleasure in storytelling, the delight he took in spinning yarns, which was rooted in his Southern upbringing. There is ample evidence that Faulkner drew heavily in his early fiction on the tales he heard as a child and young man, and that he genuinely enjoyed telling stories to children himself. Moreover, in spite of his radical experiments, particularly in his novels, with fragmented, disjunctive narrative, with temporal dislocations, with complex, shifting points of view, he knew, long before he put it into the words of his Nobel Prize speech, that his primary function as an artist was to tell stories about "the human heart in conflict with itself." Faulkner knew that his identity, his very being, whatever gave a measure of stability and meaning to his life, was dependent on the narrative process. Hence he felt obliged not just to tell stories but to dramatize that process itself, to raise some basic questions within his fiction about the complex and problematical nature of *telling*. By its very nature, first-person narration, with its use of an "I" (or sometimes a "we") who is a "teller" within the framework of the work itself, speaking or writing in presumably his or her own voice to an implied audience, calls attention more immediately and directly than does the third person to that process.

It seems clear that the thematic concerns dominating Faulkner's work—solipsism, loneliness, obsessiveness, the failure to love, the dominance of abstractions—relate to and strongly influence his use of first-person narration. For Faulkner knew that stories are a way of reaching out beyond the self to others, of attacking the barriers between the teller and the audience, of relating *my* experience to *your* experience, of suggesting, by means of the coherence and the existential immediacy of a narrative, patterns of meaning and value transcending the limitations of the individual human being and the abstractions by which people mold their lives. Stories are also a way, as John Irwin has so perceptively indicated, of revenging oneself on time (1); they imply that it is not irreversible, that it can be transcended through the creation of another, "superior" time: that of controlled, meaningful narrative. And the ironies and tensions that are implicit in first-person narration can, on the level of technique, underlie and dramatize these concerns. For it is not just the author who is wrestling with these problems; it is also the "I," the narrative voice of the story.

But the use of the first person poses greater problems than do the other narrative modes. It is clearly not as flexible as omniscience because of its confinement to a single consciousness, nor can it achieve the effects of the third-person limited because it cannot, in a very precise sense, employ the voice of the author (although many of Faulkner's more intelligent narrators do, of course, use his rhetoric). Perhaps the most basic problem with which writers must contend when employing this point of view is the extremely complex question of credibility. They must attempt, at least if they are using the conventions of realism, to justify the viewpoint character's knowledge of the events he or she is narrating. They must anticipate the fundamental questions that may be raised at any time by an intelligent reader: "How could this person possibly know this? Where did he or she get this information?" As we shall see, Faulkner sometimes got into trouble in his handling of this problem.

In discussing the ways in which the first person may be employed in a narrative, Friedman develops two categories: the "I" as Witness and the "I" as Protagonist. In the first case, the character is more or less peripherally involved in the action; in the second, the character is the chief agent or one of the chief agents of the plot. Friedman goes on to note that the former mode is most effectively employed when the author's aim is to develop and reveal, little by little, the basic situation, as in a mystery story or, say, *Lord Jim*. On the other hand, the protagonist-narrator's point of view will prove most useful if the intent is to study the growth of a sensibility of some intelligence and refinement, as in *Great Expectations* ("Point of View" 1174–76, 1181). These suggestions are quite useful and can certainly be applied to Faulkner's short fiction, but they must be qualified and augmented in the light of his individual concerns and themes and of his approach to technique.

For one thing, many of Faulkner's protagonists are eccentrics, grotesques. To permit them to tell their own stories would, more often than not, lead to effects that would be hyperbolic, nightmarish, too unrelieved in their intensity. In these cases, Faulkner sensed the need for more distance between his protagonists and the reader—a distance that could be achieved through the use of the third person or of a witness-narrator. Hence only a few of his short stories are narrated by their protagonists. Moreover, while he was fascinated by the archetype of initiation, Faulkner was not as interested as some writers in the developmental process, in the gradual growth of a sensibility. And, of course, it is difficult to treat such a process within the confines of short fiction; the subject virtually requires a novel.[7]

In his necessarily brief analysis, Friedman fails to note that certain ironic effects can be achieved through the use of the "I" as Protagonist. Faulkner did, as we shall see, occasionally attempt such effects through the use of naive or unreliable viewpoint figures who are also protagonists. But he is generally more successful in his short stories when a narrator attempts to understand or at least make some sense out of the central character's motivations by telling us about him or her, and, therefore, in the very act of narration, dramatizing the limitations of the human consciousness. The narrator, Faulkner's surrogate, is struggling, like his creator, with the mystery of human existence by trying to *tell*.

Even in those stories in which the basic narrative mode is the third person, Faulkner will often employ a considerable amount of direct, first-person narration. The point of view of "Thrift," the story of the incredibly frugal Scotsman, MacWyrglinchbeath, during World War I, is selective omniscience, but a considerable portion of the exposition is given to us in the first person by Ffollansbye, the man who first recommended MacWyrglinchbeath for promotion. To cite only one more example, much of the exposition of the far more complex third-person story, "Fox Hunt," is supplied in what an unnamed valet tells a chauffeur in a dialogue extending over about half of the work.

The uses of this device in these stories suggest several problems Faulkner, like many other writers, had with first-person narration. In "Thrift" Ffollansbye tells his auditors that MacWyrglinchbeath, having learned of the advantages of being in the Flying Corps, got out of the infantry by deliberately burning his foot. But is it credible that the canny, taciturn Scotsman would have imparted this information to Ffollansbye? If what the man did to his foot were generally known, he would, without doubt, have been court-martialed. In "Fox Hunt" Faulkner seems more aware of this problem of the sources of information a character has, but he solves it in a rather clumsy fashion. Consider the following exchange between the valet and the chauffeur about Blair's wife's attempts to learn horseback riding:

> "So she goes to Callaghan, riding them practice plugs of his with the children and the chorines that have took up horse riding to get ready to get drafted from the bushes out in Brooklyn or New Jersey to the Drive or Central Park. And her hating a horse like it was a snake ever since one day when she was a kid and gets sick on a merry-go-round."
> "How did you know all this?" the chauffeur said.
> "I was there. We used to stop there now and then in the afternoon to see how she was coming on the horse." (*CS* 596)

A little later, in reference to the woman's visit to her mother to complain about her life with the sadistic Blair, another such exchange occurs:

> "So the gal goes to the old dame (she lives on Park Avenue) and the gal . . ."
> "Was you there too?" the chauffeur said.
> "Cried . . . What? Oh. This was a maid, a little Irish kid named Burke; me and her used to go out now and then. She was the one told me about this fellow, this Yale college boy, this Indian sweetheart." (*CS* 597; ellipses Faulkner's)

Here Faulkner takes great pains to establish the credibility of his character, but he is too obviously doing so. Because the skeletal underpinnings, the mechanisms of his craft are too much in evidence here, these passages seem contrived and artificial.

In "Dull Tale" we have another but quite different manifestation of this kind of problem. The story contains a lengthy scene in which Gavin Blount discusses with a friend, an old woman, Dal Martin's attempts to bribe him. Now the use of the confidant as a means of imparting necessary information to the reader is a perfectly reputable and sometimes essential device in good fiction; Henry James has a great deal to say in his criticism about the particular uses of what he calls a *ficelle*. Blount might very well have such a friend and might feel the need to confide in her about the bribe attempt. However, he does much more than this: he tells her the entire life story of Martin, including the incident of his being turned away at the front door of a mansion by a black servant and being told always to come to the back door. Is it believable that the cold, unscrupulous, and taciturn Martin (who resembles Flem Snopes more than any other character in the Faulkner canon) would have confided such things to Blount? It is almost inconceivable that Blount could have known this much about his antagonist.[8]

A few of Faulkner's stories consist largely or almost entirely of first-person narration but are framed by an authorial voice in the third person. In "Snow" the technique is very clumsily handled; we are shifted suddenly from a scene in the third person in which a child asks her father, "What was Europe like before all the people in it began to hate and fear Germans?" (*US* 665), to a first-person narrative involving a villainous German.[9] But for our purposes the most interesting work in this category is "Pennsylvania Station." The primary reason the story fails is probably the handling of point of view.

Faulkner sets up the frame elaborately by describing Pennsylvania Station during a snowstorm and then focusing on two vagrants, through whose conversation the story of Danny, the older bum's criminal nephew, and his long-suffering mother is developed. It is a tale of ingratitude and duplicity on the part of the boy and of self-sacrifice and incredible naiveté on the part of the mother and the uncle. But Faulkner is so interested in dramatizing the narrative process itself, in establishing the setting for the frame, and in suggesting the gullibility of the narrator in his exchanges with his companion, that the story of Danny himself never comes alive. Faulkner does not achieve an effective balance here between the telling and the told; the former almost swallows the latter. We don't really care about Danny and his mother because we are too far removed from them; they are insufficiently dramatized. As we shall see, this kind of problem recurs in some of Faulkner's other short stories.

Considerably more important and characteristic than the stories we have just been considering are those written entirely in the first person. As early as the New Orleans period, Faulkner experimented with protagonists as narrators: in the effusively "poetic" "The Cobbler" and in "Cheest," the wish-fulfillment story about the young jockey. But, as I have indicated, Faulkner's protagonists rarely tell their own stories, and when they do, it is likely that they will be naive or unreliable narrators. The most obvious examples of such characters are children: the monstrously greedy protagonist of "That Will Be Fine," the courageous little Grier boy in the sentimental "Two Soldiers," and the young companion of Mister Ernest in "Race at Morning."

A rather special case of this kind of point of view is "The Leg." In this piece it is the protagonist-narrator—or, more precisely, his doppelgänger—who perpetrates a series of terrible evils. But because of the strong element of mystery in the story, it is necessary that the narrator hold back from the reader certain essential elements of the plot as long as possible and that his culpability not be fully revealed until the end. We are therefore likely to feel cheated when we have finished the work, as some of Agatha Christie's readers may feel when they discover that the narrator of *The Murder of Roger Acroyd* has committed the crime.

The stories of initiation that Faulkner wrote in the middle and late thirties are—in at least their early versions—sometimes narrated by their protagonists. Such is the case with "The Old People," whose original protagonist suggests Quentin Compson. But when Faulkner incorporated the story into *Go Down, Moses*, he changed the narrative perspective to the third person for the sake of consistency, as he also did with "Was" and "Lion," and changed the protagonist to Ike McCaslin in order to integrate the piece more effectively into a work that he always considered a novel. In doing so he was able to use his own narrative voice, whose rhythms and modulations do so much to enhance the rich texture and archetypal complexities of *Go Down, Moses*.

However, he made no such effort to change the basic point of view of the somewhat earlier stories that in their revised versions were to become *The Unvanquished*. Bayard Sartoris narrates all these stories in their original forms and in the book itself. Friedman's assertion that first-person narration is most appropriate for tracing the growth of a sensitive and intelligent personality certainly applies to *The Unvanquished* when it is considered as a totality. Obviously the Bayard of "An Odor of Verbena" is a thoughtful and mature human being, very different from the child of "Ambuscade." But there is little evidence of the growth *within* the individual stories, particularly in their magazine versions. Indeed, Bayard is not really even the protagonist of the middle stories: "Raid," "The Unvanquished," and "Skirmish at Sartoris." In these pieces Bayard is a somewhat shadowy figure, more of a device than a living human being. Nevertheless, we are dealing here with stories which Faulkner from the beginning very consciously wrote as a series. The fact that they cannot be evaluated as totally autonomous works is a complicating factor in the criticism of their technical aspects. I shall have more to say about such matters in chapter 5 of this study.

There is another closely related problem in the handling of point of view in the magazine versions of these stories: the difficulty of where to place the narrative voice in time. We assume that Bayard Sartoris is telling us about these events at some time after they have occurred, but it is not clear how long after. Except in "An Odor of Verbena," Bayard speaks to us in the voice of the child or adolescent who has just experienced these things; the point of view does not suggest any distance at all between the occurrence of any event and its narration. Now this is a convention we can readily accept because it does give us a relatively direct and immediate sense of the impingement of a series of extraordinary happenings on an immature mind. The styles of these stories, with their use of short, simple sentences and compound sentences, many coordinate conjunctions, and a somewhat elementary vocabulary, are clean and clear and economical, and admirably convey the sensibility of young Bayard. Yet while such a convention is appropriate for these works, we do have a right to expect that it be consistently employed. However, Faulkner does slip up in his handling of narrative voice in "The Unvanquished" (which was to be retitled "Riposte in Tertio" when it was revised for inclusion in the book). Consider the following paragraph, which recounts a visit by the Yankees as a result of Granny's and Ringo's skullduggery in the selling of mules:

> It was just a lieutenant; by this time Ringo and I could tell the different officers' ranks better than we could tell Confederate ranks, because one day we counted up and the only Confederate officers we had ever seen were father and the captain that talked to us with Uncle Buck McCaslin that day in Jefferson before Grant burned it. And this was to be the last time we would see any uniforms at all except as the walking symbols of defeated men's pride and indomitable unregret, but we didn't know that now. (*US* 87)

In this passage the point of view and the language of a child are well maintained until the final sentence, which not only clearly establishes the retrospective nature of the narration but is also obviously the voice of a much older Bayard. Any careful reader should be disturbed by this kind of inconsistency, which is by no means the only such slip in Faulkner's short fiction. (The problem is, as we shall see, far more acute in the revised versions of Bayard's stories in *The Unvanquished*.)

Faulkner's most interesting viewpoint characters are his witness-narrators—to which we might add the category of auditor-narrators, for reasons that will become apparent shortly. The roles of such characters in the stories they tell are widely varied. They range from being most importantly implicated in the action to being totally removed from, or "outside," the narrative they recount. Sometimes they have experienced at first hand what they tell us about; sometimes they have observed at a considerable distance the events they narrate; sometimes they themselves have simply been told about them. A few of these narrators are fully realized human beings in their own right, but others are very shadowy presences. Faulkner is by no means always successful with this kind of narration, but he is able to achieve some memorable effects with it.

As he did with virtually every kind of narrative device, Faulkner experimented in the New Orleans sketches with this kind of point of view. He wrote several pieces for the *Times-Picayune* in which an unnamed narrator, but one who should probably be closely identified with Faulkner himself, has some sort of experience with one of the eccentrics of New Orleans: the alcoholic in "Mirrors of Chartres Street," the race-track tipsters in "Damon and Pythias Unlimited," the young wanderer in "Out of Nazareth," the old couple in "Episode," and the young son of the prostitute in "Peter." It is not altogether clear whether we should even apply the term *fictional* to all these sketches; some of them may be more or less accurate recountings of experiences Faulkner and his friend Spratling had in New Orleans. In any case, all these pieces have a rather characteristic tone: of wonder, bemusement, detachment, and, regrettably, condescension. These characters—even the sweet young innocent of "Out of Nazareth"—seem to be treated by the young Faulkner as *specimens* of some of the more extraordinary vagaries of human nature, who must be examined with tolerance, amusement, and pity.

Faulkner continued for a while to use this kind of approach in some of his more fully developed stories. The narrators of "Black Music" and "A Dangerous Man" rather obviously patronize their protagonists. The case of *Idyll in the Desert* is somewhat more complex. This story, like "Black Music," is developed by means of a conversation between two characters. The "I" of *Idyll in the Desert* listens to Crump, the Mail Rider, with occasional comments suggesting amusement and condescension. However, when Crump gets to the central matter of the work—a tale in which he played a most important role, a story of love, self-sacrifice, and the blackest ingratitude—it becomes clear to the discerning reader that, rather than being a garrulous fool, Crump is a decent, loving, and compassionate human being. Yet, while the "I" seems temporarily caught up in the tale told by Crump, he returns to his joking, patronizing tone at the end. Here Faulkner achieves a rather deft ironic effect.

The point of view of "Hair," the story of the great love of the barber Hawkshaw's life, is a kind of variation on this technique. Hawkshaw seems, until the very end, one of those lonely souls doomed to empty, frustrated, and unfulfilled lives. The traveling man who tells us his story—he reminds us vaguely of Suratt-Ratliff—regards Hawkshaw with the proper degree of wonder and compassion. And the reader who has some acquaintance with the best of Faulkner's short fiction and with the traditions of twentieth-century American literature, with its long line of desperate "little people" destroyed by the sterility of small-town life, will assume that the barber's existence will be as futile and meaningless as those of all these other characters. But, no, Faulkner deceives us; his narrator is nonplussed when he learns from Gavin Stevens (in one of his earliest appearances) that Hawkshaw, after a life of dedicated self-effacement, has won Susan Reed's hand

and left Jefferson. The dénouement of "Hair," I like to think, implies Faulkner's awareness that the conventions of realistic fiction can become as banal as those of sentimental commercial fiction.

"Hair" is, for another reason, considerably more interesting than those other stories with witness-narrators to which I have so far referred. In contrast to the narrators in the sketches and those who establish the frames in "Black Music" and *Idyll in the Desert*, the viewpoint figure here is a real human being, a relatively individualized person, with a job, a family, health problems (like Ratliff in *The Hamlet*), and some very specific views of his own. In "Hair" the narrator is something more than just a device. On the other hand, we are too conscious, I think, that the Bayard Sartoris of, say, "Skirmish at Sartoris" or "My Grandmother Millard," the unnamed narrators of "Divorce in Naples" or "Ad Astra," or Chick Mallison in several of the stories in *Knight's Gambit* function in these works as viewpoint characters and as little else. But while the undifferentiated "we" narrators of "A Rose for Emily" and "Death Drag" have no real substance as human beings either, they do serve significant thematic functions because the very use of "we" emphasizes the contrast between the values of the community and of the outsiders who are the subjects of these stories.

However, some of Faulkner's most fascinating short fiction involves witness- or auditor-narrators who are as important or virtually as important in their stories as are the ostensible protagonists. Such works as "Mistral" and "Snow" are certainly as much about the reactions of the narrator and his companion to the strange events they witness as they are about the events themselves. And just as the two young men try *within* the framework of the narrative to make sense of what they are experiencing, so too does the retrospective "I" narrator make another effort to find some kind of meaning in these events. Such stories have at least three narrative levels: the level of action (in "Mistral," for example, the events involving the priest, his ward, and her lover); the experience, either direct or indirect, of those events by the witness or witnesses; and the attempt, at some unspecified later time, to recount that experience. It is the oscillating relationship between these levels that gives such stories, imperfect as they are, their density and fascination.

That relationship is brilliantly manifested in "That Evening Sun," which employs a witness-narrator in a most striking and unusual way—so unusual that Faulkner never used anything quite like this technique again. Surely "That Evening Sun" is as much the story of Quentin Compson as it is of the terrified black woman, Nancy, who is certain she will be murdered by her vengeful husband, Jesus. Quentin tells his story fifteen years after the events he is recounting, at first in the language of a very literate and intelligent adult:

> Monday is no different from any other weekday in Jefferson now. The streets are paved now, and the telephone and electric companies are cutting down more and more of the shade trees—the water oaks, the maples and locusts and elms—to make room for iron poles bearing clusters of bloated and ghostly and bloodless grapes, and we have a city laundry which makes the rounds on Monday morning, gathering the bundles of clothes into bright-colored, specially-made motor cars: the soiled wearing of a whole week now flees apparitionlike behind alert and irritable electric horns, with a long diminishing noise of rubber and asphalt like tearing silk, and even the Negro women who still take in white people's washing after the old custom, fetch and deliver it in automobiles. (*CS* 289)

But as Quentin moves more deeply into the past, the language is gradually simplified, until, within only a few pages it becomes that of a child (much like that of Benjy in the first section of *The Sound and the Fury*): "Dilsey was still sick in her cabin. Father told Jesus to stay off our place. Dilsey was still sick. It was a long time. We were in the library after supper" (*CS* 292). The narrative voice continues in this vein throughout the work.

Faulkner has been taken to task for this apparently inconsistent handling of language. In a very early article on "That Evening Sun," Evans Harrington argued that Faulkner erred in having Quentin narrate the story fifteen years after it occurred, maintaining that he should have told it very soon after it happened so that Faulkner could have naturally employed the language of a nine-year-old (55). However, Harrington failed to understand that as Quentin gets into his narrative, he is not simply telling a story but *reliving* it; he becomes again the child who, in contrast to the other members of his family, understands at some basic, intuitive level the anguish of Nancy. But this nine-year-old is incapable of articulating the complex emotions that Nancy's plight arouses in him. Therefore the point of view becomes almost purely dramatic; what we have in most of the story is essentially only dialogue and stage directions.

But is the frame really necessary? Why must Quentin begin the story fifteen years later? The earliest version of the material we have, "Never Done No Weeping When You Wanted to Laugh," does not have the frame; Faulkner clearly added it relatively late in the process of composing the story. However, I think he did so for very valid reasons. For the frame only adds to the extraordinary complexity of the finished work of art. The contrast between the Quentin who narrates the story and the Quentin who lives it is one means of enhancing the basic thematic concern of "That

Evening Sun": the conflict between youth and maturity, innocence and corruption. It is also a means of dramatizing the effects of time on perception, as epitomized in two very different Quentins, and thereby indirectly pointing to the epistemological problems that underlie the story, to the barriers between the consciousness of Nancy and those of the people who futilely strive to understand her. And the fact that Quentin is telling us about events that occurred fifteen years ago is another means of emphasizing Faulkner's concern with the storytelling process itself: as a means of reliving the past, revenging oneself on time, trying to come to terms with temporal realities through narration.

The technique of "A Justice" has some interesting parallels with that of "That Evening Sun." Again, Quentin establishes the frame in an introductory section in which he tells us about his Saturday visits as a twelve-year-old to the farm and describes Sam Fathers, the narrator of a marvelously wry, sardonic tale about Indian life and about the strange name he once had. But here there is an interesting reversal of the technique of "That Evening Sun." In the frame at the beginning the language is that of a twelve-year-old:

> Until Grandfather died, we would go out to the farm every Saturday afternoon. We would leave home right after dinner in the surrey, I in front with Roskus, and Grandfather and Caddy and Jason in the back. Grandfather and Roskus would talk, with the horses going fast, because it was the best team in the country. (*CS* 343)

Contrast this with Quentin's narrative voice when we return to the frame after Sam has completed his story of sexual jealousy, murder, and revenge. Quentin tells us that he did not understand what Sam told him at the time and then describes leaving the farm:

> We went on, in that strange, faintly sinister suspension of twilight in which I believed that I could still see Sam Fathers back there, sitting on his wooden block, definite, immobile, and complete, like something looked upon after a long time in a preservative bath in a museum. That was it. I was just twelve then, and I would have to wait until I had passed on and through and beyond the suspension of twilight. Then I knew that I would know. But then Sam Fathers would be dead. (*CS* 360)

Obviously this is not the voice of a twelve-year-old. And, just as obviously, the Quentin who narrates the story now understands the frightening implications of what Sam has told him. The contrasting narrative voices at the beginning and end of the frame symbolically suggest the two very different Quentin Compsons with whom the story is concerned. Even though the voices are in reverse order from those of Quentin in "That Evening Sun," they also imply his initiation into the tensions and passions of the adult world—a world Sam has told him about in his strange tale. Again, in "A Justice," Faulkner's control of point of view greatly enriches the story; here technique and theme, the telling and the told go hand in hand.

In one sense the point of view in "A Justice" is even more complex than that of "That Evening Sun." For Quentin is only told about the events that transpire in the tale of the Indians; he does not experience them directly. And Sam Fathers has, in turn, been told the story by Herman Basket. Because the reader is at several removes from the action of the internal narrative, Faulkner is, in the manner of some of Conrad's works or of *Absalom, Absalom!*, raising some basic questions about the problem of getting back into the past in any kind of authoritative way, about the validity of the narrative process itself.

The "I" of another story, "Uncle Willy," is of even greater importance than Quentin in "That Evening Sun" or in "A Justice." The young man who narrates "Uncle Willy" is perhaps as much the central figure as the title character, the drug-addict druggist. However, Faulkner's management of the narrative voice here is by no means as successful as it is in "That Evening Sun" or "A Justice." The stylistic inconsistency in "Uncle Willy" seems to derive from Faulkner's uncertainty about the placement of that voice in time and cannot be justified, as in the other two stories by its symbolic significance. The narration here is also retrospective; that the "I" is recounting the events in at least his early adulthood is implied by what he has to say about Uncle Willy's alcoholic binges: "and Secretary learned to drive in Memphis pretty quick, too, because they went every Saturday, returning Monday morning with Uncle Willy insensible on the back seat, with his clothes smelling of that smell whose source I was not to discover at first hand for some years yet" (*CS* 236). Yet the language and point of view of "Uncle Willy" are, for the most part, those of the adolescent idealist who admires and loves his older friend:

> But the ice cream tasted all right to us, especially when we came in hot from the ball games. We had a league of three teams in town and Uncle Willy would give the prize, a ball or a bat or a mask, for each game though he would never come to see us play, so after the game both teams and maybe all three would go to the store to watch the winner get the prize. (*CS* 226)

However, in the very next sentence, when the narrator is describing the injections Uncle Willy gives himself, he refers to "the little blue myriad punctures" (*CS* 226) on his arm. *Myriad* is one of Faulkner's favorite words, but it certainly seems out of keeping with the language that has just pre-ceded it and with that of most of the rest of the story. Such inconsistency is disturbing because there is no real rationale for it, as there is in "That Evening Sun" and "A Justice."

Problems of consistency in the management of the narrative voice are fairly common in Faulkner's short fiction. The temptation to use one of his favorite words or to put just a touch of Faulknerian rhetoric into the language of a narrator whom it clearly does not suit was sometimes too great for the writer to overcome. Or, to put it more bluntly, in spite of his commitment to craftsmanship, he was occasionally simply careless.

A really egregious example of carelessness in the handling of point of view is "Centaur in Brass." This story is narrated by a first-person witness who occasionally surfaces but about whom we know nothing. In the first paragraph we are told that: "In our town Flem Snopes now has a monument to himself, a monument of brass, none the less enduring for the fact that, though it is constantly in sight of the whole town and visible from three or four points miles out in the country, only four people, two white men and two Negroes, know that it is his monument, or that it is a monument at all" (*CS* 149).

As Joanne Creighton notes (50), the two white men must be Flem him-self and Harker, the night engineer at the power plant where most of the action takes place. But the narrator has apparently forgotten about him-self! Surely there are *three* white men who know about Flem's theft of the brass, which so disastrously backfires on him. Furthermore, the narrator gives us information concerning things he could not possibly have known about—for example, a scene involving one of the blacks, Tom Tom, and his wife. Clearly, the handling of point of view in "Centaur in Brass" is rather thoroughly botched.

But perhaps the strangest instance of this kind of problem in Faulkner's short fiction is the management of narrative voice in "Artist at Home." Who narrates this story about the triangular relationship involving the writer Roger Howes, his wife, Anne, and the poet who visits them and falls in love with Anne? In the opening pages we assume that the point of view is omniscient, that the voice is simply Faulkner's. Gradually, however, a somewhat sardonic tone, unlike that employed by any omniscient narrator in Faulkner's fiction, makes its appearance, and we have the sense that a person who is somewhat privy to the strange goings-on in the story is tell-ing us about them. After the exposition has been completed and just before the poet decides to embrace Anne, the narrator says: "Now get this. This is where it starts" (*CS* 634). A little later, after the two embrace again, he says:

But that's not it. That can be seen in any movie. This is what it is, what is good.

About this time, coincident with this second clinch, Roger happens to come out from behind this bush. He comes out kind of happen-so; pleasant and quiet from taking a little stroll in the moonlight to settle his supper. They all three stroll back to the house, Roger in the middle. (*CS* 636)

Obviously this is not the voice of Faulkner in any of its many manifestations. We have the sense that we are being told these things orally by a witness-narrator, even though he never identifies himself, never uses the word "I." But how could he possibly have the information he imparts about the intimate scenes involving these three people?

Joseph Reed has suggested an ingenious solution to this problem (41–42). About halfway into the story, Howes goes to his office, puts some paper in his typewriter, and begins to write. He continues to do so until nearly the end, when he completes his manuscript and sends it to a publisher: "And what was it he had been writing? Him, and Anne, and the poet. Word for word, between the waiting spells to find out what to write down next, with a few changes here and there, of course, because live people do not make good copy, the most interesting copy being gossip, since it mostly is not true" (*CS* 644). Reed indicates that what Howes has been writing is the very story we are reading, "Artist at Home," that Faulkner is perpetrating a kind of elaborate joke on us by making the work self-reflexive, an example of "metafiction" long before the term came into vogue.

It is tempting to agree with Reed, for the story would be a technically brilliant tour de force if he were correct. If the point of view were Howes's, the strangely sardonic tone would be appropriate. And clearly Howes would have access to most or all of the information that the narrator reveals. But unfortunately Reed's theory is not completely convincing. For Howes does not write a short story about the relationship but apparently writes a complete book—one that enables him to make enough money to buy his wife a fur coat. Moreover, an examination of an earlier manuscript version of "Artist at Home" reveals that the narrator was originally much less literate, much less grammatical than he is in the final version. He says at one point, for example: "Because it seems like Anne dont get to see this poet a-tall hardly" (13–pp. ms. 5; *WFM 24* 324). This suggests a Ratliff-like character. It is possible that Faulkner revised the language to the relatively sophisticated level of the final version because the idea of making Howes the narrator occurred to him at a late stage in the composition of the story. But why then didn't he change the book Howes was writing to a short story? No, it seems likely that the pleasure Faulkner took in employing the first person, particularly if it suggested oral storytelling, got him into some rather serious trouble in the composition of "Artist at Home."

Fortunately, that pleasure was, on other occasions, manifested in some of Faulkner's more successful and enjoyable short fiction. His management of language in the comic dialect stories that owe so much to the oral traditions with which he grew up is generally quite effective. Such works as "Fool About a Horse," the *Scribner's* version of "Spotted Horses," and "Shingles for the Lord" (in spite of some stylistic inconsistencies in the latter) are not as complex in their narrative perspectives as are many of the stories I have been discussing, but they reveal, at the most obvious level, that exuberant delight in oral storytelling that is so basic an aspect of Faulkner's art. The pleasure these works give us surely derives as much from the telling as from what is told, from the sense they convey of not just the fun in but the joy of storytelling. And what a joy it is to *listen* as Faulkner's narrators spin their yarns:

> Yes, sir. It wasn't Pap that bought one horse from Pat Stamper and then sold two back to him. It was Mammy. Her and Pat jest used Pap to trade through. Because we never left home that morning with Mammy's cream separator money to trade horses with nobody. And I reckon that if Pap had had any notion that he was fated to swap horses with Pat Stamper, they couldn't even have arrested him and taken him to town. (*US* 118)

Nothing conveys as well as this kind of language how acutely Faulkner himself listened.

Perhaps he sometimes listened too well. The only real defects in these dialect stories are of the kind I have already noted in discussing another, very different work: "Pennsylvania Station." Here too Faulkner focuses our attention so much on the narrative process itself that we sometimes find ourselves at a considerable distance from the substance of the story; again we may find that what is told is virtually submerged in the telling. Even the most cursory comparison of the first-person narration of "Spotted Horses," for example, with the omniscient treatment of the same material in *The Hamlet* should surely reveal that the latter is incomparably richer.

Nevertheless, the *Scribner's* version of "Spotted Horses" is a fine work in its own right, as are the other dialect stories to which I have referred. Indeed, the language and syntax of many of the works I have already mentioned in this chapter strongly suggest that they are "told," not "written." Faulkner's ability to transform the speech of his native land into the rhythms of fictional oral narration is an achievement of a very high order.

If this brief survey of Faulkner's handling of point of view in his short fiction has suggested anything, it may simply be the difficulty of making generalizations about this astonishingly varied achievement. But it should also be emphasized that an analysis of this nature is necessarily somewhat artificial. While there is no technical factor of greater importance in the writing of fiction than point of view, it cannot be dissociated from the many other elements of the art of narrative: plotting, characterization, language, and other formal considerations. I know of no short story by Faulkner that is inferior *solely* because of his mismanagement of point of view. On the other hand, his skillful solution of the problem of narrative perspective in his very best works in the genre does greatly enhance their effectiveness but is also indissolubly linked with all those other factors of Faulkner's craft that he managed so brilliantly in these stories. I shall return to this subject in the next chapter.

Faulkner was rarely inclined to take the kinds of risks in the stories that he took in the novels. Superlative as the best of the short fiction is, it is almost never as experimental in terms of point of view as are *The Sound and the Fury*, *As I Lay Dying*, or *Absalom, Absalom!*. Faulkner could, with impunity, daringly violate principles of verisimilitude in the handling of point of view in *As I Lay Dying*, but, because of the limitations of the genre, it was very difficult for him to do so within a piece of short fiction.

Obviously, Faulkner's handling of point of view in his short stories is anything but uniformly successful. But one of the reasons it is uneven is that it is so extraordinarily varied. While his approach to the problem is more cautious than it is in the novels, his treatment of point of view in the short fiction is still far more wide-ranging and daring than it is in the work of his contemporaries. It is hardly surprising, therefore, that Faulkner did sometimes mismanage his narrative strategies. Moreover, while the effectiveness of such stories as "Dr. Martino" or "Centaur in Brass" is certainly vitiated by their points of view, Faulkner's occasional carelessness about such matters as consistency in the handling of narrative voice in other works is rarely a major matter. In this discussion I have not mentioned or passed lightly over the uses of point of view in many of Faulkner's stories because they pose no problems at all, because he made the appropriate technical decisions about the perspectives from which they should be narrated.

In balance, Faulkner's achievement in his handling of point of view in the short fiction, uneven as it is, is impressive. At his best he was able to strike an effective balance between his concern with the matter, the substance of the stories he wanted to tell and his fascination with the nature of storytelling. Particularly in his use of first-person narration, he was able to dramatize the narrative process itself and thereby not only to anticipate the self-reflexive fiction being produced a generation after his death but also to add to the best of his short fiction dimensions of density and complexity virtually unmatched in American literature. But unlike some of those post-modernist writers whose work he was to anticipate, he never conceived of the narrative process as a kind of end in itself divorced from the messy contingencies of life, but as a means of confronting and grappling with the most basic of human issues.

# CHAPTER 4

# *Form*

My intent in this chapter is to focus primarily on the technical problems Faulkner faced in writing his stories, problems peculiar to the genre of short fiction—particularly those of an organizational nature. A short story is, of course, anything but a novel in miniature; the structural considerations with which one must deal when writing a piece of 5,000 words are very different from those confronting the author of a novel of 100,000 words. Faulkner learned about these differences through a long process of trial and error, although he tended to forget some of the lessons he had learned about his craft when his creative energies flagged late in his career. What he had to say about short and long fiction at the University of Virginia in answer to a question about how he began his stories is most interesting:

> Sometimes with a person, sometimes with an anecdote, but the short story is conceived in the same terms that the book is. The first job the craftsman faces is to tell this as quickly and as simply as I can, and if he's good, if he's of the first water, like Chekhov, he can do it every time in two or three thousand words, but if he's not that good, sometimes it takes him eighty thousand words. But they are similar, and he is simply trying to tell something which was true and moving in the shortest time he can, and then if he has sense enough stop. That is, I don't believe the man or the woman sits down and says, Now I'm going to write a short story, or Now I'm going to write a novel. It's an idea that begins with the thought, the image of a character, or with an anecdote, and even in the same breath, almost like lightning, it begins to take a shape that he can see whether it's going to be a short story or a novel. Sometimes, not always. Sometimes he thinks it'll be a short story and finds that he can't. Sometimes it looks like it's to be novel [sic] and then after he works on it, he sees that it's not, that he can tell it in two thousand or five thousand words. No rule to it. (*FU* 48–49)

Much of this is simply common sense. The student of Faulkner's work will probably not quarrel with the general tenor of this statement, with the idea that the genetic impulse for a short story may not be different in kind from that giving rise to a novel. But the student will also know that Faulkner, more often than not, deliberately set out from the beginning to write either a short story or a novel. He will also know that the quality of fiction is not solely dependent on the writer's ability to compress, that Chekhov was doing very different things in his stories from what his great contemporaries in the novel were doing. And he will know that the statement tends to minimize the notably significant differences between the two genres—an awareness of which is certainly revealed in Faulkner's best fiction.

## Learning the Genre

Faulkner did have difficulty ascertaining what material was right for short fiction. The tension in him between the poetic and narrative impulses, which I have argued is so basic to an understanding of his fiction, is manifested in much of his early work. However, as Faulkner discovered that his proper métier was prose fiction and that he could satisfy his impulse toward the static, evocative wholeness of poetry in the resonance and complexity of first-rate narration, this aspect of the problem of genre selection ceased to be of very great importance. But he still had to decide whether the material on which he was working at any given time was appropriate for short fiction or for the novel.

This problem is quite apparent in his apprentice fiction. One of several reasons why the very early "Love" is so laughably inept is that Faulkner has crammed so much into it. The story is much too brief to bear the weight of its complex plot. The subject matter of "Adolescence" was obviously more congenial for Faulkner than the absurd melodrama of "Love," but perhaps the most severe failing of "Adolescence" is the curious sense of disproportion it gives. The core of the piece—Juliet's disillusionment and loss of innocence when her grandmother discovers and misinterprets her innocent relationship with Lee Hollowell—could have been treated with great success within the limited scope of a short story, but the panoramic exposition, with its survey of the history of the Bunden family, seems to prepare the reader for a novel.

Again, perhaps the most basic flaw of *Miss Zilphia Gant*, aside from its febrile, hyperbolic nature, is that it is essentially novelistic. Faulkner is too ambitious here: within about 5,000 words in the final version of the story, we learn about the marriage of Jim and Mrs. Gant, his betrayal of her, and her cold-blooded killing of him; the manner in which she raises Zilphia; her discovery of the girl lying beneath a blanket with a boy; Zilphia's abortive marriage with the housepainter and the death of Mrs. Gant; Zilphia's long, fruitless wait for her husband to return to her, her agonies of sexual frustration, her discovery of the painter's death, and her adoption of his daughter. Clearly there is ample material here for at least a novella.

As Faulkner gradually acquired practical knowledge of the exigencies of magazine publishing through the admission, acceptance, and rejection of stories and through correspondence with editors, it is surprising that he did not acquire a more acute sense of what was feasible for publication in either the mass-circulation or quality periodicals. One wonders how he could have expected to place "Victory," which would have been the length of a novella if it had included the material he eventually excised from it and turned into the separate story, "Crevasse." Even the version of "Victory" printed in *These 13* and *Collected Stories* seems to require a more expansive treatment because the changes that transform Alec from an innocent young Scotsman to first a vicious killer and then to a dour, cold stereotype of the British officer tradition seem insufficiently motivated.

Faulkner's stories of the sadly ineffectual Gavin Blount have a far greater potential than "Victory," but again there is simply too much in all these works for the compass of short fiction. Stylistically, "A Return" is a fine achievement, containing some of the richest prose Faulkner ever wrote, but, like the much earlier "Adolescence," the work lacks balance and proportion. The climactic scene—the dinner at which Lewis Randolph, the old lady whom Blount worships because of her experiences in the Civil War, throws a soup plate at him—is much too slight to bear the weight of the lengthy, leisurely, and detailed exposition.

There are examples of the same kinds of problems in other works of short fiction Faulkner attempted: in the much too long "Mistral," in the ambiguities of the too heavily plotted "Dr. Martino," and in the wildly formless "Portrait of Elmer," with its vulgar and silly ending. But, to give him his due, Faulkner did sometimes recognize that his original choice of genre was incorrect, that material he once thought right for a short story could only be adequately developed in novel form. Thus "Twilight" became *The Sound and the Fury*, "Wild Palms" became *The Wild Palms*, and, most interestingly of all, "Evangeline" was ultimately transformed into *Absalom, Absalom!*. "Evangeline" is a failure as a short story for several reasons: shadowy characterizations, inadequate motivations, and Faulkner's inability to find the right general tone. But obviously the material fascinated him, and his attempts to master it, which gave him more difficulty than any other writing project except the composition of *A Fable*, finally led to the creation of his masterpiece, one of the greatest examples of technical virtuosity in American literature.

We should not exaggerate the problems this tendency to employ essentially novelistic material in short fiction caused Faulkner; it is not apparent in at least the final versions of most of his stories. However, it does suggest that, like so many of his fellow authors and so many critics of fiction, Faulkner did have difficulty understanding what a short story *is,* what the boundaries and confines of the genre should be. On the other hand, while the writing of his novels did not come easily to him, he did reveal from the beginning a fundamental understanding of the genre, a kind of confidence that is not always apparent in the stories.

Perhaps the most important reason for Faulkner's problems with the latter is that he had difficulty understanding that the essence of short fiction is compression, economy, concentration. Now such a principle should be obvious; by definition, a short story must be *short.* But Faulkner did not always know what *makes* a short story short.[1] Hence the use of essentially novelistic material in several of his stories. Moreover, the evidence of the manuscripts and typescripts of several of his shorter works, including some of the more successful, suggests that he labored long to achieve a better sense of the proper confines of the genre, that he cut, condensed, rewrote in order to attain that concentrated unity of effect and the concomitant subtlety and indirection that are almost always characteristic of the very best short fiction.

I have already briefly noted what Faulkner learned about his craft in writing "A Rose for Emily" and "That Evening Sun." I have also touched on some significant differences between the manuscript of "Drouth" and the story that Faulkner was to publish under the title of "Dry September." But it may be helpful here to discuss this latter manuscript somewhat more thoroughly.

Instead of plunging us into the midst of the action, as Faulkner does so brilliantly with the barber shop scene in the final version, the manuscript begins in a rather leisurely and certainly undramatic fashion with background material on Minnie's life, in what was to become the second section of the published story. Then, after we are introduced to Plunkett (later renamed McLendon), Hawkshaw, and the others in the barber shop, Faulkner begins the third section of "Drouth" by describing the town. He tells us that it is a hill town "where an old strong simple economical patriarchate had been violently slain 60 odd years ago" (8–pp. ms. 4; *WFM 9* 264). Then he goes on to tell us that "Life in such places is terrible for women" (4). These passages are quite unnecessary and, of course, much too explicit. They are eliminated from the typescript and the final version.

Of even greater interest are certain changes Faulkner made on the manuscript itself. He had some trouble in the fourth section of the story, after the murder of Will, with the comments of the townspeople and drummers about Will and Minnie. In his description of Minnie's passing the hotel, he originally wrote of "the coatless drummers in chairs along the curb trying to look at her. 'That's the one: see? The one in pink in the middle'" (7; *WFM 9* 270). He then resumed the description of Minnie's walk to the picture show. However, it apparently soon occurred to him that, since "Drouth" was really the story of an entire community, not merely of certain isolated individuals within it, he had to do more with the reactions of the townspeople and the drummers. In the left-hand margin of the page he added:

> "They'll send him away. A long way. Where there dont any trains come back."
> "Who are they?" "I dont know. I dont want to know. Do you want to know?"
> "No. Well it has to be done. Glad it aint me that has to, though."[2] "Yes, it has to be done. We got to keep them in their places. Got to protect our wives and mothers and daughters." "Sure, it's got to be done." (7; *WFM 9* 270)

But, because this exchange is much too obvious, Faulkner crossed it out and added above it the far more subtle and economical passage which appears (with one minor change) in the typescript and the printed version: "What did they do with the nigger? Did they—?" "Sure. He's all right." "All right, is he?" "Sure. He went on a little trip" (19–pp. ts. 17; *WFM 9* 289; *CS* 180–81).

Two more differences between the manuscript and the final version should be briefly noted. In the final paragraph of the fourth section of the manuscript, when Minnie's friends are ministering to her after the disastrous trip to the movie, they refer to "The black brute" (7; *WFM 9* 271)— an unnecessarily explicit allusion that Faulkner wisely cut out of the printed story. Finally, the very last sentence of the manuscript reads: "The dark world and all that dwelt in it lay cursed and stricken beneath the moon-pall and the insane and lidless stars" (8; *WFM 9* 272). This is clearly too intense; the final version is tighter and more controlled because of the elimination of several words and particularly the addition of *seemed:* "The dark world seemed to lie stricken beneath the cold moon and the lidless stars" (*CS* 183).

We have all heard the cliché that the very best fiction seems "inevitable," that it is difficult to imagine it in any other form but the final one. "Dry September" is such a work, but the evidence of the manuscript of "Drouth" suggests how hard Faulkner worked to attain this effect—as he did with all his major achievements. We also find the same efforts to compress and condense when we compare the manuscripts and typescripts of some of his less successful stories with their final versions. In composing several of these pieces, Faulkner learned that sometimes economy of effect can be achieved only at the expense of drama, that there are occasions when a writer must "tell" and not "show," in spite of the pronouncements of some critics to the contrary.

To return for a moment to "There Was a Queen," one of the problems in this story, aside from the handling of point of view, is the difficulty Faulkner had with the necessarily rather complex exposition, with the need to give the reader considerable background on the Sartoris family—more information than can be easily accommodated in so short a piece. Faulkner never solved the problem completely, but the exposition is considerably more economical in the printed story than it is in several manuscript and typescript versions because in the former it is presented panoramically, as filtered through the consciousness of the black servant Elnora. In earlier versions it is developed in a long and rather tedious dialogue between Elnora and her son Isom (e.g., 8–pp. ms. 2–5; *WFM 11* 106–9), only a portion of which is retained in the second section of the final version.

Essentially the same principle is apparent in Faulkner's work on other stories. In a manuscript version of "Death Drag," there is a long expository dialogue between Captain Warren and the "tall man" (11–pp. ms. 4–7; *WFM 11* 70–73). In the final version Warren simply *talks about* this conversation in the barber shop after the plane has left, and hence is able to sum up rather quickly what he has learned from the man (*CS* 193–97). Similarly, there are several scenes that are presented directly in an early manuscript version of "Dr. Martino" but in the printed story are either eliminated or reported in conversation (14–pp. ms.; *WFM 11* 1–14). Again Faulkner improves the work by deliberately sacrificing drama for economy, but he is unable to solve the many other problems posed by the material.

I have suggested that one of the reasons for the failure of "Victory" is that it is too novelistic, yet surviving manuscript and typescript versions are even more diffuse. The very gradual expository development in the final version, with its complex use of a double flashback, is far superior to the much too explicit exposition of one of the typescript versions at the Alderman Library, which begins with the following introductory paragraph:

> Alexander Gray's background, like his life, falls into three phases, each of which is summed up in an individual who not only typifies each a generation with all a generation's surface differences from the preceeding or succeeding one, but who being interchangeable one with another, sums up and typifies a manner, a habit of thought and conduct that dates back to the first ship ever built on Clyde. It is necessary to say something of Alexander Gray's background, for without this background there might well have been an Alexander Gray, but this story would not be his. (51–pp. ts. 1; *WFM 9* 3)

This exceedingly clumsy introduction suggests a date for this version that may be as early as 1926.

In working on another piece Faulkner attained greater economy by eliminating an unnecessary frame. In manuscript and typescript versions of "Fool About a Horse," there is a narrator (probably Quentin Compson) who sets the stage and introduces us to the storyteller Suratt (10–pp. ms., *WFM 15* 1: 135–44; 21–pp. ts., *WFM 15* 1: 145–65; 33–pp. carbon ts., *WFM 15* 1: 166–98). The frame also includes the narrator's grandfather, Doc Peabody, and the servant Roskus. This setting is very elaborately developed and also includes, among other things, several descriptions of Suratt and his background and of the enormously fat Peabody. Suratt does not begin the story itself until page 5 of the thirty-three-page carbon typescript, but Faulkner interrupts the story of the horse trading on two occasions by bringing us back to the frame. All of this achieves virtually nothing and is irritating and distracting. We don't need to know the setting in which this wonderful tall tale is told; here the story itself should be all. In other works, of course, Faulkner does employ frames, and sometimes he achieves stunning effects with them, but only when they contribute in some meaningful way to the ironies and tensions of the stories for which they are established.

The works with which I have been concerned here in discussing Faulkner's efforts to achieve economy have generally been relatively early. We do not, of course, have all the manuscripts and typescripts of the stories that were composed later, but an examination of what we do have suggests that Faulkner probably made fewer false starts and that he found it easier to achieve the appropriate concentration and compression as he gained confidence in his handling of the medium. But not always. A typescript version of "Hand Upon the Waters," written in 1939, is much longer, much more verbose than the relatively tight story in *Knight's Gambit* (30–pp. ts.; *WFM 18* 4–33). A typescript version of "Shingles for the Lord" (1942) contains an unnecessary conversation between Pap and Maw, deleted from the final version probably because it puts too much emphasis on the rather unimportant character of the mother (21–pp. carbon ts. 14–15; *WFM 24* 519, 521). Faulkner did sometimes forget the lessons he learned about economy in his early creative struggles. He always had a tendency toward verbosity, which he found difficult to curb, particularly in the very late fiction. How much better a story "My Grandmother Millard" would be if Faulkner had cut it by at least one third!

## Handling Time

Writing good short fiction requires, of course, more than an understanding of the limitations of the medium and of the importance of economy. Faulkner also had to learn how to achieve coherence. What he discovered about the management of point of view helped him solve some very pressing formal problems, but the selection of the appropriate narrative voice hardly guarantees the success of a piece of fiction. Faulkner also had to acquire a sense of how to plot effectively and of how to achieve structural harmony and balance.

It will be necessary, before continuing this discussion, to make some simple definitions. When I use the term *fabula,* I mean the raw materials of any given piece of fiction, the basic narrative, the actions of the story in strict chronological order.[3] By *plot* I mean the selection and ordering of the events of the *fabula* in order to emphasize the causal relationships among them. But I want to stress, in particular, the credibility of the writer's handling of character motivation. *Structure* in this context refers to the organization of the materials of the story in terms of their sequential ordering—their placement in time, the use of temporal dislocation, flashbacks, narration of a portion of the action by a character within the story, etc.—and the relative amount of emphasis given the events of the *fabula* through the use of fully dramatized scenes (the scenic method) or of summary (the panoramic method). The *fabula* of "Red Leaves," for example, begins with the background material about Doom, continues with the story of Issetibbeha and his apparent murder by Moketubbe, and concludes with the events of the present time of the story: the flight, pursuit, and capture of the body servant. The plot is set in motion by the events generated by the death of Issetibbeha and the community tradition necessitating the ritual murder of his body servant. It is carried along by the slave's consequent attempt to resist execution and is resolved by his capture. Structurally, the story begins *in medias res* with the scene involving Three Basket and Louis Berry. This is followed by the elaborate "historical" flashback, partly scenic and partly panoramic. The next section, which is almost entirely scenic, ends with the decision that Moketubbe shall lead the hunt for the slave. In the fourth section, we move back in time to the slave's perception of Issetibbeha's death, even further back to a brief panoramic treatment of his background, and then into the chase itself. The final two sections detail in a series of vivid scenes the pursuit, capture, and imminent execution of the black.

It should be obvious to anyone with even a superficial acquaintance with Faulkner's work that some memorable *fabulae* underlie his fiction. Because of his delight in storytelling and because he had perhaps the most vivid imagination of any of the major writers of our century, the core materials of Faulkner's stories, their basic narrative elements, are often totally engrossing. The *fabulae* of all the Indian stories—"Red Leaves," "A Justice," "A Courtship," even "Lo!"—are particularly impressive, especially if we bear in mind that there is virtually no historical basis for the situations Faulkner created; he made them up out of whole cloth. Almost as memorable, although not as originally conceived, are the *fabulae* of those tales developed from the traditions of Southwestern humor: "Spotted Horses," "Fool About a Horse," "Lizards in Jamshyd's Courtyard," "Shingles for the Lord." To these lists we can add a number of other works that fascinate us because of the originality of the fundamental narrative situation: "Mountain Victory," "Turnabout," "Was," some of the Bayard-Ringo stories, etc. It can even be argued that the *fabulae* underlying some of Faulkner's less successful works of short fiction—"My Grandmother Millard," *Notes on a Horsethief*, "A Name for the City"—are marvelous tales, even though he was unable to bring them to life because of the diminution of his narrative drive late in his career. Of course, Faulkner wrote many works of short fiction whose *fabulae* are less complex, less inherently interesting, and hence these stories are more dependent for their effects on structure, motivation, and other elements of fictional craft. But one cannot overemphasize the importance of the impelling narrative ideas that are the generating force in much of Faulkner's best work. The genetic power of those ideas often gave him an invaluable head start.

Still, it was only a head start. In any *fabula,* in any narrative idea, there is already implicit a kind of rudimentary form, if only the sequential order of a progression of events in time. But, like every master of fiction, Faulkner learned very early that such a form was not sufficient, that he could not simply let a story tell itself. He learned not only that he had to solve the problem of point of view, that he had to find a medium, a voice, a perspective through which to filter the basic narrative, but also that he had to manipulate the element of time in the *fabula* in order to create a genuinely coherent work of fiction. He had to find the proper proportion for each story between the scenic and the panoramic, and he had to find the best temporal sequence for the arrangement of the events of the *fabula.* It is in this latter aspect of what I have defined as *structure*—the handling of chronology, particularly the employment of temporal dislocation—that Faulkner made one of his most original contributions not only to the novel but also to the short story.

In a very simple work of fiction there may be little distinction between the chronology of the *fabula* and of the finished work. There is virtually none in some of the more simply constructed of the New Orleans sketches: "Jealousy," "Chance," or "The Kid Learns." Nor is there a great deal in more mature stories like "Artist at Home," "Turnabout," "Two Soldiers,"

"Shingles for the Lord," or "Mr. Acarius." However, it is very difficult to write a story whose chronology is precisely the same as its *fabula*. For a work of fiction cannot begin *in vacuo*. The characters and situations with which a writer deals cannot spring full-blown out of nowhere; they obviously have antecedents, backgrounds that must be at least suggested but that are, in the vast majority of cases, rather explicitly developed in the course of a work. However, in contrast to the often very complex handling of time in the longer fictional modes, the ordering of chronology in short fiction is likely to be relatively straightforward. But in Faulkner's stories, like his novels, the presence of time and the reality of its effects are often dramatized by means of the manipulation of chronology. Faulkner's experiments with time in his short fiction, as with point of view, are never as radical as they are in the great novels simply because he does not have the *room* for this kind of maneuvering in the stories. Nevertheless, he does achieve some memorable and original effects in them.

I have already touched on some of these effects in my analysis of point of view, most obviously the two dimensions of time in first-person narration, those of the telling and the told, which are perhaps most brilliantly dramatized in "That Evening Sun." My brief discussions of "Red Leaves" and of "Dry September" also point toward one of the most characteristic of the structural patterns that may be found in Faulkner's short stories. Both works begin *in medias res* with a climactically disruptive situation,[4] brought on by some kind of obsessive commitment, some kind of idée fixe: in the case of "Red Leaves," the Indians' commitment to the ritual murder; in the case of "Dry September," Minnie's sexual pathology and the racism of the community. Faulkner then moves back into the past to develop the backgrounds of the situations and finally focuses on the effects of the crises upon the lives of the protagonists. Because of the limitations of space and the consequent need for compression, Faulkner is far more likely to begin his short stories than his novels with such conditions of extreme disequilibrium. In this manner, by beginning rather late in the *fabula* at a moment of maximum tension, Faulkner is able, at his best, to achieve a powerfully concentrated intensity and to dramatize the role of time in the lives of his characters.

This kind of structural pattern can be found in stories produced throughout Faulkner's career. It is present in embryonic form in some of the New Orleans sketches: in the crises confronting the protagonists of "Home" and "Jealousy." It is apparent not only in such mature stories as "Red Leaves" and "Dry September" but also in "The Brooch," which begins with the phone call that will destroy Howard Boyd's life; and in "Elly," the opening pages of which are concerned with the desperation of the title character after her attempt to trap the ruthless Paul de Montigny into marrying her has failed. The comic crisis in "Mule in the Yard" is precipitated in the first paragraph by old Het's "Miss Mannie! Mule in de yard!" (*CS* 249). "Pantaloon in Black" begins with the burial of Rider's wife, which will lead all too soon to his lynching; "Hand Upon the Waters" with the discovery of the body of Lonnie Grinnup; "An Odor of Verbena" with Bayard's discovery that his father has been killed. All these stories begin at a focal point, a moment of intense crisis, with an *effect,* the causes of which Faulkner traces by moving back in time into the earlier stages of the *fabula*—sometimes quite briefly through panoramic exposition, sometimes more elaborately (in the cases of "Elly" and "The Brooch," for example) through detailed flashbacks.

Other stories begin at virtually the ends of their *fabulae:* "Sunset" with the newspaper report of the black's death; "A Rose for Emily" with Miss Emily's death; "Lizards in Jamshyd's Courtyard" with Armstid's digging for the "buried treasure"; "Tomorrow" with the hung jury that causes Gavin Stevens to inquire into the pathetic life of Jackson Fentry; "Honor" with Monaghan's quitting his job. Present time is at a minimum in these works, which are developed largely by means of elaborate flashbacks. Still other works—"Mountain Victory," "Death Drag," "Divorce in Naples," "Dull Tale"—begin more conventionally with scenes generating or suggesting the basic tensions of the plots but also including a considerable amount of panoramic background information.

In none of Faulkner's short stories is time handled in a more complex way than in "A Rose for Emily," as the numerous attempts by scholars to unscramble its *fabula* by means of elaborate chronologies attest. After the brief description of the funeral and of the house in the opening paragraphs, there is an allusion to the remission of Miss Emily's taxes in 1894, followed by a scene occurring many years later near the end of Emily's life, the visitation of the deputation about the taxes. This episode establishes the basic motivating force in the woman and the central theme of the work: the refusal to acknowledge the reality of time. There follows an episode that occurred thirty years before the deputation: the problem of the smell caused by the rotting body of Homer Barron. But after this the narrator carries us even farther back into the *fabula* to give us the necessary information about Emily's family, her relationship with her father, and her refusal for three days to acknowledge his death. By these means Faulkner stresses her alienation from the community, suggests that an Electra complex underlies her motivations, and emphasizes her inability to deal with change. From this point on, the story follows a roughly chronological order, dealing first with the affair with Barron, the purchase of the poison, and his disappearance, and then rapidly covering the remaining forty or so years of Emily's life—but in the process carefully preparing the reader for the revelation in the final paragraph. When we reach the fifth and final section of the story, we are back where we began: with Emily's death and her funeral. Shortly thereafter we are introduced to that room upstairs, and the story ends.

By employing this circuitous and oblique approach to the *fabula*, Faulkner *implicates* careful readers more fully than he could possibly do by using a more straightforward chronology. This kind of narrative manipulation of time calls attention *to* time, to the encroachment of the past on the present, to the complexity of causative factors, because we can make no real sense out of the story unless we confront these issues. We are involved more actively and intensely in the narrative process because it is up to us to re-create the *fabula*. Faulkner was, of course, to develop these techniques far more radically in the novels—above all else, in *Absalom, Absalom!* In the longer fictional modes he had the space he needed in order to follow through on the structural implications of such narrative strategies. But they are of considerable importance not only in the stories to which I have referred but in a number of others as well, most obviously in the complex manipulation of chronology in somewhat longer works, the published version of "Knight's Gambit" and "Portrait of Elmer."

We need not linger long on that other aspect of time in Faulkner's short fiction to which I have referred—the proportion of scenic to panoramic development—for he handles it in a relatively conventional way. In the criticism of fiction from the time of James to the present, emphasis has quite rightly been placed on the need to achieve drama and immediacy through a high proportion of vividly realized scenes and as little narrative summary as possible. Such criticism has been largely concerned with the novel, but it should be obvious that it applies even more to the short story. The novelist has more ground to cover and more space in which to do it; hence, it is more likely he or she will, of necessity, have to resort to a considerable amount of panoramic development. But because the writer of short fiction must deal, in a brief amount of space, with a generally more confined *fabula*, he or she simply does not have room for the leisurely handling of material. He must attain his effects as rapidly and dramatically as possible through concentrating on scenic development. Even the most cursory examination of the *Collected Stories*, by simply leafing through the volume and noting the passages of dialogue, should give some indication of the fairly heavy proportion of scenic to panoramic material in Faulkner's short fiction. Of course, such an approach is anything but scholarly because it ignores the fact that many vivid scenes contain no dialogue at all. The descriptions of the flight of the slave in "Red Leaves," of the murder of Houston and its aftermath in "The Hound," of the grief of Rider in "Pantaloon in Black" contain a number of such scenes. The ratio of scenic to panoramic development in Faulkner's short fiction is certainly not as high as it is in Hemingway's, but, on the other hand, it is much higher than it is in many of Faulkner's novels, most obviously *Absalom, Absalom!*, *The Hamlet*, and the very late works.

After his early struggles to master the genre, Faulkner was generally quite successful when he was at the height of his powers in striking an effective balance between these two kinds of treatments of time in his short stories. Occasionally—particularly in the Memphis material—the amount of panoramic development makes the movement of some works ponderous and turgid. On the other hand, a story with a preponderance of the panoramic is certainly not necessarily inferior. Because of the quiet, reflective, retrospective nature of "A Rose for Emily" and because its *fabula* covers about half a century, the largely panoramic approach to that story is not only effective but essential. In Faulkner's late short fiction, however, his sense of the pace and drive necessary for successful narration sometimes deserted him almost entirely. Several of these works—the published version of "Knight's Gambit," "Hog Pawn," "By the People"—seem dull and lifeless because of the preponderance of panoramic material, particularly in their early portions. They seem sadly flat and empty, containing almost no evidence of the drama and intensity of the great stories.

## Beginnings and Endings

In what I have so far said about Faulkner's treatment of the formal elements of his short fiction, I have touched on a number of aspects of his handling of beginnings and endings—particularly the former. But it is necessary to focus a bit more intensively on this area because of its obviously great importance in any consideration of what constitutes successful short-story writing. While it goes without saying that beginnings and endings are always important in any form of written discourse, they are of greater significance in the short story than in the novel because compression and singleness of effect are so essential in the former genre. Hence, beginnings and endings are more likely, considering the limitations of the genre, to call attention to themselves and to linger in the memory.[5]

In my discussion thus far of characteristic structural patterns in Faulkner's stories, I have stressed those works which begin *in medias res* and thereby achieve powerfully dramatic effects. However, it is interesting that several of the problematical passages to which I have referred in my analysis of Faulkner's revisions—in the various versions of "Dry September," "There Was a Queen," "Death Drag," and "Victory"—are essentially expository in nature. In spite of Faulkner's sense of what a good story is, it was not easy for him to find the right way into a narrative; it was much easier for him to find the way out. To some degree, I suppose this is true of most writers. Perhaps nothing is more difficult in the process of composition than beginnings—whether for a novel, a short story, a freshman theme, or a critical study of Faulkner's short fiction! In any case, we can sometimes find Faulkner floundering in the opening pages of stories that are otherwise relatively compact. About half of the very slight second version of "Moonlight" is introductory, and about a third of the first two detective stories in *Knight's Gambit*, "Smoke" and "Monk," is exposition. The problem is also strikingly evidenced in the title story of that volume, which is anything but "relatively compact." After the initial scene of that turgid novella, there is an expository flashback covering about thirty pages—a good third of the entire work.

In one sense, Faulkner may have had more difficulty with exposition than some other writers precisely because he had so much material at hand, because he knew so much about his stories *even before he began to write them*. Because he wrote sequential fiction and because so many of his works are anything but discrete though they are related in many complex ways to other works, he had to confront special kinds of difficulties in several stories. He knew that most of the readers of "There Was a Queen" would not have read *Sartoris*, and he was therefore compelled to devote an inordinate amount of space to filling them in on the background of the story. However, if we consider the piece, as we ultimately must, as an autonomous work of art, we realize that the exposition is not only clumsy but also somehow incomplete; the story works for us only if we have read *Sartoris* (or *Flags in the Dust*) and perhaps *Sanctuary*.

The same problem is apparent in such stories as "Lizards in Jamshyd's Courtyard," "Spotted Horses," and "Centaur in Brass," which are concerned with the Snopeses. All these stories are fairly successful, but some of the drama deriving from the immediate situations with which they deal is vitiated by the need to give the reader considerable background information about the rise of the Snopeses in Yoknapatawpha County. The situations in at least the first two stories are far more convincingly and powerfully portrayed when they are incorporated into the trilogy and achieve, because of their new context, a thematic and symbolic resonance that Faulkner could not attain in the individual works.

At his best, however, he was able to solve this problem of beginnings with stunning success: by the simple expedient of reversing the first two sections of what was to become "Dry September"; in the marvelous opening dialogue between the two Indians in "Red Leaves"; in the drama of the first trial scene in "Barn Burning," together with the richly evocative description of Sarty's reaction to the setting; in the tension generated in "Mountain Victory" as the Tennessee family watches through the cabin window the intruders who will disrupt their lives. These works begin scenically and dramatically, with a powerful and telling immediacy, but when it suits his purposes, Faulkner can draw us back and distance us from the action in the beginnings of his stories, as he does with the very quiet initial paragraph of "A Rose for Emily": "When Miss Emily Grierson died, our whole town went to her funeral: the men through a sort of respectful affection for a fallen monument, the women mostly out of curiosity to see the inside of her house, which no one save an old manservant—a combined gardener and cook—had seen in at least ten years" (*CS* 119). The story depends for its effects on the slow, steady accretion of detail, on the pieces gradually but inexorably falling into place, with a kind of peaceful, slow-motion stillness, until the reader is jolted into a full realization of the horror—and the meaning—in the final sentence. Hence the casual, quiet distance of that opening sentence. There is a similar quietness in the initial paragraph of "That Evening Sun." Or, to cite one more example from "A Courtship," where the "pastness" of the story is everything, where dramatic immediacy would be destructive, Faulkner sets up the appropriate distance and establishes the basic tensions of the entire story in a remarkable first sentence: "This is how it was in the old days, when old Issetibbeha was still the Man, and Ikkemotubbe, Issetibbeha's nephew, and David Hogganbeck, the white man who told the steamboat where to walk, courted Herman Basket's sister" (*CS* 361).

Although Faulkner did rather frequently have trouble with beginnings, he rarely had difficulty ending his short stories. Once he had found a way into his material, once the work had started to flow, he had an almost unerring sense of the proper way to conclude it. He achieved a strong sense of closure in several ways. Most obviously, there are the O. Henryesque surprise endings of several of the relatively early works: "Jealousy," "A Rose for Emily," "Hair," and "The Big Shot." Aesthetically more satisfactory are those endings in which Faulkner conveys a sense of circularity, of recurrence by essentially bringing us back to the beginning. He does this occasionally in the New Orleans sketches. The final two sentences of "The Cobbler," for example, "You getta thees shoe today. Si, si" (*NOS* 69), are virtually a reprise of the first two sentences. The myth of the "eternal return" is suggested in the final image of the title character of *Miss Zilphia*

*Gant,* which recalls an earlier image of her mother: "her open coat, stirring in the wind, revealing her sewing apron of black oil cloth, and the straight thin glints of needles in her black bosom and the gossamer random festooning of the thread" (*US* 381). In "A Courtship" after Ikkemotubbe and David Hogganbeck have lost Herman Basket's sister to Log-in-the-Creek, the story gently and nostalgically ends as it began: "That's how it was in the old days" (*CS* 380).

In other stories Faulkner achieves closure by returning to and strongly stressing a controlling symbol: that marvelous image of the verbena on Drusilla's pillow in "An Odor of Verbena" or Ike's melancholy "It was a doe" (*US* 280) in "Delta Autumn." Sometimes a final scene will sum up in encapsulated form the basic tensions of the work: McLendon's return home in "Dry September," Bland's "mopping at his face" and crying for his "poor little wife" (*CS* 429) in "Ad Astra," Armstid's insane digging in "Lizards in Jamshyd's Courtyard," or the slave's fruitless efforts to drink water in "Red Leaves." But some effects Faulkner achieves in his endings—effects that seem as conclusive and powerful as a tonic chord—are virtually impossible to classify. Consider the final argument between the children in "That Evening Sun"; the crouching black, with his eyes "like those of a cornered animal" (*CS* 777), waiting for Vatch to shoot him in "Mountain Victory"; or the lovely final two sentences of "Barn Burning": "He went on down the hill, toward the dark woods within which the liquid silver voices of the birds called unceasing—the rapid and urgent beating of the urgent and quiring heart of the late spring night. He did not look back" (*CS* 25).

Occasionally the endings of Faulkner's stories do leave something to be desired. The concluding banter in that tale of love and self-sacrifice, *Idyll in the Desert,* seems somewhat flat, and nothing in "Artist at Home" adequately prepares us for the final "Because it was Christmas soon, and then spring; and then summer, the long summer, the long days" (*CS* 646). In "Victory" Walkley's final contemptuous reference to Gray—"My God . . . . I think I am going to vomit" (*CS* 464)—seems crude and achieves very little. But such aberrations are relatively rare in Faulkner; his management of closure is almost always effective.

Why? I can find no satisfactory explanation. The years Faulkner devoted to poetry did not apparently teach him much, in any obvious sense, about the necessity for economy in short fiction, but perhaps his largely unsuccessful efforts to achieve wholeness and harmony in his poems taught him something about the vital importance of closure. In his efforts to master metaphor in his poetry (which were to come to fruition only in his best fiction), he may have acquired some sense that there should be an essentially synecdochic relationship between the conclusion of a work of literary art and the entire piece. Perhaps in his poetic experiments he also learned something about the importance of repetition, recurrence, cyclical effects, essentially musical techniques in achieving certain kinds of closure. Perhaps. But it is sufficient to say that Faulkner's ability in this area is most impressive.


## Achieving Coherence

A writer who can handle point of view effectively, who understands the importance of compression in short fiction, who can deal with the complexity entailed in the manipulation of time, and who has solved the problem of getting into and out of his stories has indeed gone a long way toward mastering the formal problems posed by the genre. If he has achieved these goals, all of which are obviously interrelated, he is probably also capable of dealing successfully with the most basic of all aesthetic problems: the achievement of balance, harmony, coherence. Like all first-rate writers, Faulkner attained these ends by a variety of means.

The most obvious of these is the creation of coherent, aesthetically satisfying plots, setting up in any given story a problem involving the tension between opposing elements, intensifying those tensions, and finally resolving them. Because of the pleasure he took in the narrative process itself, Faulkner was more interested in achieving coherence through the relatively conventional devices of plotting than many of his significant contemporaries, who were more consistently concerned about mood, atmosphere, the revelation of character, the creation of epiphanic effects, etc. This interest in basic plot devices is obvious throughout Faulkner's career. While many of the New Orleans sketches are static mood pieces, several contain rudimentary or even fairly complex plots. In "Home" Jean-Baptiste is torn between his desire to make some rather easy money by criminal means and his memories of the golden days of his childhood in his homeland, but the conflict is resolved when he hears the tune played on the musical saw, which reminds him of his early life in France. The narrative line of "Country Mice" is more complex because it is dependent on those comic reversals that owe so much to the traditions of Southwestern humor and that Faulkner employed in so many of his lighter stories.

The most conventionally plotted of Faulkner's works are probably the detective stories. They satisfy the most elementary of our aesthetic expectations—the need for a kind of stasis and order—because the condition of disequilibrium inevitably brought about by the perpetration of a crime is resolved through its solution. Very closely related are such stories as "The Hound" and "Vendée," which are not concerned with the process of detection but with bringing the criminal to justice. All such works owe a great deal to the expectations engendered in us by the archetype of the hunt, embodied in such stories as "Sunset" or "Lion" or "Red Leaves," in which the quarry is run down, or in those stories like the *Saturday Evening Post* version of "The Bear" or "Race at Morning," in which ironic reversals are achieved because those expectations are played on but not satisfied by Faulkner.

He was often able to resolve the tensions in his plots through other relatively conventional means. As in the case of *Mayday*, many of his stories end with the deaths of a protagonist or antagonist; we can find such resolutions in "There Was a Queen," "Red Leaves," "Mountain Victory," and a number of other works. Departures or returns, signaling the end of some kind of effort, attempt, or project, figure prominently in the plotting of "Mistral," "Snow," "Divorce in Naples," "Death Drag," etc. Faulkner even employed the time-honored device of a marriage to resolve conflicts in two of his stories: "Knight's Gambit" and "My Grandmother Millard." The resolution of the latter story is also interesting because it is one of the few cases in his fiction in which a character is actually *cured* of an idée fixe that has set a plot in motion; the wedding of the renamed Lieutenant Philip Backus to Cousin Melisandre neatly resolves the problem caused by the young man's obsession with the overwrought young lady. But this kind of resolution is very rare in Faulkner's work; his obsessed characters almost always remain obsessed.

Faulkner achieved some of his most memorable effects in stories whose plots (as distinct from their *fabulae*) are relatively simple. At issue in both "Barn Burning" and "An Odor of Verbena" is a moral choice. While that choice in both cases involves extremely complex issues, the resolutions of the tensions in these works are solely dependent on the decisions that must be made by the protagonists—on Sarty's decision to betray his father and on Bayard's refusal to continue the blood code of revenge by killing Redmond. Hence there is a kind of cleanness and economy in such plots. On the other hand, Faulkner loved the kind of complexity that we associate with games, strategems, tricks, reversals, puzzles, or surprises, and such elements are of considerable importance in very heavily plotted stories: in such works as "Love," "Was," "Shingles for the Lord," "My Grandmother Millard," and, of course, all the comic swindle stories.

At the opposite end of the spectrum are those stories that are not, in any conventional sense, plotted and that Faulkner therefore attempted to make coherent by other means. In such mood pieces as most of the New Orleans sketches, "Crevasse," "Golden Land," and "Ad Astra," not a great deal happens; here the evocation of atmosphere and the revelation of theme are primary. The extremely vivid imagery of "Crevasse"—visual, tactile, olfactory—conveys an overpowering sense of the reality of death in war. Whatever coherence the largely unsuccessful "Golden Land" has is thematic: at the most obvious level, Faulkner's contempt for Hollywood as a false and meretricious Eden; at a deeper level, the idea that we define ourselves as human beings only through our willingness to acknowledge and confront the harsher realities of life. These are truths that the protagonist, Ira Ewing, has long since forgotten but that his mother understands until, at the very end of the story, she seems to give up her attempts to escape California and says to herself, "I will stay here and live forever" (*CS* 726).

Perhaps the most interesting of these pieces technically is the complex "Ad Astra." Like "Crevasse," like all the pieces in "The Wasteland" section of *Collected Stories*, it is made coherent in part by its evocation of the futility and stupidity of war. But the themes of "Ad Astra," in contrast to virtually all the other stories written during the most productive years of Faulkner's career, are not only implicitly and dramatically developed—in the portrayal of the disillusionment of the soldiers and the brawl started at the bistro because of the presence of the captured German lieutenant— but are also presented discursively and explicitly in the ruminations of the narrator and in the platitudes uttered by the German and the subadar. In this respect, "Ad Astra" looks forward to Faulkner's tendency in the late stories to spell out his themes rather than to permit their implications to emerge from the dramatic context of the narrative.

A far more sophisticated device for making the story cohesive is the use of the leitmotif. The term, which, of course, derives from Wagnerian opera, has been variously defined, but I am employing it here in a relatively narrow sense to mean the kind of technique used by such writers as Tolstoy or Thomas Mann: the deliberate repetition of a word, a phrase, an allusion to a physical mannerism or an article of clothing, etc., with which we associate a character, situation, or idea and which serves to make the work coherent because, whenever it is used, it brings to mind earlier contexts in which the character, situation, or idea appeared.[6] In "Ad Astra" the leitmotifs are largely verbal: Comyn's offers to fight for a shilling, Bland's allusions to his make-believe wife, Monaghan's emphasis on his shanty-Irish origins, and the German's references to Bayreuth. The device is used rather sparingly in "Ad Astra," but it does help to characterize and also to give a degree of coherence to a somewhat flabby work. Faulkner occasionally used the technique elsewhere in his short fiction: in the sky-blue coat of the poet in "Artist at Home," the phrase "tolled away" in "Uncle Willy," the batting eyes of characters in "Gold Is Not Always" and "Was," the bright eyes of

Gavin Stevens in "Tomorrow," and the descriptions of Ratliff as "bland," "affable," "tieless" in "By the People."

Perhaps the most memorable single instance of this device in the short fiction is the imagery of stiffness used in characterizing Abner Snopes in "Barn Burning." In an early description of Ab at the conclusion of the initial trial scene, Faulkner writes: "His [Sarty's] father turned, and he followed the stiff black coat, the wiry figure walking a little stiffly from where a Confederate provost man's musket ball had taken him in the heel on a stolen horse thirty years ago" (*CS* 5). A little later we are told that: "[Sarty] followed the stiff back, the stiff and ruthless limp, up the slope and on to the starlit road where, turning, he could see his father against the stars but without face or depth—a shape black, flat, and bloodless as though cut from tin in the iron folds of the frockcoat which had not been made for him, the voice harsh like tin and without heat like tin" (*CS* 8). Still later, as Abner and Sarty visit the de Spains' mansion for the first time, Faulkner uses the word *stiff* in reference to Abner's back, his foot, and his stance on about half a dozen occasions. At the conclusion of the scene, Faulkner drives home the image implacably with the phrase "planted stiffly on the stiff foot" (*CS* 12). All of this serves to characterize a person who is not only fiercely dedicated to the maintenance of what he considers to be his integrity but is also, as a moral being, profoundly *unnatural* because of his commitment to abstractions, his refusal to bend to or with the rhythms of life. One of the master touches of this extraordinary story occurs in the final paragraph when the leitmotif is applied to Sarty: "He was a little stiff, but walking would cure that too as it would the cold, and soon there would be the sun" (*CS* 25). This suggestion of Sarty's heritage, of his blood ties, carrying with it the implication that there is something in him that must always be loyal to Abner Snopes, is one of the most moving moments in all of Faulkner's work.

One more brilliant instance of this kind of device is the hammerlike repetition of the word *dust,* with its connotations of death and sterility, in portions of "Dry September." This effect has an almost hypnotic power in the final two paragraphs of the third section of the story, which describe the barber after he has jumped out of the car containing the lynch party:

> The impetus hurled him crashing through *dust*-sheathed weeds, into the ditch. *Dust* puffed about him, and in a thin, vicious crackling of sapless stems he lay choking and retching until the second car passed and died away. Then he rose and limped on until he reached the highroad and turned toward town, brushing at his clothes with his hands. The moon was higher, riding high and clear of the *dust* at last, and after a while the town began to glare beneath the *dust*. He went on, limping. Presently he heard cars and the glow of them grew in the

*dust* behind him and he left the road and crouched again in the weeds until they passed. McLendon's car came last now. There were four people in it and Butch was not on the running board.

They went on; the *dust* swallowed them; the glare and the sound died away. The *dust* of them hung for a while, but soon the eternal *dust* absorbed it again. The barber climbed back onto the road and limped on toward town. (*CS* 179–80; emphasis mine)

This is one of many passages in Faulkner that must be read aloud in order to comprehend their full power.

On the other hand, anyone who has read much of Faulkner's work knows that he often carries what some scholars have rather kindly called "incremental repetition" too far. There are many, many instances in the stories of the overuse for no apparent purpose of some of Faulkner's favorite words: *motionless, sibilant, myriad, outrage, terrific, diffident, sourceless, avatar, impotence, effluvium, attenuation, infinitesimal, erect, immolation, indomitable, gaunt, quizzical, bemused, inscrutable, rigid, immobile, apotheosis, moiled, static, endure,* and *ammoniac,* among others. Sometimes, when one senses that Faulkner is not at ease with his material, when he has lost control, when he is floundering, he will begin to employ, with maddening repetitiveness, some of these words. In "Beyond," which is probably one of the weakest stories of his great period, he constantly uses *outrage, impotence, quizzical,* and *bemused.* But even the effectiveness of some of his very best stories can be somewhat vitiated by this device. "Mountain Victory" is marred by the needless and pointless repetition of such words as *quizzical* and *motionless.*

We cannot use the term *leitmotif* to characterize this kind of ineptitude in the handling of language. However, there is an instance in "Beyond" of an apparently conscious attempt by Faulkner to use a leitmotif. The Judge is constantly rolling his own cigarettes, gazing at the finished products, and asking for a match. Perhaps this device was intended to humanize the Judge and to add a realistic little touch to his strange situation in the afterlife. But it hardly helps to characterize the old man, nor does it seem to make the story more coherent. Here we have something that is not analogous to musical form but is like a fussy instance of stage business—a device that achieves little except to irritate the reader.

Many critics use musical terminology in discussing Faulkner's work, as he did himself in some of the things he said about the organization of *Collected Stories* and *The Wild Palms* (*SL* 278; *FB* 2 980). And it is certainly true that such literary masters of our age as Mann, Joyce, Proust, and Eliot consciously used musical techniques. However, I find no concrete evidence that Faulkner did to any great extent. For one thing, there is little in his biography, his fiction, his poetry, or his statements about his work that suggests he knew much about music. Moreover, it can be argued that when we examine works of literature from the standpoints of their "musical" forms, we are simply using a different kind of language to describe what are fundamentally literary techniques—or, at least, techniques common to both arts, deriving from some elemental aesthetic principle. On the other hand, it is certainly true that the forms of fiction have, within the past century, moved closer to those of music; a writer's use of patterns of cyclical repetition, of complex networks of symbols and themes in which the organization of thematic relationships is more important than the temporal, sequential progression of conventional narratives, does at least vaguely suggest the structural principles of music. In such a sense as this I think we are justified in using musical terminology in assessing the techniques of Faulkner's short fiction.

What I have said earlier in this chapter about Faulkner's achievement of closure in such pieces as "The Cobbler," *Miss Zilphia Gant*, and "A Courtship" through the suggestion of circularity and recurrence brings to mind obvious analogies in the forms of music. There is a comparable kind of effect near the beginning and end of "Gold Is Not Always." In the second paragraph of the story,

> [Lucas] went on up the hill and mounted the gnawed steps beside which a bright-coated young mare with a blaze and three stockings stood under a heavy comfortable saddle, and entered the commissary, with its ranked shelves of tinned food and tobacco and patent medicines, its hooks from which hung trace chains and collars and hames, and where, at a roll-top desk beside the front window, his landlord was writing in a ledger. (*US* 226)

In the first paragraph of the third and final section of the story, after he has completely outwitted the gold machine salesman,

> [Lucas] mounted the gnawed steps beside which the bright mare stood beneath the heavy saddle, and entered the commissary, with its ranked shelves of tinned food, the hooks from which hung collars and trace chains and hames and ploughlines, its smell of molasses and cheese and leather and kerosene. Edmonds swiveled around from the roll-top desk. (*US* 236)

Obviously the effect of recurrence that Faulkner achieves in this way could hardly be more deliberate.

There is occasionally a certain symmetry in the organization of Faulkner's stories that reminds us vaguely of musical forms. The patterning of the five sections of "Dry September," with its alternation of passages in which McLendon and then Minnie are the center of attention, suggests a kind of ABABA form. The elaborate parallels in "Turnabout" between the experiences of Hope on the plane and those of Bogard on the torpedo boat suggest a kind of "theme and variations" form. Perhaps one could also apply this term in a rather different sense to the structure of "A Rose for Emily." Floyd C. Watkins has most interestingly pointed out Faulkner's symmetrical use of the motifs of isolation and intrusion in the five sections of the story (46–47). In the first, there is the invasion of the Board of Aldermen. In the second there are two forced intrusions, in which four men use lime on Emily's property to cover up the odor and the townspeople prevail on her to part with the body of her father. In the third part, the middle of the story, Miss Emily's isolation is totally intact. The fourth section, paralleling the second, contains two intrusions: the visit by the Baptist minister in an attempt to mitigate the scandal caused by the affair with Barron and the descent upon Emily of her relatives from Alabama. In the fifth and final section there is the breaking down of the upstairs door after Emily's death and the discovery of the corpse.

But in this case we may be pushing the use of musical terminology too far. For the organizational device that Watkins so cleverly analyzes is obviously an instance of a very basic *literary* technique: the achievement of coherence by means of symbolism. Of course, Faulkner often very deliberately uses symbols and symbolic patterns in his short fiction to attain cohesion. It would be beyond the scope of this study to analyze these attempts in detail. I have already noted some of them in various contexts, and much of the limited amount of criticism that has been devoted to the stories is concerned with symbolism. All that I can do here is to note a few relatively clear-cut examples.

Several of the stories have rather obvious controlling symbols, some of which are suggested by their titles. Clearly the weather plays such a role in several stories. In "Mistral" the wind symbolizes the force of sexual passion; the snow in the story of that name evokes the icy power of lovelessness and hatred; the drouth in "Dry September" brings to mind the archetypal wasteland, the death in life of Jefferson, and, implicitly, therefore, the need for the scapegoat, the killing of whom can restore the land to fertility.[7] The rabbit in "Dr. Martino," the deer in "The Old People," "Delta Autumn," and "Race at Morning," the verbena in "An Odor of Verbena," the leg, the brooch, and hair in the stories bearing those titles: all of these are very consciously and deliberately employed symbols. One thinks also of the rather complex but ultimately much too explicit handling of the related symbols of chess, knights, and horses in "Knight's Gambit" (to which I shall return later). A different kind of technique, one that brings to mind the use of

Christian symbolism in *The Sound and the Fury* and *Light in August*, is the ironic backdrop of the Christmas season in "That Will Be Fine" and the little boy's use of *Jesus* as a curse word.

Some readers will be dubious about being excessively concerned with Faulkner's *intent* in these matters, but it seems obvious that these symbols were quite consciously contrived—some would say *too* consciously contrived. Even Faulkner himself, who in his public pronouncements seemed to be quite suspicious of such interpretations, conceded that his bear was a symbol (*FU* 280). However, when we touch on Freudian symbolism in the short fiction, we are moving into a murky and controversial area. The unreconstructed Freudian would have no difficulty in finding a sexual basis for virtually all the imagery in Faulkner's stories. We need not go quite that far. And because we are largely concerned here with the conscious craftsmanship of Faulkner, we involve ourselves in all kinds of difficulties if we attempt to sort out the deliberate from the unconscious use of sexual symbolism in the stories. But I have already noted in other contexts the feverish sexuality underlying much of the fiction Faulkner produced in the twenties. It seems reasonable to assume that in at least those stories overtly concerned with sexual repression—"Don Giovanni," "Mistral," *Miss Zilphia Gant*—Faulkner was consciously employing Freudian symbolism. In "Don Giovanni" the sexual imagery is all too obvious; we find such phrases as "he ejaculated" (*US* 482) (after the protagonist spills water all over himself), "a swelled head" (483), "turn the trick" (483), and "ravished of quiet" (484), together with female images of darkened windows and streets, and rhythmical activities, such as climbing stairs, typing, dancing, and mastication, which suggest intercourse or masturbation. Nothing could be more overt (or adolescent) than the following exchange between the protagonist and his host:

> "You are kidding me now. But dont you really think this scheme is sound?"
>
> "Air tight. You have thought of everything, haven't you?"
>
> "Certainly. That's the only way to win battles, you know. Napoleon taught us that."
>
> "Napoleon also said something about the heaviest artillery, too," his friend remarked wickedly.
>
> He smiled with complacence. "I am as I am," he murmured. . . .
>
> "Especially when it hasn't been used in some time," his host continued. (*US* 483–84; ellipsis Faulkner's)

Fortunately Faulkner's use of sexual imagery in such mature stories as "A Rose for Emily," "Fox Hunt," "Mountain Victory," and "The Brooch" is far more subtle than this. The latter story has grave deficiencies, but, as Sharon Hult has demonstrated so well, "The Brooch" reveals a most sophisticated awareness of Freudian theory. The situation it depicts, involving the sadly ineffectual Howard Boyd, his wife Amy, and his possessive mother, is a classic oedipal triangle. Howard's inability to dance, the reiteration of the words *impotent* and *impotence* in regard to him in what is only ostensibly their more general sense; his prodding of the fire with a poker (far more prominently featured in early manuscript and typescript versions of the story),[8] his fascination with what Faulkner explicitly calls his "cave-symbol" (*CS* 663) in *Green Mansions*; and his killing himself in the bathroom by sticking the muzzle of his pistol between his teeth after covering his head with Amy's blanket—all these things and a number of other details surely suggest a conscious use of Freudian imagery. But Faulkner would never have admitted to it!

## Weaknesses

I have been dealing here with various *attempts* by Faulkner to achieve coherence in his short fiction. Considering the wide range of quality of the stories used as examples, he was anything but successful in all those attempts. There are obvious technical weaknesses, caused by a variety of factors, not only in several of the works to which I have just referred but in a number of others as well. I have already discussed at length the problems caused by a faulty or uncertain handling of point of view, by clumsy expositions, by the failure to attain an effective balance between the scenic and the panoramic methods. There are other problems as well.

One of the reasons "A Return" fails is that the early material on the lives of Lewis Randolph and her son is not effectively integrated with the story of Gavin Blount. There seems to be no organizing principle at all aside from the character of the protagonist in the strangely inchoate, almost meaningless "A Dangerous Man," and the same thing seems to apply to Faulkner's much more ambitious attempt to cannibalize his abortive novel in "A Portrait of Elmer." "Monk" is not cohesive because we lose sight of the title character too soon. The relationship between the story of Gavin Stevens's love for Melisandre Harriss and the other material in "Knight's Gambit" is not well developed. Moreover, several of the stories, particularly the very late pieces, are badly in need of cutting.

However, I do not believe that such organizational problems as these are the major flaws in Faulkner's handling of the genre. His greatest weakness lies in his treatment of plot: in the sometimes unconvincing motivation of his characters and in his curiously careless handling of detail. A conscientious reading of Faulkner's short stories will raise many questions about these matters.

We can begin by returning once more to "There Was a Queen." The plot of this story turns on the obscene letters Narcissa had received from Byron Snopes before he absconded with the money he took from the Sartoris bank. On the night of the theft he broke into her house and stole the letters (as anyone who has read *Flags in the Dust* or *Sartoris* knows). But is it credible that the letters would turn up twelve years later and that the federal government would still be working on the case? Moreover, while Narcissa is certainly capable of giving herself to the Yankee agent in order to get the letters back, I find it difficult to believe that she would tell Miss Jenny what she has done. Some readers would argue that she is trying to relieve herself of intense feelings of guilt by confessing in such a manner; they would point out that her sitting in the creek with her little boy Bory before the conversation with Jenny implies her need for some kind of purgation. But I wonder if this episode at the creek doesn't suggest an almost *literal* need to cleanse herself of the dirt of the "Yankee Jew" rather than any real feelings of guilt. Nothing in the casual manner in which she tells Miss Jenny about her fling indicates any deep-lying moral concern about what she has done. It is quite true that she is too insensitive to realize what effect this kind of knowledge might have on the old lady, but surely her strong sense of propriety, if nothing else, would prevent her from telling Jenny. Her motivations are quite unconvincing.

In "Elly" we are asked to believe, in the first place, that the protagonist could prevail on her fiancé Philip, another one of Faulkner's all too decent, self-effacing men, to let her go to a distant city with another man to pick up her grandmother and yet permit her family to believe that Philip will be with her. She starts on the trip with Paul de Montigny, knowing that her grandmother, who has earlier discovered her in the bushes with Paul and believes the man to have Negro blood, will be at the other end. On the way, they pause at a clump of trees and have sex for two hours because Elly apparently believes Paul will then marry her, even though he has repeatedly said he won't under any circumstances. On the return trip, believing that her grandmother will tell her father about what she has done, she apparently kills both Paul and the old woman by wrenching the steering wheel out of Paul's hand and causing an accident. How credible is this?

There are several such problems in the Bayard-Ringo stories. The business about the requisitioning of the mules in "Raid" and "The Unvanquished" is certainly amusing but wildly implausible. Nor is it believable, in the latter story, that the cagy Granny Millard would allow herself to be lured into Grumby's lair by Abner Snopes. The motivation of Grumby in "Vendée" makes little sense; it is incredible that this vicious murderer would allow Bayard, Ringo, and Uncle Buck to pursue him without ambushing the would-be avengers and killing them.

In "Turnabout," considering Bogard's uncertainty about Hope and the contempt that the rest of the airmen have for him, is it credible that they would allow him to man a machine gun on their bombing flight to Germany? In "Go Down, Moses" can we believe that a census taker would be allowed to visit a condemned man a few hours before his execution and that Samuel Worsham Beauchamp would still be dressed in his street clothes? Finally, considering the fact that telephones are very much in evidence in "Knight's Gambit," and that the wealthy Harrisses would surely own a phone, we wonder why Gavin Stevens does not simply call Captain Gualdres, the Harrisses's houseguest, to warn him that a dangerous stallion has been placed in the stall of his gentle mare. But, of course, a phone call would have prevented that dramatic last-minute drive to save Gualdres's life.

Sometimes simple ignorance gets Faulkner in trouble. In "Dr. Martino" he seems to have rather peculiar ideas as to what goes on in college psychology classes. One day Jarrod hears his instructor talking about the mysterious phases through which young girls go:

> "A blind spot, like that which racing aviators enter when making a fast turn. When what they see is neither good nor evil, and so what they do is likely to be either one. Probably more likely to be evil, since the very evilness of evil stems from its own fact, while good is an absence of fact. A time, an hour, in which they themselves are victims of that by means of which they victimize." (*CS* 568)

I suppose anything *could* be said in a college classroom, but this is a most peculiar disquisition for a teacher of psychology.

A more serious instance of Faulkner's ignorance is the symbol system of "Knight's Gambit," more specifically the chess symbolism. Early in the novella he implies that a castle is a different piece from a rook (*KG* 140). Later we are told that Chick "checked his uncle's queen and her castle both with the horse" (*KG* 176). The only piece one can "check" in a chess game is the king; Faulkner is referring here to a fork. Moreover, no one with more than a nodding acquaintance with the game would call a knight a horse, in spite of the fact that the piece generally does have the configuration of the animal. Of course, the use of the word *horse* does serve to relate the chess symbolism to the horses that play so important a role in the plot of the novella. And Faulkner does employ this symbolism, as it relates to the human relationships of the work and Stevens's maneuvering of those relationships, in an interestingly complex way. Still, it seems he could have been more careful about his terminology.[9]

We need not linger long over the question of obscurity in Faulkner's short fiction. That battle has long since been won. Most astute readers of Faulkner's works and of those of his great contemporaries find the pleasure of wrestling with the difficulties of modernist fiction one of its most rewarding aspects. Knowing the delight Faulkner took in mystifying his readers, we like to rise to his challenge. Furthermore, Faulkner's short stories rarely pose the problems in this regard that such novels as *The Sound and the Fury* and *Absalom, Absalom!* do. Yet we *can* grow a little irritated occasionally with what seem to be unnecessary ambiguities in a few of the stories. "The Leg" is a very difficult story to unravel, as is the Christ symbolism in "Beyond," and the question of the apparent murder in "Mistral," not to mention the obscurity of the conversation with the waiter that takes place near the end of that story. One special case is the famous second poker game in "Was." Attempts have been made by several scholars to resolve the complexities of that game, which, on the surface, seems to make no sense at all to those who know anything about poker.[10] Perhaps the most convincing interpretation is that of Sharon Leahy, who argues that we can understand the game if we realize that there is a curious semantic literalism in the betting, that the precise meanings of the words Uncle Buddy and Hubert employ are crucial. I find Leahy's closely reasoned interpretation as convincing as any can be. But even it is anything but easy to understand. One wonders if Faulkner really achieved anything by this kind of complexity, if indeed the general effect of this otherwise delightful story is not seriously vitiated by the difficulties even the most careful, astute, and conscientious readers would have in trying to unravel what Leahy calls in her title that "Gordian knot."[11]

Faulkner lovers may find the preceding few pages of this study marred by a kind of excessive fastidiousness, by a niggling attention to trivia, by irritable carping. Perhaps. Yet I do find the flaws I have noted dismaying. In a sense, they seem less forgivable in a short story than they do in a novel because in the shorter span of the story they call attention to themselves more readily than they do in the longer fictional modes; one expects even the most careful of novelists to slip up occasionally. Moreover, it is surprising that Faulkner, who revised his work so indefatigably, who labored so tirelessly on even some of his most trivial pieces, had so much trouble with plot and detail. Of course, his occasional lack of concern for these matters is evidenced in other ways throughout his career, notably in his inconsistency in the handling of characters and situations from work to work—in the Snopes trilogy, for example. But what he had to say in his prefatory note to *The Mansion*, to explain the contradictions in the trilogy, about his changing views of "the human heart and its dilemma," is, I think, a valid justification for the inconsistencies in those works and in others on which he labored so long. I find considerably less justification for the kinds of problems with which I have been concerned in the last few pages.

If we move back to a broader perspective on the techniques Faulkner employed in his short fiction, which I have been discussing in this chapter and the preceding one, the evidence does seem to corroborate what I have said in several contexts before: that Faulkner's work in the genre is quite uneven. He is at his best in his handling of first-person narration, in his manipulation of time, in the creation of his *fabulae*, in his general handling of the larger organizational elements of short fiction. He is less effective in his treatment of plot motivation and in his concern for detail. But when he was able to put it all together, he was a master. His very best stories—"Red Leaves," "That Evening Sun," "A Justice," "Dry September," "Mule in the Yard," "Barn Burning"—are technically virtually flawless.

CHAPTER 5

# *Stories and Books*

It is now necessary to assess the role of Faulkner's short fiction in his career by discussing the relationships between his stories and books. After examining Faulkner's efforts to organize his various collections of short fiction, I will discuss his methods of revising the stories he incorporated into the novels. I also want to consider what light the themes and techniques of the short fiction can throw on those employed in the novels. By these means it should be possible to gain not only a clearer sense of the complex and problematical relationship between the stories and the books but also of the aesthetic underlying Faulkner's total achievement.

## Collecting Stories

There has been a considerable amount of critical interest in Faulkner's efforts to organize his collections of stories. Some distinguished work has been done in this area by critics of the stature of Michael Millgate and Arthur F. Kinney, who have demonstrated with considerable acuity that at least two of the volumes, *These 13* and *Collected Stories*, are most carefully organized.[1] In his correspondence Faulkner himself indicated how deliberate his intentions were in this regard, particularly in the well-known statement to Malcolm Cowley about the organization of the *Collected Stories*: "even to a collection of short stories, form, integration, is as important as to a novel—an entity of its own, single, set for one pitch, contrapuntal in integration, toward one end, one finale" (*SL* 278).

But one or two caveats are in order here. In attempting to assess Faulkner's intentions in organizing these collections, we run far greater risks of excessive critical ingenuity than we do when we examine the symbolic structure of an individual short story or of a novel. In the first place, to argue that the stories an author has chosen to collect in any one volume have a fundamental unity of theme or imagery is really to say very little, for the same thing can almost always be said, in one sense or other, of a purely random selection by a critic of the works of that writer. Every literary figure—from the greatest to the most insignificant, from Shakespeare to the most untalented of hacks—has characteristic themes, preoccupations, and patterns of images, as "cluster" critics have so well demonstrated. Hence I am not always convinced when one of Faulkner's readers points to the recurrence of a theme or image in several stories in one of his collections as evidence of the care he took in structuring that book. Of how much value, for example, is the assertion that one of the patterns unifying "The Village" section of the *Collected Stories* is the motif of the trapped woman? Faulkner's use of the pattern suggests some most interesting things about his art and his values, as I have noted elsewhere, but the fact that the theme can be found in several of the stories collected in that volume tells us nothing about Faulkner's craft in putting the book together. Only if those stories are arranged in such a way that their placement sets up a kind of rhythm or counterpoint that causes them, through the reiteration of such themes, to comment on, qualify, or modify each other and thus enrich our experience of them, is the critic justified in making his case.

In examining the work Faulkner did on his collections, more than one critic has tended to forget that the writer had to deal with material *already at hand,* that there is little evidence he wrote the stories with their ultimate arrangement in a book in mind. The general tenor of more than one analysis of Faulkner's collections has strongly implied that he organized these books almost as carefully as he did the novels. However, it should be obvious that it was impossible to do so. Only if he had revised the stories extensively, as he did with those he incorporated into *The Unvanquished* and *Go Down, Moses,* could he have begun to approach the kind of unity in his collections that he attained in his best novels. But there is not much concrete evidence of such revision for the collections. It is possible that Faulkner did do some work of this nature in preparing previously unpublished stories for these volumes. Because of H. L. Mencken's editorial work on "That Evening Sun Go Down" before its publication in *The American Mercury,* Faulkner did make some extensive alterations in that story for *These 13,*[2] but the changes he made in other previously published stories were generally relatively minor, certainly not significant enough to justify the supposition that he was revising these works with the same kind of care that he was to take when he was working on *The Unvanquished* or *Go Down, Moses.*

With these strictures in mind, let us briefly examine, first of all, the organization of *These 13*. The stories in that book are arranged in the following order:

I
Victory
Ad Astra
All the Dead Pilots
Crevasse

II
Red Leaves
A Rose for Emily
A Justice
Hair
That Evening Sun
Dry September

III
Mistral
Divorce in Naples
Carcassonne

There is not a great deal that I can add to Millgate's admirably judicious and restrained analysis of this volume. Obviously the stories in the second section—those dealing with Yoknapatawpha, which are by all odds the best in the book—are framed by the first four stories in the first section, which deal with World War I or its effects, and by the stories in the final section, concerned, as Millgate suggests, with Americans abroad who are undergoing some kind of enlarging of experience (*Achievement* 262). Faulkner probably decided to make "Victory" the first story in the volume because it is so ambitious in its scope; it is almost a novella and ranges in time from the beginning of World War I to several years after the end of the war. In its portrayal of the effects of war on one person, Alec Gray, who becomes a kind of zombie, "Victory" also looks forward to the more explicit development of this theme of the living dead in the next two pieces in the volume, "Ad Astra" and "All the Dead Pilots." In the former story, the subadar says to Bland, "What will any of us do? All this generation which fought in the war are dead tonight. But we do not yet know it" (*T13* 69; *CS* 421). In the latter, the narrator expresses the same sentiments: "Because they are dead, all the old pilots, dead on the eleventh of November, 1918" (*T13* 81; *CS* 511).

The positioning of "All the Dead Pilots" in *These 13* suggests a principle Faulkner used in all three of his major collections of short stories. While it deals with some of the same themes as "Victory" and "Ad Astra" and is also linked to the latter story by the presence of John Sartoris in both, "All the Dead Pilots" develops its themes somewhat more lightly. Although its framing sections, the first and the seventh, are quite melancholy in tone, the basic modality of the piece is comic, in contrast to the deadly seriousness of the first two works. We can find this kind of alternation, in one form or other, again and again in Faulkner's collections.[3] In the case of *These 13*, the tonal contrast is all the more apparent when we consider that the next and last story in this section of the book is a tale of unmitigated horror, the concentration and intensity of which are set off against the more panoramic scope of the other three stories in the section, thus bringing this first part of the volume to a powerful conclusion.[4]

The technique of variations in tonality is also apparent in the arrangement of the stories in the second section of *These 13*. The horror engendered by the first two stories, "Red Leaves" and "A Rose for Emily," can be contrasted with the comedy of the middle stories, "A Justice" and "Hair," comedy in turn giving way to the bleak emptiness and despair of "That Evening Sun" and "Dry September." But there is also a kind of balance and symmetry suggested by various parallels between the stories: the emphasis on corruption and degeneration in the first two pieces, the theme of love and courtship in the middle two, and the conflict between the races in "That Evening Sun" and "Dry September." As James Watson has noted, there is a further parallel between "Dry September," the last story in the section, and "Red Leaves," the first, in that both deal with ritual murders ("Faulkner's Short Stories" 216). Moreover, there are obvious similarities between the alienated female protagonists of the second and the penultimate stories, "A Rose for Emily" and "That Evening Sun." Faulkner therefore succeeded admirably in integrating this middle portion of *These 13* by means of the complex contrapuntal development of tone and theme.

In the third section of the volume both "Mistral" and "Divorce in Naples" are obviously concerned with the archetype of initiation, but again the mood of the first story, with its pathos and intensity, can be sharply contrasted with the humor, slight as it is, of the second. Although these two works are both concerned with attempts by young men to achieve some kind of breakthrough to the fullness of human life, the reader, in the light of the experience he or she has had of the first two stories in the collection, must take a highly ironic view of these endeavors—a view that is, I think, enhanced by the final piece, "Carcassonne."

Most of the critics who have attempted to deal with the ambiguities of "Carcassonne" have concluded that it is some sort of allegory about the role of art in human life. But Noel Polk, in perhaps the most interesting reading of the piece ("Carcassonne"), maintains that such an interpretation is much too limiting, that the protagonist is a kind of Prufrock or one of Eliot's Hollow Men, who has completely failed to achieve what he aspired to do and is now content to live in his dreams. Polk may well be right. But however one chooses to interpret "Carcassonne," it is certainly, on the most basic level, about the tragic gap between flesh and spirit, mind and body, "reality" and dream. In this sense, it serves as a fitting climax to *These 13*, all of whose stories are concerned, in one way or another, with the inadequacy of the dream, with the pathos or comedy engendered by the solipsistic failure to acknowledge human limitations.

However, Polk sees "Carcassonne" as having a far more complex and subtle relationship to the rest of the volume, largely because of the parallels between symbols and images in this work and those found in the other stories in *These 13*. These parallels are fascinating and certainly suggest Polk's most astute, careful, and meticulous reading not only of the story but also of the entire book. But, for reasons noted elsewhere in this chapter, I am not altogether convinced by Polk's explication. For it is valid only if it can be demonstrated that "Carcassonne" was specifically written to serve as a kind of capstone to the volume, only if Faulkner deliberately set out to make the piece a kind of recapitulation of the symbols and motifs in the rest of *These 13*. However, as I have already noted,[5] internal evidence suggests that Faulkner was at work on the prose poem in 1926 or 1927, around the time of the composition of *Mosquitoes*.

The two extant typescript drafts are very different from the final version, and hence it is possible that Faulkner worked on the piece off and on over a period of years and perhaps put the finishing touches on it while preparing *These 13* for publication. Nevertheless, Polk's case would be stronger if the images appearing in the published version of "Carcassonne" could not be found in the earlier ones. He makes much of the fact that in an early scene of "Victory" Gray sleeps in a garret in a village of "tarred paper roofs made in America" (*T13* 4; *CS* 432), an image that seems to look forward to the sleeping arrangements of the protagonist of "Carcassonne." Yet in the very earliest extant drafts of the prose poem, the character lies "beneath an unrolled strip of tarred paper roofing" (7–pp. ts. 1 [item 7a]; *WFM 9* 382). The similarity of these descriptions does not therefore point to a high degree of deliberate craftsmanship on Faulkner's part but to the predilection he shared with virtually every writer for repeating images which, for some reason, he found interesting. *These 13* is certainly a most skillfully integrated volume, but we must beware of exaggerating the tightness of its organization.

On the other hand, *Doctor Martino and Other Stories* may not be quite so casually organized as most critics have assumed. Millgate can find no discernible pattern in the arrangement of the stories in the volume (*Achievement* 265), and while Arthur Kinney does find some interesting parallels between situations in the stories, he devotes only a portion of a paragraph to them ("Narrative Poetics" 59). There is little reason to believe that *Doctor Martino* is as well integrated as *These 13*, but I think there is some order, some pattern in the volume.

The stories are arranged as follows:

Doctor Martino
Fox Hunt
The Hound
Death Drag
There Was a Queen
Smoke
Turn About
Beyond
Wash
Elly
Black Music
Leg
Mountain Victory
Honor

The fact that "Doctor Martino" is the first story and that it gives the title to the collection implies that Faulkner had an undeservedly high opinion of this piece. But it *is* a complex work containing many themes found in other stories in the volume, and in this sense it serves as a rather effective introduction to the rest of the book. Most obviously, it is concerned with alienation, a theme we can find in virtually every story in the collection, and with initiation, a triangular love relationship, and one of Faulkner's trapped women. The fact that Martino tries to live in and through Louise, to make up for the deficiencies in his own existence by attempting to mold her into the kind of person he is himself incapable of being, also looks forward to a theme of the greatest importance throughout the volume: the solipsistic desire to achieve justice, the need to attain some kind of quid pro quo.

The second story, "Fox Hunt," picks up on several of the patterns that can be found in the first: the archetype of initiation, the triangle, the struggle over a young woman. Furthermore, the killing of the fox by Blair and his wife's giving herself to Gawtrey suggest a kind of symbolic quid pro quo. This motif of justice, in various manifestations, becomes dominant in the next few stories: in Cotton's revenge against Houston in "The Hound"; in Ginsfarb's insistence on getting his money for his "death-defying" feat in "Death Drag"; in the measures Narcissa takes to reclaim her letters and in her ritual cleansing in "There Was a Queen"; and in the more literal achievement of justice in Stevens's solving of the crime in "Smoke." In "Turn About" the quid pro quo is achieved in another, perhaps even more literal sense: in the elaborate parallels between the two dangerous missions, the bombing raid and the torpedo boat attack.

In the next story, "Beyond," there is a very different attitude toward the achievement of justice. The Judge is offered a vision of life in which equity *is* built into the nature of things, in which the quid pro quo can be achieved, but he refuses to accept this kind of order, preferring to find his identity in contingency, loss, bereavement. In this sense the Judge is in revolt, as are the protagonists of the stories immediately following "Beyond": "Wash," "Elly," "Black Music," and "Leg."

The penultimate story of this collection, "Mountain Victory," is, like the first story, "Doctor Martino," a most ambitious work containing several of the themes developed throughout the volume: alienation (in the portrayal of Weddel), a kind of abortive initiation in the characterization of the boy, a young woman at the focal point of conflict, and the attempt to achieve the quid pro quo in Vatch's murder of Weddel because of their differing allegiances in the Civil War and Vatch's concern about his sister's attraction to the older man. Because "Mountain Victory" is an excellent story, perhaps the strongest and most complex in the volume, one might think that Faulkner should have ended *Doctor Martino* with this work. But had he done so, he would have violated a fundamental aesthetic principle. If we recall the final scene of "Mountain Victory" and the last sentence ("Crouching, the Negro's eyes rushed wild and steady and red, like those of a cornered animal" [*DRM* 354; *CS* 777]), it seems obvious that the level of intensity is very high—appropriately so for the conclusion of this story but too high for an effective closure to the entire volume. A very short work can end at such a level, but anything of greater length and complexity, anything involving a considerable range of tonalities and emotional effects—a tragedy, an epic poem, a novel, or a collection of stories—requires some diminution of intensity in order to achieve effective closure. Such a principle may partly explain why Faulkner chose to conclude with the rather slight "Honor."

Perhaps there is another reason. It can hardly be said that either "Mountain Victory" or "Honor" is, in toto very affirmative in its implications. But both stories do contain positive elements: the portrayal in "Mountain Victory" of the devotion of Weddel to his black servant and the decency and courage of Rogers in "Honor." These somewhat affirmative aspects of the two stories hardly cancel out the overriding pessimism of the entire volume, but they do offer a gleam of hope.

The table of contents of *Collected Stories* is as follows:

I. THE COUNTRY
 Barn Burning
 Shingles for the Lord
 The Tall Men
 A Bear Hunt
 Two Soldiers
 Shall Not Perish

II. THE VILLAGE
 A Rose for Emily
 Hair
 Centaur in Brass
 Dry September
 Death Drag
 Elly
 Uncle Willy
 Mule in the Yard
 That Will Be Fine
 That Evening Sun

III. THE WILDERNESS
 Red Leaves
 A Justice
 A Courtship
 Lo!

IV. THE WASTELAND
 Ad Astra
 Victory
 Crevasse
 Turnabout
 All the Dead Pilots

V. THE MIDDLE GROUND
 Wash
 Honor
 Dr. Martino
 Fox Hunt
 Pennsylvania Station
 Artist at Home
 The Brooch
 My Grandmother Millard
 Golden Land

Because of Faulkner's correspondence about the matter, we have considerably more evidence about the arrangement and selection of the stories in this volume than we do about the planning of the other collections. Faulkner's letters to Robert Haas are particularly interesting in this regard. Haas sent him a letter in March 1948, suggesting a new collection and including a list of stories that volume might contain (*SL* 266). Faulkner apparently lost the list and in a letter he wrote in September asked for another copy, indicating that "I would like to mull over it, try to give this volume an integrated form of its own, like the Moses book if possible or at least These 13" (*SL* 273). Several weeks later, when he had the list, which at this stage consisted only of stories that had not previously been collected, he again wrote Haas about the projected volume (*SL* 274–75). This lengthy letter is one of the most intriguing Faulkner ever wrote because it contains his assessments of several of his stories—assessments that indicate a generally good critical sense of his own work. His opinions of such stories as "Monk," "Pennsylvania Station," "Thrift," "The Brooch," "Shall Not Perish," and "Snow" are not high, and most critics of Faulkner would probably agree with these evaluations. It is interesting that by November 1948, when Faulkner wrote to Malcolm Cowley about the nearly completed selection and arrangement of the stories, none of these pieces had been included (*SL* 277–79). For some reason that is not clear, "Shall Not Perish" was added quite late to *Collected Stories* and placed after "Two Soldiers" as the concluding story in "The Country" section. "Pennsylvania Station," "Artist at Home" (which both Faulkner and Haas had apparently forgotten in their earlier correspondence), and "The Brooch" were also later inserted in "The Middle Ground" section between "Fox Hunt" and "My Grandmother Millard." One wonders if the relatively late addition of these pieces might have had a slightly deleterious effect on the "form, integration" that Faulkner described in the same letter to Cowley as being as important for a short-story collection as for a novel.

Nevertheless, Faulkner did organize his *Collected Stories* with consider-

able care. There is an obvious unity—geographical or thematic—in each
of the first four sections of the volume: "The Country," "The Village,"
"The Wilderness," and "The Wasteland." The unity of the final two parts
of the volume, however, is somewhat more problematical. To consider the
"Beyond" section first, Millgate is probably right in arguing that the three
stories of the supernatural beginning this section and the last three in the
volume (the same stories in the same order which end *These 13*) all deal
with initiation, with the discovery of new dimensions of the self (*Achievement* 274). Another unifying theme in the section is a very intense dualism,
which I have already noted in discussing the role of "Carcassonne" in *These
13*. All the stories in "Beyond" are marked, in one way or other, by an
awareness of the dichotomy between mind and body, spirit and flesh.

Even Millgate has conceded that it is difficult to find a unifying theme
in "The Middle Ground," the fifth section of *Collected Stories* (*Achievement*
273). In analyzing this part of the volume, we must remember that Faulkner
had a very real problem in assembling his short fiction: his range of subject
matter and theme was so great that a sizable number of his stories could
not be neatly categorized and classified; they simply didn't belong in one
of the other five sections. But since they were certainly worthy of inclusion
in the book, they had to be placed somewhere. Hence, Faulkner had no
recourse, I think, but to construct a section fundamentally miscellaneous
in nature and to give it a title vaguely implying its somewhat amorphous
quality. However, it was still possible to imply some interesting parallels
and to achieve some contrapuntal effects by a careful arrangement of the
stories within the section.

It is now necessary to return to the beginning of the book and to consider
in a little more detail Faulkner's efforts to organize the stories. There is, as
Philip Momberger notes, a rather basic contrast between Faulkner's generally positive portrayals of life in "The Country" and the darker tonality of
the stories in "The Village" (103–91). However, it is easy to exaggerate the
contrast, considering, on the one hand, the somewhat negative characterizations of Ab Snopes and Res Grier in the first section and, on the other
hand, the affirmation that is implicit in the second section in the portrayals
of Hawkshaw in "Hair," the blacks in "Centaur in Brass," and Miss Mannie
in "Mule in the Yard." Furthermore, we should bear in mind that the pieces
in "The Country" were, on the whole, written much later than those in
"The Village" and hence reflect the more positive orientation of Faulkner's
later work. But I think we *can* argue that the placement of the stories in
the first section, with their celebration of the simple virtues of integrity,
courage, honesty, and endurance, gives the reader certain norms that he or
she can use in assessing values in the rest of the volume.

Millgate has written most persuasively of the parallels between the stories in "The Country," particularly of the motif of the poor whites visiting the de Spain mansion in "Barn Burning" and "Shall Not Perish" and of the very different consequences of those visits (*Achievement* 271). We should also note the characteristic alternation of tonalities in the stories of this section. The first and third, "Barn Burning" and "The Tall Men," are quite serious; the second and fourth, "Shingles for the Lord" and "A Bear Hunt," are comic. Pathos dominates the tonalities of the final two stories, although there are certainly comic elements in "Two Soldiers." But we must remember that "Shall Not Perish" was a late addition to the book, and perhaps for that reason it somewhat mars the symmetry of the arrangement. Finally, we should note that the placement of "Barn Burning," with its strongly initiatory elements, at the beginning of the section and of the two Grier stories about the effects of World War II at the end strongly suggests a kind of expansive movement out and away from the constraints of rural life, positive as the values embodied in that life may be, and thus serves to prepare us for what is to come in the rest of the volume.

There is an impressive unity in the stories of the second section, all of which are dominated, in a variety of ways, by the theme of the relationship between individual and communal values. The conflicts between the needs of selfhood and the imperatives of the social order are quite apparent in the stories of Miss Emily, Hawkshaw and Susan, the defeat of Flem in "Centaur in Brass," the alienation of Minnie, Will, and Hawkshaw in "Dry September," etc. Again we can find a kind of tonal symmetry in the arrangement of the stories. The horror of "A Rose for Emily" is succeeded by the essentially comic modes of "Hair" and "Centaur in Brass." These are followed by four intensely serious stories—"Dry September," "Death Drag," "Elly," and "Uncle Willy"—but they are, in turn, succeeded by the much lighter "Mule in the Yard" and "That Will Be Fine" (although the comedy of the latter story is very sardonic indeed). Finally, the dark pessimism of the last story of the section, "That Evening Sun," effectively parallels the perversity of "A Rose for Emily," the first story. Thus, if I may use somewhat unscholarly and imprecise terminology, the order of the tonalities of the ten stories is: heavy, light, light, heavy, heavy, heavy, heavy, light, light, heavy. It is also interesting that Faulkner chose to begin and end this section with two of his most effective and powerful stories. If we remember that he had an especial fondness for some stories that have not been widely acclaimed—"Lo!" and "All the Dead Pilots," for example—there is some evidence that he generally followed this principle in the arrangement of *Collected Stories*.[6] (Again we must stress that "Shall Not Perish" was a late addition and that he originally intended to end "The Village" with "Two Soldiers," a work he clearly liked.)[7]

We need say only a few things about the next two sections, "The Wilderness" and "The Wasteland." The titles and, to some extent, the contents of the two do suggest a kind of contrast between the natural and the primitive, on the one hand, and, on the other, the corruption engendered by a decadent civilization. But I cannot agree with Momberger's argument that Faulkner is setting up a dichotomy between the positive values celebrated in "The Wilderness" and the degeneration and chaos of "The Wasteland" (191–219). For the Indians Faulkner portrays are anything but noble savages; they seem as corrupt as the whites whose customs they parody. If anything, the juxtaposition of the two sections may point to ironic *similarities* between the abstractions by which the inhabitants of the wilderness and the wasteland live.

However, there is, in both sections, a kind of progressive lightening of tone. This is most obvious in the movement from the tragic spirit of "Red Leaves" through the black comedy of "A Justice" to the nostalgic warmth of "A Courtship" and the broader comedy of "Lo!" "The Wasteland" begins in characteristic Faulknerian fashion with a story focusing on effects: "Ad Astra." The causes of the disillusionment and cynicism that permeate that piece are then traced in the grim "Victory" and "Crevasse," works that are overwhelmingly pessimistic. But the positive view of the courage of young men that is so apparent in "Turnabout" serves to balance the more negative views of the two stories preceding it, and the section is brought to a close with the seriocomic nostalgia of "All the Dead Pilots." Generalizations about such matters are clearly suspect, but if we contrast the arrangement of the war stories here with that of the first section of *These 13* and also take into account what I have said about the placement of stories in terms of their tonalities in other sections, the *Collected Stories* is surely a far more affirmative volume than the earlier collection.

In attempting to find some kind of organizational principle in the arrangement of the stories in "The Middle Ground," one can very easily be excessively ingenious; the temptations are great because there is certainly no readily discernible pattern. However, if one begins at both ends of the section and works toward the middle, rather intriguing parallels can be found. The framing stories, "Wash" and "Mountain Victory," the best pieces in the section, are both concerned with the aftermath of the Civil War and with the relationships between a young girl and an older man. The second and tenth stories, "Honor" and "There Was a Queen," both deal with conceptions of honor that are tested by sexual liaisons. The third and ninth stories, "Dr. Martino" and "Golden Land," focus on older people who are trying by very different means to hold on to life. The fourth and eighth, "Fox Hunt" and "My Grandmother Millard," are concerned respectively with the problems engendered by an unhappy marriage and with the resolution by marriage of an otherwise insoluble problem. The fifth and seventh, "Pennsylvania Station" and "The Brooch," are about the consequences of a stupidly unrealistic selfless devotion. Finally, the middle story, "Artist at Home," is perhaps the most positive work in the section because it suggests a means of coming to terms with and transcending—if only temporarily—the tensions of human life by incorporating them into the timeless world of art, as Howes does when he writes his novel about the triangular relationship involving Ann, John Blair, and himself.

It is unnecessary to add much to what has already been said about the "Beyond" section of *Collected Stories* except to note that the same principle of tonal counterpoint that I have pointed out in discussing other parts of the book is again in evidence here. The section is framed by two serious pieces, "Beyond" and "Carcassonne," which contain the broadest and most far-reaching implications of the six stories. "Beyond" is followed by the comic "Black Music," which is, in turn, followed by the feverishly intense "The Leg" and "Mistral." Another comic story, "Divorce in Naples," precedes "Carcassonne," which, like "Artist at Home," at least suggests the possibility of a kind of transcendence through art.

It seems clear that Faulkner worked very hard to integrate *Collected Stories*. Whatever reservations we may have about the quality of some of these works, the volume is a most important book, one of the great achievements of Faulkner's career. And the form he was able to give it certainly enhances its impressiveness.

We can refer only in passing to the other two collections of his short fiction on which Faulkner worked. The detective stories in *Knight's Gambit* are simply arranged in the chronological order of their publication, although Faulkner did greatly expand the title piece, which had not been previously published, for inclusion in the volume.[8] On the other hand, he labored very hard on *Big Woods*, and the result is a well-unified, lyrical, and moving study of the meaning of hunting, a kind of elegy for the lost wilderness. It deserves more attention than I can give it here.[9]

We can never know, apart from what he said explicitly, what Faulkner's aims were in organizing his more important collections of short fiction in the ways he did. Certainly some of my speculations about these matters will not convince everyone. But whatever reasons Faulkner had for the arrangement of the stories he chose to collect, there is ample evidence in these volumes of his integrative abilities, of his sensitivity to form.

## Stories into Novels

Until fairly recently, the only aspect of Faulkner's short fiction that had repeatedly received close, concentrated, and careful attention was his revision of stories for incorporation into books.[10] Those critics who have dealt extensively with this aspect of his art have generally been quite positive in their assessments of the results. They have argued strongly and persuasively that the revised versions in the novels of material based on the short stories are, for the most part, considerably better than the original stories. On the other hand, Marvin Klotz in his article "Procrustean Revision in Faulkner's *Go Down, Moses*" takes the opposite perspective and has some very harsh things to say about Faulkner's revisions for that book. Klotz's assessment is, I think, much too severe. Furthermore, like several critics with more positive attitudes toward the revisions, Klotz made some assumptions about Faulkner's work in this area that later scholarship has proved to be invalid—notably that Faulkner revised the *Saturday Evening Post* version of "The Bear" for incorporation into *Go Down, Moses* when, in fact, he extracted it from the longer version he was working on at the time and specifically tailored it for the *Post*'s audience (*FB* 2: 1086).

Nevertheless, if we are to make any really just evaluation of Faulkner's skill in his reuse of material from his stories, we cannot ignore the kind of attitude represented by Klotz. For while Faulkner, at his best, was brilliantly successful in this kind of revision, it sometimes caused very real problems. Most of this material in his novels is considerably richer and more complex than it is in its original versions, but it is not always fused with complete success into these works.

One of the reasons for this problem is Faulkner's extreme economy in the use of what he had already written. He clearly hated to let go of anything until he had extracted all he possibly could from it, no matter how inherently trivial it might be. Once he had found a subject, he almost invariably worked on it until he had made *something* of it. And he was often able to transform apparently most unpromising material into something approaching sublimity. Sometimes, on the other hand, when he attempted to fuse old material with new, the result was a troubling inconsistency, an incoherence of style or tone. We can sense stresses, tensions, almost a kind of violence in this yoking together. The problem is apparent in some portions of not only *Go Down, Moses* but in a number of other works as well.

In Faulkner's earliest novels, we can find much material that derives from the stories: from the New Orleans sketches, "Adolescence," *Mayday*, etc. However, it was not until the mid-thirties, when Faulkner's interest in writing autonomous short fiction waned, that his practice of incorporating his short stories into novels became particularly important. His revision of "Wash" for *Absalom, Absalom!* is a triumphantly successful instance of this practice. "Wash" is, in its own right, a superlative story—moving, evocative, beautifully written. But in the revision of the material for the novel, Faulkner achieved an extraordinary density because of the parallels between Sutpen and his retainer that suggest they are doubles. Both come from poor-white stock, both are turned away at the front doors of mansions by blacks, and the tragedies that they both undergo derive from their concern for female progeny.[11] When Faulkner wrote "Wash," the story of Thomas Sutpen, which he had already attempted unsuccessfully to deal with in "Evangeline," had already taken hold of him. It continued to fascinate him until, after the most arduous creative struggles, he completed *Absalom, Absalom!* Nothing in Faulkner's career is more engrossing than the genesis of that great novel. And it may be that the transmutation of "Wash" into *Absalom* is the single most successful instance in Faulkner's work of the revision of a piece of short fiction for incorporation into a novel.

I have more reservations about the reworking of the Bayard-Ringo stories for *The Unvanquished.* There is no question at all that the revisions in that volume of the original magazine pieces—particularly of the first three, "Ambuscade," "Retreat," and "Raid"—are far more complex and stylistically considerably richer than the original stories. As Creighton indicates, the narration in *The Unvanquished* is clearly retrospective; the voice is that of a mature man rather than that of an adolescent (74). Bayard is therefore better able to judge from the perspective of time what he has lived through. There are ironies in *The Unvanquished* in the treatment of John Sartoris, of the war, and of the problems of race that are hardly even suggested in the original stories. We can also sense that as Faulkner worked on the series, he saw possibilities in it of which he had been quite unaware when he began; hence there is a darkening of tone in the later stories, which required much less revision. *The Unvanquished* is by no means as slight a book as some critics have claimed.

However, I *am* troubled by stylistic inconsistencies, by a kind of awkward double perspective caused by the revisions. Consider, for example, the beginning of the novel, the opening lines of the revised "Ambuscade":

> Behind the smokehouse that summer, Ringo and I had a living map. Although Vicksburg was just a handful of chips from the woodpile and the River a trench scraped into the packed earth with the point of a hoe, it (river, city, and terrain) lived, possessing even in miniature that ponderable though passive recalcitrance of topography which outweighs artillery, against which the most brilliant of victories and the most tragic of defeats are but the loud noises of a moment. To Ringo and me it lived, if only because of the fact that the sunimpacted ground

drank water faster than we could fetch it from the well, the very setting of the stage for conflict a prolonged and wellnigh hopeless ordeal in which we ran, panting and interminable, with the leaking bucket between wellhouse and battle-field, the two of us needing first to join forces and spend ourselves against a common enemy, time, before we could engender between us and hold intact the pattern of recapitulant mimic furious victory like a cloth, a shield between ourselves and reality, between us and fact and doom. (*U* 3–4)

Clearly such a passage is an instance of high Faulknerian rhetoric—orotund and grandiloquent. But contrast it with a passage occurring near the end of the story, which is exactly the same in the original magazine version and *The Unvanquished*. Bayard and Ringo are hiding from the Yankees under Granny's skirts:

We couldn't see; we just squatted in a kind of faint gray light and that smell of Granny that her clothes and bed and room all had, and Ringo's eyes looking like two plates of chocolate pudding and maybe both of us thinking how Granny had never whipped us for anything in our lives except lying, and that even when it wasn't even a told lie, but just keeping quiet, how she would whip us first and then make us kneel down and kneel down with us herself to ask the Lord to forgive us. (*US* 12; *U* 32)

Could the voice that narrated the first passage also have narrated this one? In this case the perspective is obviously that of a child—not the mature and thoughtful master of language whose voice we hear in the other quotation.

Two more contrasting passages from "Retreat," the second "chapter" of *The Unvanquished*, should be sufficient for our purposes. The first is a description of a scene in the kitchen that occurs near the beginning of the story, which again is the same in the *Post* version and in the book:

Joby and Loosh were in the kitchen. Joby was sitting behind the stove with a plate on his knees, eating. Loosh was sitting on the wood box, still, with the two shovels between his knees, but I didn't see him at first because of Ringo's shadow. The lamp was on the table, and I could see the shadow of Ringo's head bent over and his arm working back and forth, and Louvinia standing between us and the lamp, her hands on her hips and her elbows spread and her shadow filling the room. "Clean that chimney good," she said. (*US* 18; *U* 44)

Only two pages later in the *Unvanquished* version there is another description of Louvinia:

Then Louvinia came in. She had already undressed. She looked tall as a ghost, in one dimension like a bolster case, taller than a bolster case in her nightgown; silent as a ghost on her bare feet which were the same color as the shadow in which she stood so that she seemed to have no feet, the twin rows of her toenails lying weightless and faint and still as two rows of faintly soiled feathers on the floor about a foot below the hem of her nightgown as if they were not connected with her. She came and shoved Joby aside and stooped to lift the trunk. (*U* 46)

In this case, the simple rhythms of the first passage seem to derive from the sensibility of a child. But no child could be capable of those remarkable similes in the penultimate sentence of the second passage. Again there is a basic inconsistency in the handling of the narrative voice—an inconsistency that becomes even more apparent when we compare the second description of Louvinia with the original one in the *Post* version: "Then Louvinia came in. She had already dressed. She looked tall as a ghost; she came and shoved Joby away and took hold of the trunk" (*US* 19). The version in *The Unvanquished* is much richer than this, but the revised passages set up a kind of dissonance when they are compared to the portions of the story which Faulkner did not see fit to alter.

One could argue that, in the case of "Ambuscade," the two disparate narrative voices are appropriate because they serve very different purposes and reflect very different aspects of the narrator's sensibility. In the case of the first quoted passage, the narrator has set up a great distance between himself and the events of his childhood, and is thoughtfully pondering their significance. On the other hand, in his description of the drama of the scene in which he and Ringo hide under Granny's skirts, he is so caught up, like Quentin in "That Evening Sun," in his memories that he again relives those moments as if he were still the child he was at the time. But Faulkner's management of the disparity between the narrative voices in "That Evening Sun" is so subtle, the modulation from the point of view of the adult to that of the child so gradual, that it creates no real sense of strain, in contrast to the much more obvious stylistic incongruities in *The Unvanquished*. Moreover, even if one makes such an argument to explain these inconsistencies in the revision of "Ambuscade," it cannot apply to the two passages I have cited from "Retreat," both of which are concerned with the same kind of experience and should therefore be treated stylistically in essentially the same kind of way. Thus while it is quite true that Faulkner's revisions greatly increase the depth and solidity, the thematic resonance of the original stories and help to unify the larger elements of the book, the reworking of the material also creates a sense of strain and incongruity. *The Unvanquished* is anything but a seamless web; the stitching is all too obvious.

*The Hamlet* is a far better book than *The Unvanquished*—superbly confident and accomplished, richly inventive, and as wildly funny as anything in American literature. Yet it too has problems deriving from Faulkner's reuse of earlier stories, although the problems are of a different kind from those we find in *The Unvanquished*. Here Faulkner's revisions do not lead to stylistic incongruities, but they do cause us to raise questions about motivation and consistency of characterization. The sheer quality of writing in *The Hamlet* is almost always far superior to the quality of the original material, but even if a sensitive reader knows nothing about the origins of the book, he or she might very well sense that it is the product of disparate elements that Faulkner had worked on over a long period of time and could not always successfully integrate.

There is, for example, the disparity between the characterization of Abner Snopes in the material deriving from "Fool About a Horse" and what we learn about Ab in the other early portions of *The Hamlet*. The Ab who is so totally outfoxed by Pat Stamper in the novel is the same person as the Pap of the original story—lazy, boastful, not very bright, but affable and decent. He does not resemble in the slightest the much older Ab, that dour, mean, ugly arsonist whom we encounter in the present time of *The Hamlet*. That Faulkner is aware of this problem is indicated by his having Ratliff explain to Will Varner that "[Ab] aint naturally mean. He's just soured" (*H* 27). In characterizing Ab, V. K. reiterates the word *soured* on several occasions. But we never get an adequate explanation for why Ab has become soured, and even if we had one, it would still be virtually impossible to believe that the horse trader and the arsonist are the same person—no matter what the passage of time has done to him. Here we sense that because Faulkner was so delighted by "Fool About a Horse" and because he knew that its mood, tonality, and subject matter were right for *The Hamlet*, he simply *had* to include it in the novel and could think of no other way of integrating it except to make it an early episode in the career of Abner. But it seems wrenched into place.

There is a similar problem in Faulkner's revision of "Lizards in Jamshyd's Courtyard," which was to become the final major episode in *The Hamlet*. As Blotner has indicated, the evidence of the manuscripts and typescripts of the various drafts of the story over a period of probably more than ten years reveals how painstaking Faulkner could be in his work on his fiction (*US* 686–88). But there is no doubt that the version in the final pages of the novel is definitive—far more confident and fluent writing than any of the drafts of the magazine version. From the beginning, however, the story of the salted treasure does not vary in any essential way, and Suratt-Ratliff and Flem Snopes are the basic antagonists. And herein lies the problem. For the Suratt of the drafts and of the magazine version is a different person from the Ratliff of *The Hamlet*. The characters are alike in many ways: in their volubility, their shrewdness, their affability. But as Faulkner worked with this figure over a period of many years, he became much fonder of him; in *The Hamlet* he gave him a really penetrating intelligence and qualities of wisdom and compassion that he did not originally have. While Ratliff is certainly a very complex character and is anything but a goody-goody, his values are surely the norms of the implied author. He has a far better understanding of the evils of Snopesism and of how Flem is able to attain his ends than any of the other personages of the novel have. It is therefore very difficult to believe that he would be taken in by Flem's scheme of the salted treasure. On the other hand, it is not at all unlikely that the Suratt of "Lizards in Jamshyd's Courtyard" would be deceived, for he is quite capable of greed and lacks the depth and breadth of understanding that Ratliff has. It is thematically appropriate for the novel that Ratliff be duped, for Faulkner's point is clearly that Snopesism is not confined to the Snopeses, that Flem succeeds because he is able to understand and use the rapacity in others. But we have lived with the wise and sagacious Ratliff too long in the novel to countenance his being taken in by so obvious a strategem. Here Faulkner seems to go astray because the characterization has become, through an evolutionary process, so rich that it can no longer fit its original mold.

The reservations I have about Faulkner's revisions of "Fool About a Horse" and "Lizards in Jamshyd's Courtyard" do not apply to the other stories he used in *The Hamlet*. The magazine versions of both "The Hound" and "Spotted Horses" are superb, but the transformation of the story of Cotton in the former, gripping and intense as it is, into that of Mink Snopes in the novel is an almost magical realization of the potential inherent in the original work, and the substitution of the omniscient point of view for the narrative voice of Suratt in the spotted horses material gives it a poetic resonance that is almost unmatched in Faulkner.

Whatever its defects, *The Hamlet* is joyous reading. It is, I think, a more successful work of art than *Go Down, Moses*. The latter contains some of Faulkner's best and most majestic writing; stylistically, there may be nothing finer in his fiction than the sonorous prose of the hunting sections of "The Bear." "Pantaloon in Black" is one of his most moving stories, "Was" one of his funniest. Yet, after many readings of the book, I find it unsatisfying, unsettling—and again one of the reasons for this dissatisfaction is my sense of the wrenching together of disparate elements.

As is so often the case in attempting to trace the process that led to the creation of Faulkner's works, one is impressed by the transformations he was able to effect in *Go Down, Moses* of seemingly trivial and unpromising material. His initial approach to the work was certainly casual. In a letter I have already noted, which he wrote to Robert Haas in 1940,[12] he told

Haas that he could build a book around "four stories about niggers" (*SL* 124). Three of those stories, "A Point of Law," "Gold Is Not Always," and "The Fire on the Hearth," which are basically comic pieces devoted to the machinations of the redoubtable Lucas Beauchamp, hardly qualify as major fiction, with their patronizing, low-comedy approach to the doings of a wily black man. But even in these early versions of the material that was to become "The Fire and the Hearth," the second "chapter" of *Go Down, Moses,* Faulkner must have sensed that the character of Lucas contained the potential for a far more serious treatment. For Lucas already has a commanding presence in the three pieces, an intense but perverse integrity. Furthermore, as Creighton has noted (103), the typescript version of "A Point of Law" in the Alderman Library contains a passage that Faulkner deleted from the *Collier's* story but later restored, in slightly modified form, to the novel. The original version reads: *I am not only looking at a face older than mine, but at a man whose race was pure ten thousand years when my own anonymous beginnings became mixed enough to produce me* (21–pp. ts. 15; *WFM 16* 33).[13] In such a passage as this one can sense the germ of the entire book.

The modifications Faulkner made in the original stories greatly increased the complexity of Lucas's characterization and the significance of his actions because of the establishment of his blood relationship to Roth Edmonds and the entire McCaslin family. The flashbacks detailing Lucas's recollections of Roth's birth, of his conflict with Zack Edmonds over Lucas's wife Molly, and the sad story of the aborted friendship between his son Henry and Roth give a depth, weight, and seriousness to "The Fire and the Hearth" that the original stories, for the most part, do not have. But again we have the sense that the new material does not quite mesh with the old. The broad comedy of Lucas's hunt for buried treasure and of his conflicts with his son-in-law over moonshining does not seem effectively integrated with the moving, poignant material in the flashbacks. And it is difficult to believe that a man of Lucas's intelligence and sensitivity would be convinced for so long that the McCaslin land contained buried treasure and would go to such lengths to attempt to find it. I am inclined to agree with Klotz that Faulkner's revisions here cause rather fundamental problems (10–13).[14]

Moreover, there may be more than a grain of truth in the concerns Klotz expresses about "The Bear" (4–10). He is wrong in his assumption that the *Post* version of "The Bear" precedes the one in *Go Down, Moses,* but he is right in pointing out that the episode of the fyce—the little dog that so gallantly attacks the bear—is not well integrated with the material Faulkner drew from the 1935 story, "Lion." When Ike rescues the fyce from Old Ben, both he and Sam Fathers have the opportunity to fire at the bear, but they do not do so. This passage and others as well establish that there is a symbolic bond of the utmost importance between Sam and Old Ben; the bear is Sam's totem. Yet only a few lines after Ike asks his mentor why he did not fire at Old Ben, the story of Sam's capture and the training of the mongrel Lion to kill the bear begins. It is all very well to argue that Sam's training of Lion makes sense because he knows that the bear—and he himself—*must* die, but the fact remains that Sam had the opportunity to kill Old Ben when the fyce attacked the bear, and he refused to do so. His motivations do not seem consistent. Again we have the sense of the rather forced and clumsy linkage of new and old material.[15]

On the other hand, the transformations that Faulkner effected in "Lion" for *Go Down, Moses* are, for the most part, very good indeed. The original story is quite weak—slow, sentimental, and strangely undramatic. But, as was so often the case when Faulkner returned to old material, he became aware of the potential it had, potential that he had failed to realize when he worked on it originally. In the version of "The Bear" in *Go Down, Moses*, he therefore enriched the characterization of Boon, expanded the episode about the buying of liquor in Memphis, introduced the material about Sam's training of Lion and the old man's death after the killing of Old Ben— in spite of the problems it was to cause—and near the end added Ike's marvelously lyrical meditation about Sam and the bear.

Of particular interest are two passages in "Lion" that achieve their full meaning only in *Go Down, Moses*. When Ike returns to the wilderness in the closing pages of "Lion" and sets out to find Boon, Ad (the black servant who becomes Ash in the novel) warns Ike about snakes: "Watch out for snakes. . . . Dey's crawling now" (*US* 199). The reader expects that something will come of this admonition, but nothing does. However, in *Go Down, Moses*, Ike has the encounter with the rattlesnake that leads to his hailing the creature in the language Sam has taught him (and which echoes the passage that Faulkner had written a decade earlier in "Red Leaves"): " 'Chief,' he said. 'Grandfather' " (*GDM* 330). The other passages, describing Boon's frenzied attempt to get his gun into working order again so that he can kill the squirrels at the Gum Tree, is the final episode in both "Lion" and the version of "The Bear" in *Go Down, Moses*. But in terms of what has preceded it, the episode is far more meaningful in the novel in what it suggests about hunting, the character of Boon, and the energy and vitality of the cyclical processes of life itself. We have not really been prepared for this striking scene in "Lion," but it is a marvelously appropriate conclusion for "The Bear." What Faulkner was able to do with both these passages is an indication of the expansive power of his imagination. In some strange way "The Bear" of *Go Down, Moses* is already present, waiting to be discovered, in "Lion."

A few more comments about Faulkner's revisions for *Go Down, Moses* will suffice. It can be argued that the metamorphosis of Don Boyd of the original "Delta Autumn" into the Roth Edmonds of the version in *Go Down, Moses* is not altogether convincing because the caustic and bitter Roth seems to be a very different person from the more thoughtful man we encounter in "The Fire and the Hearth."[16] But, on the whole, Faulkner's transformation of the original "Delta Autumn" for *Go Down, Moses* is one of his most striking and memorable revisions. The fact that there is McCaslin blood in the veins of Roth and that he and Ike are distantly related to the woman with whom he has an affair and who confronts Ike in the closing pages of the story makes the conclusion of this penultimate "chapter" of *Go Down, Moses* among the most moving passages in all of Faulkner's works. The repetition of the pattern of incest and miscegenation, the sense that we are beginning all over again, that the cycle must be played out at least once more gives this passage a tragic depth that is memorable for its power and irony.

The revisions of Faulkner's stories for incorporation into his later novels are generally superior to their original versions.[17] For the leisurely qualities, the slow tempos, the lack of narrative drive in the material contained in *Notes on a Horsethief,* "By the People," and "Hog Pawn" make it more appropriate for the expansive form of the novel than for the concentration and intensity we expect of the best short fiction. However, more generally speaking, it seems that what I have attempted to establish about Faulkner's handling of technical matters—point of view and other formal aspects of his stories—also applies to his reuse in the novels of material in the short fiction; it is characterized by a troubling unevenness. Some readers of Faulkner have been rather uncritical in their assessment of these revisions, which are anything but uniformly successful. But in spite of this unevenness, Faulkner was often able to effect magical transformations in his material. Few things in the study of his work are more exciting—or moving—than a close analysis of the revisions that produced the superb writing we can find in *The Hamlet* or *Go Down, Moses.*

## Novels and Stories: Patterns

Because a novel is longer and necessarily more complex than a short story and because the generally much more extensive period of time involved in its creation inevitably leads to significant transformations in the impulses that initiated it, it is more difficult to get at what a first-rate novel is doing than it is to understand a short story. The very process it takes to create a novel puts us at a greater remove from it than from a comparable work of short fiction. Since even a very subtle and refined short story is, in this sense, more elemental than a comparable novel, the story can be a most useful tool in analyzing the longer fiction of a writer. The thematic patterns and techniques of the stories that I have analyzed in preceding chapters can throw a considerable light on Faulkner's novels.

In the chapter on patterns in the short fiction, I argued that the overriding concern, under which Faulkner's other themes can be subsumed, is solipsism, that his more significant characters cannot, for the most part, come to terms with their limited, contingent status and with the reality of otherness. In the novels this theme is manifested in the lovelessness of the Compsons, in the self-serving emptiness of Temple Drake and of Popeye, in the denial of the humanity of Joe Christmas by those who mold him, and in Flem Snopes's ruthless manipulation of his fellow human beings. But perhaps the most impressive instance in Faulkner's work of this concern lies in the character of Thomas Sutpen, who in his obsession with his "design" totally fails to understand the contingent particularity of other men and women. The theme is somewhat less obvious in Faulkner's later works because of their more affirmative qualities. The younger Ike of *Go Down, Moses*, Ratliff in the trilogy, Nancy in *Requiem for a Nun*, the Corporal in *A Fable* are all able, in one sense or other, to acknowledge their own limitations and the reality of others. But even in these works the force that seems to motivate most people, that destroys the wilderness, that leads to the execution of the Corporal, and that to which Gavin and Ratliff are implicitly referring when, in their characterization of the human condition, they speak of the "pore sons of bitches" (*M* 429), is solipsism.

I have devoted a considerable amount of space to the embodiment of this theme in Faulkner's short stories that are concerned with the archetype of initiation. It should be obvious to even the most casual reader of Faulkner how important initiation themes are in the novels: in *Elmer*, *The Sound and the Fury*, *Sanctuary*, *Light in August*, *Intruder in the Dust*, etc. One of the purest and most consciously contrived examples of the archetype in American literature is Faulkner's very last novel, *The Reivers*. In discussing the patterns in the short fiction, I somewhat arbitrarily divided Faulkner's initiation stories into those that deal, more or less overtly, with sexual themes and those that do not. If anything, such a categorization seems even more arbitrary when applied to the novels, but sexual themes do seem to be more obviously involved in the initiations in the earlier works—in *The Sound and the Fury*, *Sanctuary*, and *Light in August*—than they are in those occurring in the later books. The distance that Faulkner was able to achieve from the sexual preoccupations of his early years is not only evident in the short fiction but is also implicit in the novels: in the contrast, on the one hand, between the aversion to female sexuality that is so intense in the characterizations of Quentin Compson, Horace Benbow, and Joe Christmas, and, on the other hand, the sense we have in the later books, particularly in Faulkner's treatment of Eula and Linda Snopes in *The Town* and *The Mansion*, of his sympathy for and understanding of women.

Faulkner's concern with children, which is so apparent in the short fiction, is obvious not only in *The Sound and the Fury* but in most of the other novels as well, particularly in the portrayals of Vardaman Bundren, of the boyhood of Joe Christmas, of Chick Mallison and Lucius Priest. But these young people either grow up in the works in which we see them portrayed, or we know that they will achieve adulthood in due time. More characteristic Faulknerian types are those figurative children who will never attain maturity. The most obvious instances of this type are, of course, the mental defectives we find in several of the novels: Benjy, Ike Snopes, Jim Bond in *Absalom, Absalom!*, Marya in *A Fable*. It is interesting that while such unfortunates can be found in a few of Faulkner's short stories—"The Kingdom of God," "Monk," and "Hand Upon the Waters"—none of these works is, by any means, a major piece, and Faulkner devoted proportionally far more attention to the retarded in the novels. He probably did so because in the novels he had the space he needed to develop the ironies suggested by the contrasts between the vision of the world afforded by this kind of innocence and that of the normal person. There is simply no room for this kind of development in a short story. Furthermore, mentally retarded characters tend to call too much attention to themselves in shorter works. Consider what a decision to give a significant role to Benjy in "That Evening Sun" would have done to that story.

There are others in Faulkner's novels, as in the stories, whom we cannot characterize as retarded but who maintain to the very end a kind of primal innocence: Elmer; the convict in *The Wild Palms*; Lena Grove; Boon Hogganbeck; and, in a very different sense, Thomas Sutpen. The pattern I have found in the short stories of the innocent or presumably innocent attaining some sort of triumph over the world of evil and corruption can certainly also be found in the novels. It is apparent in the story of Lena Grove and, in a sense, in that of the convict of *The Wild Palms* (who does, after all, get back to the security of his prison). But it is far more likely to occur in the later, more sentimental novels: in the roles played by Chick and Lucas in *Intruder in the Dust*, by Nancy in *Requiem for a Nun*, and by Uncle Ned and Lucius Priest in *The Reivers*. Consider also the contrast between the defeat and frustration experienced by Boon in "Lion" and *Go Down, Moses* and the complete triumph of his marriage to Corrie in Faulkner's last novel. However, this pattern is most memorably developed in *The Mansion* in Mink Snopes's obsessive, dogged, and finally successful efforts to kill Flem Snopes.

There are proportionally as many triangles in Faulkner's novels as in the short stories, and they again seem to suggest a basic lack of parity and equity in the sexual relationships he portrays. Curiously, while there are many triangles involving parental figures in the short fiction, there are very few in the novels. The most obvious of these are suggested in the various relationships in *The Town* and *The Mansion* involving Gavin Stevens, Eula and Linda Snopes, and the men who are attracted to them. The archetype of the "Terrible Mother" that figures so prominently in the short stories also occasionally appears in the novels in such figures as Mrs. Compson and perhaps Addie Bundren, but these characters do not play as prominent a role in the love relationships of their children as in the short stories. On the other hand, the incestuous attractions of siblings toward one another that are so obvious in *Flags in the Dust*, *The Sound and the Fury*, and *Absalom, Absalom!* can hardly be found in the short stories.

What can we make of these differences in Faulkner's handling of triangular relationships in his shorter and longer fiction? Perhaps they derive in part from the greater distancing and detachment from his raw materials that the more complex process of creating a novel helped Faulkner to attain. Hence, the short fiction may more obviously reflect Faulkner's oedipal feelings, on the one hand, and, on the other, his hostility toward the very strong maternal figures in his family. The use of incestuous attractions in the novels signals not only a Freudian displacement of these feelings but also Faulkner's developing sense, as he struggled to master the materials of such novels as *The Sound and the Fury* and *Absalom, Absalom!*, of the rich symbolic possibilities of the incest motif. And, of course, on a purely pragmatic level, it was probably considerably easier to sell a story with thinly disguised oedipal implications than it was to market a piece containing even the vaguest suggestion of incest.

In any case, while there are some relatively "normal" triangular relationships in the novels—for example, those involving Lena, Byron, and Lucas in *Light in August* or Harry, Charlotte, and Rittenmeyer in *The Wild Palms*—Faulkner's triangles are generally as curious in the novels as in the stories. In *Absalom, Absalom!* the relationship of Henry, Charles, and Judith not only involves incestuous longings but also the homosexual feelings of Henry for Charles. There is also the literal impotence of Flem and the figurative impotence of Gavin Stevens vis-à-vis Eula in *The Town*; the sexless rivalry for the dying Donald Mahon in *Soldiers' Pay*; and the strangely casual and blasé relationship of Roger, Laverne, and Jack in *Pylon*—so casual that no one knows who the father of Laverne's child is.

There are probably also proportionally as many wronged or trapped women in the novels as in the stories: Caddy Compson and her daughter Quentin, Addie Bundren, Temple Drake, Lena Grove (although it is doubtful that she ever considers herself wronged), Judith Sutpen, Eula Varner, etc. The pattern of such a person striking back in an effort to achieve vengeance can be found in Miss Quentin's theft of Jason Compson's money, Addie Bundren's adultery and the promise she extracts from Anse that he will bury her in Jefferson, and the role Linda plays in the murder of Flem Snopes. Nevertheless, there is a difference between Faulkner's treatment of such women in the short fiction and in the novels. In the stories, particularly the relatively early ones, sexual pathology is stressed. While Temple Drake and Joanna Burden clearly have problems along these lines, Faulkner's characterizations of the trapped women in his novels generally seems more muted, less shrill, more compassionate. It may be that his portrait of the frustrated Joanna in *Light in August* was so definitive that he no longer felt any need to return to that type. But again the greater length of the process involved in the creation of the novels and the opportunity Faulkner was thereby afforded to achieve more distance from his preoccupations and obsessions is probably a significant factor in explaining this difference.

In the novels the insistence of Faulkner's characters on justice, on a cosmic quid pro quo is apparent in Jason Compson's furious efforts to get back at Caddy for what she has done to his prospects, in Quentin's longing for hellfire, in Percy Grimm's murder and castration of Joe Christmas, in Thomas Sutpen's baffled incomprehension of the failure of the "design" created to satisfy the little boy who was turned away at the door of the mansion. In these novels of Faulkner's greatest period the ironic mode is dominant, and the kind of justice these characters want is generally *not* achieved. But again, as in the case of the later stories, Faulkner's handling of the pattern becomes more sentimental in the novels of the last two decades; the wrongs are righted in such works as *Intruder in the Dust* and *The Reivers* and especially in Mink Snopes's triumph in the concluding pages of *The Mansion*.

However, Faulkner's treatment of the theme of justice in the late novels or in any of his major works is not simplistic. Mink's murder of Flem is hardly a triumph of the good guys over the bad guys. Faulkner's handling of the dichotomy between the legal and the just is very complex in the trilogy and in *Intruder in the Dust*, as it is in such earlier works as *Sanctuary* and *The Wild Palms*. In *The Hamlet*, the only one of the novels deriving largely from the traditions of Southwestern humor—the theme of the biter bit seems more appropriate for the shorter fictional forms—it is clear that everyone is tainted with Snopesism, that guilt is universal. And Faulkner is as concerned in his great novels as he is in such stories as "Barn Burning" and "Mountain Victory" with the anguish involved in moral choice and with the terrible wrongs perpetrated in the name of *somebody's* conception of justice.

The closely related theme of the idée fixe is even more apparent in the novels than in the short stories. Bayard Sartoris's fixation on his dead brother, the obsession of the Compson brothers with the departed Caddy and of Hightower with his grandfather, the various compulsions of the Bundren family, Labove's passion for Eula, and Stevens's love for Eula and Linda—the list seems endless. While Mink Snopes does succeed in killing Flem and Lena Grove has apparently succeeded in her dogged search to find a father for her baby, Faulkner's characters are rarely able to satisfy their obsessions.

Faulkner's self-abnegating characters can be found in proportionally greater numbers in the novels than in the stories. In these terms we think of Dilsey, of Cash, of Byron Bunch, of Judith Sutpen, of Rat Rittenmeyer, of Nancy in *Requiem for a Nun*, and the Corporal in *A Fable*. Perhaps the more obvious prominence of these characters in the novels derives from Faulkner's sense of the greater importance of achieving some kind of moral balance in his longer works, of suggesting through such personages a way out of an otherwise overriding and oppressive solipsism.

In the concluding pages of the chapter on patterns, I stressed the limitations of any one thematic approach to Faulkner's short fiction and pointed to his concerns with the dangers of abstraction as another means of getting at what he was attempting to do. Clearly, the destructive abstractions of race, of class, of honor, of the integrity of the community play at least as great a role in the novels as in the stories. The theme is most memorably portrayed in Addie Bundren's concern with the gap between language and life, in the characterization of Joe Christmas as "nigger" by his community, and in Thomas Sutpen's failure to understand that people will not very readily allow themselves to be subordinated to a "design."

It should now be obvious that there is no great disparity between the themes we find in Faulkner's short stories and in the novels. The differences we find can be accounted for, in large measure, if we remember that the genetic impulses that led to the creation of the stories were rawer, more immediate, more direct than those that resulted in the novels. In this sense, the stories seem more basic, closer to the roots of Faulkner's mind and art, and hence worthy of the most concentrated and tenacious scrutiny.

## Novels and Stories: Techniques

While the patterns Faulkner employed in his short stories and novels are more notable for their similarities than for their differences, we are far more aware, when we consider technical matters, of the contrasts between his approaches to the two genres. There are several reasons for these differences. I have already noted Faulkner's greater interest in the novel as an art form. Furthermore, after the initial stages of his career he was by no means as concerned about the marketability of his long fiction as he was about that of his short fiction and therefore more inclined to take chances with the former; he *knew* his novels would be published. Because the novel, through its greater range and complexity, offered more opportunities for innovative techniques, he was more willing to experiment with it, to attempt daring, even radical solutions to the formal problems it posed. Faulkner's handling of point of view in the novels is an obvious instance of this difference.

Aside from Faulkner's far more daring and experimental treatment of point of view in his great novels, probably the most striking contrast between his handling of technique in the two genres is the greater frequency of first-person narration in the stories. As Millgate has noted, only two of the novels, *The Unvanquished* and *The Reivers*, are narrated by a single character ("The Problem of Point of View" 182). In two others, *As I Lay Dying* and *The Town*, the point of view is entirely in the first person but there are multiple narrators. In at least portions of all the other novels the authorial voice is present. Thus, while more than half of Faulkner's short stories are in the first person, the third person is in evidence in the vast majority of the novels. But to put the differences in terms as stark as these is to be somewhat deceptive. For the "I" narrator is obviously of very great importance in many of the longer works of fiction. In spite of the authorial voice in the fourth section of *The Sound and the Fury* and its use to frame the different narrative voices we hear in *Absalom, Absalom!*, the first person is, of course, the dominant mode of both these great novels. It is also used in about half of *The Mansion*, and there is much first-person narration by characters within the other novels—most notably in *Light in August*.

Nevertheless, it is clear that Faulkner used the third person more extensively in the novels than in the stories. He probably did so for a variety of reasons, but perhaps the most basic was his growing sense, as he experimented with various kinds of point of view, of the limitations that an extended use of the first person imposes within the framework of the novel. In the smaller scope of short fiction, the use of a witness- or protagonist-narrator can help to give a story concentration, intensity, irony—the kinds of effects that make such pieces as "That Evening Sun" and "A Justice" such fascinating works of art. Faulkner proved conclusively, in his management of many different narrative voices in *The Sound and the Fury* and *As I Lay Dying*, that he could manage the first person with stunning virtuosity in the novels. It is doubtful that there is anywhere in fiction a more compelling handling of an unreliable narrator than in the Jason section of *The Sound and the Fury*. But, as Millgate notes, the very fact that Faulkner felt impelled to complete that novel with a fourth section in the third person suggests his awareness of the problems deriving from the exclusive use of the first person in a work of such scope ("The Problem of Point of View" 184–85). Perhaps also Faulkner's clearly very conscious and deliberate use of language beyond the capabilities of his narrators in *As I Lay Dying*, particularly in the monologues of Darl, Vardaman, and Dewey Dell, implies a kind of straining attempt to transcend the limitations of the first person.

Faulkner was certainly very conscious of the advantages for his art of the use of the "I" narrator. But he came to realize that he needed the range, the flexibility, and the authority that a judicious use of an authorial voice can supply. He therefore tried to achieve the best of both worlds in the management of point of view in *Light in August* and *Absalom, Absalom!* In the former novel the use of selective omniscience, together with a considerable amount of material narrated by the characters, gives us a greater sense of range and variety than we have in any of Faulkner's other works. It allows us to hear the voice of Faulkner—his poetry, his rhetoric at its most restrained—and at the same time, to become aware, from the many different narrative perspectives, some in the first person, some in the third, of the moral and epistemological complexities which are the thematic matter of the novel. In *Absalom, Absalom!* Faulkner went one step further. The "I" voices we hear in *Light in August* are still distinctly those of the characters. In the later novel their language becomes essentially Faulkner's own. Even though there are significant differences in tonality and emphasis in what Miss Rosa, Mr. Compson, Quentin, and Shreve say, even though they are all, like Jason in *The Sound and the Fury*, unreliable narrators, it is clear that their language, in marked contrast to Jason's, is that of Faulkner. Thus he was able to dramatize his themes of the inadequacy of human knowledge and the limitations of history through these different points of view but also to infuse the entire novel and every narrative perspective in it with the rich, sweeping complexity of his rhetoric.

These contrasts between Faulkner's management of point of view in the stories and novels point toward what may be the most significant of the formal differences in his handling of the two genres. While there are exceptions, most of Faulkner's stories are devoted to a single narrative line, to the development of one coherent action. They are, to use a musical analogy again, homophonic, in contrast to the polyphony characteristic of Faulkner's greatest novels. It is a critical truism that Faulkner developed his aesthetic effects in his longer works through the juxtaposition of apparently relatively discrete material, the playing out of different story lines, different narrative voices, different perspectives against each other. This principle is apparent, in a variety of forms, in most of the novels: in the relative autonomy of the four sections of *The Sound and the Fury*; in the multiplicity of the voices we hear in *As I Lay Dying*; in the development in *Light in August* of the three stories of Lena, Joe, and Hightower; in the contrasting attitudes of the narrators of *Absalom, Absalom!* toward the Sutpens; in the alternation of the chapters of "Wild Palms" with those of "Old Man" in *The Wild Palms*, etc. While Faulkner generally wants in his short fiction the kind of intensity that can best be achieved through the use of a limited point of view, he is not, by and large, interested in that kind of effect in his longer works—in contrast to many of his great contemporaries. Because he has a broader canvas with which to work in the novel, he is interested in developing in it the kinds of ironies that derive from juxtaposition, particularly those suggesting his awareness of the unbridgeable gaps between separate human consciousnesses. In Faulkner's terms, the use of very different points of view within a single work suggests this problem far more effectively than the use of only one. Furthermore, multiple narrative perspectives can give a richness, range, and variety to a work that would be difficult to attain in any other way. That wonderful sense of profusion that *Light in August* conveys surely derives, to a large extent, from the many very different minds into which the reader is allowed to enter, whether in the first person or the third: those of Armstid, Lena, Byron, Joe, Hightower, the dietitian, the Hineses, Lucas Burch, Percy Grimm, Gavin Stevens, and unnamed townspeople, among others. In this respect the novel reminds us, as does *The Hamlet*, of those great nineteenth-century works written long before critics became concerned about the advantages of limited points of view.

On the other hand, Faulkner did sometimes use a more restricted point of view in the novels when it suited his purposes—particularly when his primary concern was the impingement of experience on a single sensibility, as it was (with the qualifications I have previously noted) in *The Unvanquished*, *The Reivers*, and *Intruder in the Dust*. He sought rather deliberately to curtail the range of the latter two works in particular, and hence the reader's experience of them is rather comparable to that of a piece of short fiction, of an extended short story or of a novella. He also used the third-person limited largely, although not exclusively, in the two narrative lines of *The Wild Palms*, both of which are essentially initiatory (although the initiation does not seem to "take" in the case of the convict), but this novel conveys a very real sense of range and scope because of the disparity between the minds and the experiences of Harry Wilbourne and of the convict.

This is not to say that one cannot sometimes quarrel with Faulkner's use of point of view in the novels. There are inconsistencies in his management of narrative voice, particularly that of Ratliff in the trilogy. One can question how successfully Faulkner employs the reporter as the central consciousness of *Pylon*. And the shifts in *The Mansion* from third person to first and back again seem clumsy. However, these kinds of problems are more apparent in Faulkner's stories than in his novels because his greater use of selective omniscience in the latter allows for more flexibility in modulating from voice to voice, and because if the reader is given the time a novel affords, he or she can find it easier to accept the conventions Faulkner employed in his management of narrative perspective. Few sensitive readers would quarrel any longer with the violations of verisimilitude in Faulkner's use of the narrative voices in *The Sound and the Fury, As I Lay Dying*, and *Absalom, Absalom!*, for, radical as these experiments are, they *work*. But they work only because the length of those books, the kinds of expectations we bring to them as novels, and our willingness as readers to defer for an extended period of time our judgments of what Faulkner is doing, enable them to work. A short story does not afford the reader the same opportunities.

It may be that the disappointment some readers of Faulkner's novels feel when they turn for the first time to the stories springs in part from the difficulty they have in adjusting what they have come to expect of Faulkner in the novels to their experience with short fiction. What we think of as most characteristically Faulknerian is that complex fusion of the poetry of the authorial voice with the irony deriving from the juxtaposition of widely varying human sensibilities. Faulkner's best short stories, superb as they are, give us very different kinds of experiences.

In the writing of fiction nothing came easily to Faulkner except narrative ideas and a facility with language. There is as much evidence of extensive revision in the manuscripts and typescripts of the longer fiction as in those of the shorter. However, from the start—from the composition of *Soldiers' Pay*—Faulkner clearly had a relatively mature sense of the contours of the novel and of the technical problems it entails. On the other hand, all the early short fiction is obviously apprentice work in every sense.

In the middle and late twenties Faulkner did discover the importance of economy of effect in the short story. What he learned about concentration and compression was to stand him in very good stead in his finest work in the genre. However, Faulkner had a kind of natural loquacity, the desire to spin a yarn out for all it was worth, a love of the sound of his own rhetoric that sometimes militated almost as much against the effectiveness of the novels as of the stories. There is much that is tedious, repetitive, long-winded not only in the early novels but also in at least a few pages of *Absalom, Absalom!*, *Pylon*, *The Wild Palms*, and most of his late work. Nevertheless, the reader can bear up under this kind of thing because he or she has almost come to expect such longueurs in the novel. In the short story, on the other hand, they generally prove fatal.

Faulkner's use of temporal dislocation did sometimes help him to solve this problem in his stories. But his experiments with time were far more radical in the novels and are, together with his handling of point of view, the most memorable and striking of his formal innovations. Any critical analysis of the treatment of time in twentieth-century fiction that ignores what Faulkner did in *The Sound and the Fury*, *Absalom, Absalom!*, and *Go Down, Moses* and, less obviously, in *Sanctuary* and *Light in August* is likely to be very deficient indeed. However, short fiction simply does not lend itself as readily as the novel to temporal dislocation because the writer has so much more room to maneuver in the novel and so much more time to defer the satisfaction of the reader's expectations. I have said that Faulkner sometimes seems to be floundering in the beginnings of his stories because of the difficulty he had in getting into his material. In the opening pages of the great novels, on the other hand, it is likely that the *reader* will be floundering because the writer is quite willing to plunge him or her *in medias res*. Yet Faulkner also seems confident that, given the necessary time and sustained attention, things will start to fall into place. The reward for the patient reader will be commensurate with his or her efforts.

We can find in the novels, as well as the stories, the structural pattern I have noted in which Faulkner begins with a climactically disruptive situation and then flashes back to develop the causes of this condition of disequilibrium. In *Intruder in the Dust* the opening sentences about the arrest of Lucas Beauchamp for the murder of a white man are immediately followed by a long flashback tracing the relationship between Lucas and Chick. We then move again into present time and to Chick's efforts to help the old man. The same pattern is apparent in *A Fable*, although we do not know for a long time what the nature of the precipitating crisis is. Generally, Faulkner is quite willing in the novels to take his time in his expositions. A disruptive situation—the murder of Joanna Burden, the death of Addie Bundren—may be in the offing, but Faulkner is as concerned in the opening pages of his novels about suggesting theme, establishing symbolic patterns, introducing necessary but sometimes rather peripheral characters, as he is about getting to the heart of the plot.

Certainly Faulkner's troubles with beginnings are not as evident in the novels as in the stories because he could afford to be leisurely in his longer fiction. Indeed, he generally had to be. In order to achieve his most characteristic effects, in order to implicate the reader fully in the experience of the book, his technique of very gradual disclosure was necessary. Faulkner does achieve considerable drama through scenic development in most of the beginnings of his novels—one thinks especially of the marvelous confrontation between Horace and Popeye in the opening pages of *Sanctuary*—but when it suits his purposes, he can, with impunity, begin a book like *The Hamlet* with the broadly panoramic development that one might expect of a Victorian novel. Martin Kreiswirth has effectively demonstrated that some beginnings of the novels that have been sharply criticized—those of *Soldiers' Pay* and *Flags in the Dust*, for example—actually serve their purposes quite well. The train ride in the former introduces us to the theme of the alienation of the returning veterans, and old man Falls's story in the first chapter of the latter gives us a real sense of what it means to be a Sartoris (42–45). The confusion we sometimes feel when Faulkner plunges us into the midst of a situation without imparting the expository information that one would conventionally expect is really quite salutary because it helps to prepare us for the strikingly different kind of literary experience the novel will give us if we can develop the skills as readers that it requires of us. On the other hand, the beginnings of the short stories, with such notable exceptions as those of "Red Leaves" or perhaps "Dry September," rarely give us this kind of preparation.

Kreiswirth also has some perceptive things to say about the means Faulkner uses to achieve closure in the novels, particularly the use of rhetorical techniques rather than those that more conventionally satisfy our need for a genuine resolution of dramatic and thematic tensions. In this regard he points to the peaceful imagery in the concluding lines of *The Sound and the Fury*, of *Flags in the Dust*, and of *The Mansion* (48–50). Certainly Faulkner's management of closure in *The Sound and the Fury*, *Absalom, Absalom!*, and particularly *Light in August*, with the very pronounced sense of circularity it affords and its humor and serenity, is masterful.[18] But I am inclined to think that Faulkner is not quite as successful with the endings of his novels as he is with those of his stories—probably because of the greater difficulty of finding closural strategies that will adequately resolve the tensions he has aroused in the longer works. He has the tendency to end the novels with "tags": in the context, rather shocking or at least surprising statements by characters that are not unrelated to the O. Henryesque twist endings that we find in some of the early stories. Consider Anse's "Meet Mrs Bundren" in *As I Lay Dying* (242), the convict's "Women ——t" in *The Wild Palms* (339), Lucas's "My receipt" in *Intruder in the Dust* (247), or Everbe's "His name is Lucius Priest Hogganbeck" in *The Reivers* (305). Such endings do convey some sense of finality, but they seem more than a little contrived and banal.

I have touched on Faulkner's "musical" techniques in what I have said about his attempts to unify his stories, but they are generally of considerably greater importance in the novels. The leitmotif, in the precise sense in which I have defined the term, may not be as often employed in the longer works of fiction as in the shorter, perhaps because Faulkner, in contrast to Mann, found it difficult to sustain such a device throughout a book. But it can be argued that Flem Snopes's bow tie, I. O.'s proverbs, and Buck Hipps's gingersnaps in *The Hamlet*, the descriptions of the clothing of Joe Christmas and of Popeye, and the repeated allusions to the quarter and the golf ball in the first section of *The Sound and the Fury* have something of the effect of leitmotifs.

Much more interesting are the analogies one can draw between the forms of Faulkner's novels and the larger structural elements of music. Several critics have called attention to the parallels between the four sections of *The Sound and the Fury* and the movements of a classical symphony.[19] Faulkner himself used the word *counterpoint* in describing what he was doing with two very different stories in *The Wild Palms* (*FB* 2 980), and the term can also be applied to the parallel development of the characters of Joe, Lena, and Hightower in *Light in August*. The sense of circularity, of recurrence that we get from the storytellers' continual return to certain crucial moments in the history of the Sutpens suggests the cyclical nature of musical form, as does also the polyphonic arrangement of the tales of love and barter in *The Hamlet*. Faulkner's use of such techniques seems to point again to his need for space and to the importance of the juxtaposition of apparently discrete materials in order to achieve his most characteristic effects.

Those problems with plot and the management of detail in the short fiction to which I have called attention are probably as frequent in Faulkner's longer works, but they may not be as obvious because they tend to be more submerged in the totality of a novel's effects. Yet many readers of *Sanctuary* have been puzzled as to why Temple perjures herself, and others have pointed to the inconsistent chronology of the novel.[20] Perhaps the most famous crux in Faulkner studies is the question as to how Quentin in *Absalom, Absalom!* comes to know the "truth" about Charles Bon's black blood—a problem that cannot be resolved by even the closest and most acute reading of the book.[21] Questions can also be raised about Jason's impossibly complex financial dealings in the third section of *The Sound and the Fury*. The various attempts to bury and to disinter the bodies in *Intruder in the Dust* seem wildly improbable. Similar questions can be raised about almost every one of Faulkner's novels.

I indicated, with some contrition, in the preceding chapter that too much could be made of this sort of thing, considering the magnitude of Faulkner's total achievement. But we cannot ignore such problems if we are to make an honest evaluation of his work. And it does seem that an awareness of the limitations and deficiencies of the short stories, because they more readily call attention to themselves, can help us to identify comparable problems in the novels.

# Conclusion

In the first chapter of this study I devoted some attention to the conflict in Faulkner's works between his poetic and narrative impulses. The differences between his short stories and novels that I have just discussed suggest another kind of conflict. Again there is, on the one hand, the simple delight he took in storytelling. On the other hand, there is an impulse that he noted in one of his more significant letters to Malcolm Cowley:

> As regards any specific book, I'm trying primarily to tell a story, in the most effective way I can think of, the most moving, the most exhaustive. But I think even that is incidental to what I am trying to do, taking my output (the course of it) as a whole. I am telling the same story over and over, which is myself and the world. Tom Wolfe was trying to say everything, get everything, the world plus 'I' or filtered through 'I' or the effort of 'I' to embrace the world in which he was born and walked a little while and then lay down again, into one volume. I am trying to go a step further. This I think accounts for what people call the obscurity, the involved formless 'style,' endless sentences. I'm trying to say it all in one sentence, between one Cap and one period. I'm still trying, to put it all, if possible, on one pinhead. I dont know how to do it. All I know is to keep on trying in a new way. (*SL* 185)

One must be cautious about inferring too much from such pronouncements. Obviously there is much that is hyperbolic in these words, and it may be that Faulkner was trying, consciously or unconsciously, to impress Cowley. Yet there is a great deal that is quite suggestive here. In the first place, Faulkner insists, as he does on many occasions, that his primary purpose is to tell stories. His emphasis on the attempt to get it all in in one sentence implies his desire to achieve the concentrated intensity of a first-rate short story or poem. However, the major idea here, strongly suggested by the comparison to Wolfe, is a kind of Faustian desire for completeness, for wholeness, the need to incorporate the full range of experience into his work. The letter implies that such an attempt is doomed to failure. But it is obvious that the kind of art that comes closest to achieving this goal, in spite of what Faulkner says about the single sentence and the pinhead, is not an art of compression but of expansion. It is not achieved by the writing of short stories but by the composition of novels. Faulkner could, and did, satisfy his simpler narrative impulses through the creation of some superb short fiction, but the larger aim that he expressed in the letter to Cowley could only be achieved through the multifaceted complexity of extremely ambitious works of long fiction.

Thus the space provided by the novel enabled Faulkner to get at least a little closer to that goal of saying it all, of getting in the whole story of "myself and the world." He was to discover, at least as early as the writing of *Flags in the Dust*, that the best method for making this attempt was through juxtaposition, through counterpoint. As I have noted, he was to use this kind of method, in various forms, in nearly all his most ambitious works. It is this technique, as much as any other aspect of Faulkner's art, even his style, that accounts for the peculiar density and richness of his novels. Because most of his short fiction necessarily involves the development of a single line, one basic strand, rather than the multiple strands of the long fiction and because Faulkner must therefore have felt constrained by the limitations of the genre, there seems to be a kind of thinness in many of the stories. By contrast, when comparing Hemingway's novels with his short fiction, one does not have this sense because the basis of Hemingway's aesthetic seems to be the supreme importance of focus and compression. Hence his best work is in the short story, Faulkner's in the novel.

While there is considerable disagreement about the assessment of Faulkner's novels, many critics would argue that very nearly half of them— *The Sound and the Fury*, *As I Lay Dying*, *Sanctuary*, *Light in August*, *Absalom, Absalom!*, *The Wild Palms*, *The Hamlet*, *Go Down, Moses*—are works of very high distinction indeed. And others have offered strong arguments for the quality of *Flags in the Dust*, *The Unvanquished*, *Requiem for a Nun*, and *A Fable*. On the other hand, of the more than one hundred twenty stories Faulkner wrote, perhaps eight or ten are masterpieces, and another fifteen or twenty have considerable merit. While there are certainly other factors involved, it is likely that the tendency Faulkner had, from the mid-thirties on, to dispense with the writing of autonomous stories is an indication of his growing awareness of where his strengths and weaknesses as a writer of fiction lay.

In evaluating the quality of Faulkner's short fiction, one cannot ignore, although they are easy to exaggerate, the purely pragmatic exigencies of his career. At certain periods of his life he needed money desperately, and selling stories was the readiest means he had of acquiring it. He had to be aware of the markets, had to know what was likely to sell and what was not. I have noted some of the instances when he was perfectly willing to revise a story drastically in order to satisfy the editors of a mass-circulation magazine. On the other hand, he almost always firmly—sometimes furiously—rejected any tampering by his editors with his novels. Although he was certainly proud of his best stories, as he had every right to be, he did often seem to have a kind of double standard in his approach to the two genres.

Nevertheless, it was the storytelling impulse that gave rise to both the short fiction and the novels. I have noted throughout this study the close and complex relationship between Faulkner's work in the two genres. We can discern in the short stories in more rudimentary form those elements Faulkner was to fuse and integrate in the novels. The genetic processes that led to the creation of the novels were far more complex than those that produced the short fiction; the distance between the original idea and the end product is considerably greater in Faulkner's novels. When we read a story, we are closer to its germinating impulse. Hence a close study of the short fiction can tell us more than a comparable study of the novels about the psychology of Faulkner the creator. Much remains to be done in this area.

Yet, as I hope this study has demonstrated, the stories deserve to be studied in their own right as significant and autonomous works of art. The best of them are superlatively good, of as high a quality as any produced in this century. Nothing Hemingway ever wrote achieved the hypnotic fascination of "That Evening Sun" or the strangely resonant complexity of "Red Leaves" or the marvelous sense of comic absurdity in the ferociously funny "Mule in the Yard." And when we consider the total body of Faulkner's short fiction, we must conclude that, like his novels, it reveals an astonishing scope and variety, a fertility, energy, and inventiveness unmatched by any other American writer.

I have devoted a considerable amount of attention, particularly in the last three chapters, to some of the limitations and weaknesses of Faulkner's art. Certainly his work is uneven, particularly when it is compared—as it deserves to be—to that of his great European contemporaries, Joyce, Proust, and Mann. The study of the short fiction reveals, as I think any comparable analysis of Faulkner's novels should, that he was not only capable of achieving and sustaining effects of the most thrilling sublimity but that he could also produce work that is careless, shoddy, banal, and inept.

Yet there is something that is almost endearing about this unevenness. Much as we admire the great fiction that our age has produced—*Ulysses*, *Der Zauberberg*, *A la recherche du temps perdu*—we may find a quality in those novels that is chilling and austere, almost inhuman because they are the products of such incredible genius. Faulkner too had genius. But his triumphs somehow seem all the greater because of his failures, his limitations, his excesses. Since he had to work so hard to achieve those triumphs, we feel closer to him, more aware of his humanity. And ultimately it is that humanity, revealed in every page of his work, that causes us to find his achievement so wondrous, so exalting, so worthy of celebration.

# Bibliography of Faulkner's Short Fiction

The following bibliography is based, in part, on my own examination of most of the documents listed below, including all the relevant manuscripts and typescripts at the Alderman Library of the University of Virginia; the Berg collection in the New York Public Library; and the Rowan Oak papers (on microfilm at the Alderman Library). However, I am heavily indebted here to the scholarship of others: especially James Meriwether's classic 1971 study, "The Short Fiction of William Faulkner: A Bibliography"; Hans Skei's enormously useful *William Faulkner: The Short Story Career*; and the authoritative introductions to the relevant volumes of the Garland Faulkner. From these sources I have borrowed much factual information. I also employ, with some modifications, the format devised by Meriwether and Skei's alphabetical listing of the stories. Essentially, this bibliography is an updating of Meriwether's pioneering work, incorporating information unavailable to Meriwether at the time.

A number of other sources have proved most useful, particularly Kinney and Fowler, and the textual-bibliographical notes by Blotner in *US* (681–712) and by Putzel in *Genius of Place* (304, 308–23). I have cited page references to the latter two sources and to the Garland Faulkner in many of the entries on specific stories. I am also indebted to Cox; *FB*; Dasher; Gresset, *Chronology*; Meriwether, *Literary Career*; and to other works cited in the individual entries. For bibliographical information on these secondary sources, see the Works Cited section that follows. (All references to Putzel in this bibliography are to *Genius of Place*.)

Listed below are data about significant publications of Faulkner's short fiction, including the incorporation of the stories into books; all the information available to me about manuscripts and typescripts; and some notes on other matters of interest. (For information about how Blotner established the texts to be used in *US*, see his introduction: xii–xiii.) See the section "Abbreviations for Faulkner's Texts" for the abbreviations employed here for Faulkner's books. The following abbreviations are used for repositories of the manuscripts and typescripts:

BC      Brodsky Collection
JFSA    Jill Faulkner Summers Private Archive
NYPL    New York Public Library
OB      Harold Ober Associates
ROP     Rowan Oak Papers, University of Mississippi
PC      Private Collection
PR      Princeton University
TU      William Wisdom Collection, Tulane University
TX      University of Texas at Austin
VA      University of Virginia

"Abraham's Children." See "Spotted Horses."

"An Absolution." See "The Fire on the Hearth."

"Ad Astra." *American Caravan IV*. Eds. Alfred Kreymborg, Lewis Mumford, and Paul Rosenfeld. New York: Macaulay, 1931: 164–81. Revised for *T13*; that version in *CS*. VA: 11-pp. ms. See Putzel 308–9; *WFM 9* ix, xii, 117–27.

"Adolescence." *US*. VA: 26-pp. ts. See *US* 704; Putzel 309; *WFM 25* x, xii, 97–122.

"Afternoon of a Cow." Originally published under the pseudonym of Ernest V. Trueblood in a French translation by Maurice Edgar Coindreau: "L'Après-midi d'une Vache," *Fontaine* 27–28 (1943): 66–81. *Furioso* 2 (1947): 5–17. *US*. The central incident of the story is incorporated in *H*, book 3, chapter 1. ROP: 7-pp. ms. VA: 17-pp. ts. PR, TX, and BC: 17-pp. carbon tss. See *US* 702–3; *WFM 15* 1: xi, xv, xvi, 199–215.

"Al Jackson" [The Al Jackson Letters]. Bungert, *humoristische* 221–26. NYPL: 2-pp. ts. fragment. Newberry Library: 2 3-pp. tss. See *US* 704–5; Putzel 309; *WFM 4* viii, x, 489–90.

"All the Dead Pilots." *T13*. Reprinted in *CS*. VA: 10-pp. ms. Original title "Per Ardua." See Meriwether, "Faulkner's Correspondence" 266–67; Putzel 309; *WFM 9* ix, xii, 128–38.

"Almost." See "Was."

"Ambuscade." *Saturday Evening Post* 29 Sept. 1934: 12–13, 80, 81. Revised for *U*. *US*. ROP: 5-pp. ms. (incomplete); 23-pp. ts. There is an incorrect identification by Kinney and Fowler of a 10-pp. ms. of "Retreat" as a ms. of "Ambuscade." See Kinney and Fowler 328 (box 2, folder 10). See also *US* 681–82.

"And Now What's To Do." *Mississippi Quarterly* 26 (1973): 399–402. *FM*. ROP: 2-pp. ms. fragment. See Putzel 309.

"Apotheosis." See "The Fire on the Hearth."

"Appendix, Compson, 1699–1945." Cowley, *Portable* 737–56. Later editions of *SF*. VA: 12-pp. carbon ts. (incomplete); 22-pp. carbon ts.

"Aria Con Amore." See "Spotted Horses."

"Artist at Home"; "An Artist at Home." *Story* Aug. 1933: 27–41. *CS.* VA: 13-pp. ms. entitled "An Artist at Home." See *WFM 24* xiii, xviii, 320–32.

"As I Lay Dying." See "Spotted Horses."

"Barn Burning." *Harper's* June 1939: 86–96. *CS.* VA: 16-pp. ms.; 32-pp. ts.; 32-pp. carbon ts. of the preceding. Originally the first chapter of *H.* See *WFM 15* 1: xi, xvi, 216–64.

"The Bear." *Saturday Evening Post* 9 May 1942: 30–31, 74, 76, 77. Extracted from *GDM. BW* (a different version extracted from *GDM*). *US* (*Post* version). OB: 20-pp. carbon ts. See Meriwether, "Short Fiction" 298–99; *US* 696; *WFM 16* 1: xiv, xviii.

"A Bear Hunt." *Saturday Evening Post* 10 February 1934: 8–9, 74, 76. *CS.* Revised for *BW*.

"Bench for Two." See "Pennsylvania Station."

"Beyond." *Harper's* Sept. 1933: 394–403. *DRM. CS.* VA: 28-pp. ts. entitled "Beyond the Gate"; 9-pp. ms. entitled "Beyond"; ROP: 1-p. ts. or carbon ts. fragment. See *WFM 11* x, xiii, 171–207.

"Beyond Love." See "Love."

"Beyond the Gate." See "Beyond."

"The Big Shot." *US.* VA: 37-pp. ts. See *US* 707; Putzel 309; *WFM 25* x, xii, 146–82.

"Black Music." *DRM. CS.* VA: 11-pp. ms. TX: 29-pp. ts. See *WFM 11* x–xi, xiii, 240–50.

"Bourbon Street." See "Jealousy."

"The Brooch." *Scribner's* Jan. 1936: 7–12. *CS.* VA: 5-pp. ms.; 15-pp. carbon ts.; 30-pp. carbon ts. ROP: various fragments (3-pp. ms.; 2-pp. ts.; 3-pp. ts.; 1-p. ts.; 9-pp. carbon ts.; 15-pp. ts. [nearly complete]; 2-pp. ts.) An early title for the story may have been "Fire and Clock"; see Skei *Short Story Career* 54–56. See also *WFM 24* xiii, xvii–xviii, 246–96. Data in *WFM 24* on ROP fragments is incomplete.

"Built a Fence." See "A Justice."

"By the People." *Mademoiselle* Oct. 1955: 86–89, 130, 131, 132, 133, 134, 135, 136, 137, 138, 139. Incorporated in *M*, chapter 13. PR: 26-pp. carbon ts.; 25-pp. ts.; 1-p. ts. fragment. See *WFM 22* 1: viii–x.

"Carcassonne." *T13. CS.* VA: 7-pp. ts.; 7-pp. ts. See Putzel 309–10; *WFM 9* xi, xii, 382–95.

"Centaur in Brass." *American Mercury* Feb. 1932: 200–210. *CS.* Incorporated in *T*, chapter 1. TU: 24-pp. ts. See Putzel 310; *WFM 21* 1: vii–ix.

"Chance." New Orleans *Times-Picayune* 17 May 1925, Sunday magazine section: 7. *NOS.* NYPL: 6-pp. carbon ts. The running head on the ts. is "The Mirror of Chartres Street." See *WFM 24* x, xvi, 82–87.

"Chartres Street." See "Mirrors of Chartres Street."

"Cheest." New Orleans *Times-Picayune* 5 Apr. 1925, Sunday magazine section: 4. *NOS.*

"Christmas Tree." See "Two Dollar Wife."

"The Cobbler." New Orleans *Times-Picayune* 10 May 1925, Sunday magazine section: 7. *NOS.*

"Country Mice." New Orleans *Times-Picayune* 20 Sept. 1925, Sunday magazine section: 7. *NOS.*

"A Courtship." *Sewanee Review* 56 (1948): 634–53. *CS.* VA: 22-pp. carbon ts. See *WFM 24* xv, xix, 466–98.

"Crevasse." *T13. CS.* See "Victory" for tss. See also Putzel 310; *WFM 9* viii, xiii.

"Damon and Pythias Unlimited." New Orleans *Times-Picayune* 15 Feb. 1925, Sunday magazine section: 7. *NOS.* NYPL: 9-pp. ts.; 9-pp. carbon ts. The running head on the first ts. is "SINBAD IN NEW ORLEANS"; on the second, "The Mirror of Chartres Street." See *WFM 24* viii, xvi, 21–38.

"A Dangerous Man." *US.* ROP: 13-pp. ts. See *US* 708–9.

"A Dangling Clause from Work in Progress." See *Notes on a Horsethief.*

"A Dark House." See "Evangeline."

"Death Drag"; "A Death-Drag"; "Death-Drag." *Scribner's* Jan. 1932: 34–42 (entitled "Death-Drag"). *DRM* (entitled "Death Drag"). *CS* (entitled "Death Drag"). VA: 11-pp. ms. ("A Death Drag"); 27-pp. carbon ts. ("A Death Drag"). See Putzel 310; *WFM 11* ix, xii, 67–104.

"Delta Autumn." *Story* May-June 1942: 46–55. Revised for *GDM*; a portion of that version revised for *BW. US.* VA: 18-pp. ts.; 7-pp. ts. draft. See *WFM 16* 1: xiii, xv, xviii, 214–39, 280–86.

"The Devil Beats His Wife." See "Two Dollar Wife."

"Divorce in Naples." *T13. CS.* VA: 6-pp. ms. with cancelled title "Equinox"; 17-pp. carbon ts. See Putzel 310; *WFM 9* xi, xiv, 358–81.

"Doctor Martino." See "Dr. Martino."

"Don Giovanni." *Mississippi Quarterly* 32 (1979): 484–95. *US.* NYPL: 9-pp. ts.; 12-pp. carbon ts. See *US* 705: Putzel 310; *WFM 4* vii, x, 468–88.

"Dr. Martino." *Harper's* Nov. 1931: 733–43. *DRM. CS* (entitled "Dr. Martino"; the other versions cited here are entitled "Doctor Martino"). VA: 14-pp. ms.; 3-pp. ms. (incomplete); 7-pp. ms. (incomplete); 5-pp. ts. (incomplete). See *WFM 11* viii, x–xii, 1–29.

"Drouth." See "Dry September."

"Drusilla." See "Skirmish at Sartoris."

"Dry September." *Scribner's* Jan. 1931: 49–56. Revised for *T13;* that version in *CS.* VA: 8-pp. ms. entitled "Drouth"; 19-pp. carbon ts. entitled "Drouth." ROP: 1-p. ts. fragment (not identified by Kinney and Fowler; see 330, folder 35.) See Putzel 311; *WFM 9* x, xii, 258–92.

"Dull Tale"; "A Dull Tale." *US.* ROP: 1-p. ms. fragment ("A Dull Tale"); 3-pp. ms. fragment ("A Dull Tale"); 11-pp. ms. ("Resurgam Two Men Memphis Anecdote Episode"); 33-pp. ts. ("A Dull Tale"); 32-pp. carbon ts. (missing p. 1). The story is a thorough revision of "The Big Shot." See *US* 707–8.

"Elly." *Story* Feb. 1934: 3–15. *DRM. CS.* VA: 6-pp. ms. entitled "Selvage"; 14-pp. ts. entitled "Selvage"; 11-pp. ms. entitled "Elly." The original idea for the story was apparently Estelle Faulkner's. See *FB* 1: 604. For another possible early title of the story, "Salvage," see Skei, *Short Story Career* 49. See *WFM 11* x, xiii, 208–39.

"An Empress Passed." See "There Was a Queen."

"Episode." New Orleans *Times-Picayune* 16 Aug. 1925, Sunday magazine section: 2.

*NOS.* NYPL: 3-pp. ts.; 3-pp. carbon ts. See *WFM 24* x, xvi, 88–90, 92–94.

"Equinox." See "Divorce in Naples."

"An Error in Chemistry." *Ellery Queen's Mystery Magazine* June 1946: 4–19. *KG.* VA: 22-pp. carbon ts. See *WFM 18* ix–xi, 86–108.

"Evangeline." *Atlantic* Nov. 1979: 68–80. *US.* ROP: 15-pp. ms.; 40-pp. ts. There is a 7-pp. ms. fragment entitled "A Dark House," which may be an early draft of the story, among the Rowan Oak papers. See Skei, *Short Story Career* 71; *US* 709.

"Fire and Clock." See "The Brooch."

"The Fire and the Hearth." See "The Fire on the Hearth."

"The Fire on the Hearth." *GDM*, chapter 3 of "The Fire and the Hearth." VA: 17-pp. ts. (incomplete) entitled "An Absolution" (an alternate title, "Apotheosis," added by Faulkner); 20-pp. ts. entitled "The Fire on the Hearth"; 21 miscellaneous ts. pp., 1 ts. p., 23-ts. pp. of *GDM* version entitled "The Fire and the Hearth." See *WFM 16* 1: ix, xvi–xvii, 81–123.

"Fool About a Horse." *Scribner's* Aug. 1936: 80–86. Incorporated in *H*, book 1, chapter 2. *US.* VA: 10-pp. ms.; 21-pp. ts. (incomplete); 33-pp. carbon ts. See *US* 684–85; *WFM 15* 1: xii, xv, 135–98.

"Fox Hunt"; "Foxhunt"; "A Fox-Hunt." *Harper's* Sept. 1931: 393–402. *DRM. CS.* (Published versions entitled "Fox Hunt.") VA: 11-pp. ms. entitled "A Fox-Hunt"; 26-pp. ts. entitled "Foxhunt." See *WFM 11* ix, xii, 30–66.

"Frankie and Johnny." *Mississippi Quarterly* 31 (1978): 453–64. *US.* (Meriwether and Blotner gave the untitled story this title.) VA: 23-pp. ts. See *US* 698–99; Putzel 312; *WFM 25* x, xii, 123–45.

"Go Down, Moses." *Collier's* 25 Jan. 1941: 19–20, 45, 46. Revised for *GDM. US.* VA: 14-pp. ts.; 1-p. carbon ts. fragment; 17-pp. carbon ts. Collection of Carl Petersen: 2 ts. sheets. See *US* 694–95; *WFM 16* 1: xi, xii, xvii, 179–213.

"Golden Land." *American Mercury* May 1935: 1–14. *CS.* ROP: 12-pp. ms.

"Gold Is Not Always." *Atlantic* Nov. 1940: 563–70. Revised for *GDM*, chapter 2 of "The Fire and the Hearth." *US.* VA: 5-pp. miscellaneous ts.; 19-pp. ts. Yale: 21-pp. ts.; corrected *Atlantic* galley proof, 7 sheets. See *US* 693–94; *WFM 16* 1: ix, xvi, 40–63.

"Growing Pains." See "Portrait of Elmer." See also Putzel 312.

"Hair." *American Mercury* May 1931: 53–61. Revised for *T13*; that version in *CS.* TU: 21-pp. ts. See *WFM 9* x, xii.

"Hand Upon the Waters." *Saturday Evening Post* 4 Nov. 1939. 14–15, 75, 76, 78, 79. *KG.* VA: 2-pp. ts. fragment; 30-pp. ts.; 30-pp. ts. (incomplete). See *WFM 18* ix, xi, 2–63.

"Hell Creek Crossing." *Saturday Evening Post* 31 Mar. 1962: pagination unclear. (This is an extract from *R* with introductory material added.) See Meriwether, "Short Fiction" 295–96.

"The Hill." *The Mississippian* 10 Mar. 1922: 1–2. *EPP.*

"Hog Pawn." *US.* Incorporated in *M*, chapter 14. VA: 26-pp. ts.; 26-pp. carbon ts. PR: 28-pp. ts. See *US* 697; Meriwether, "Short Fiction" 314; *WFM 22* 1: viii–x; 4: 39–67.

"Home." New Orleans *Times-Picayune* 16 Aug. 1925, Sunday magazine section: 3.

*NOS*. NYPL: 6-pp. ts.; 5-pp. carbon ts. Running head on the 6-pp. ts. is "SINBAD IN NEW ORLEANS"; on the 5-pp. ts. "The Mirror of Chartres Street." See *WFM 24* viii, xvi, 39–49.

"Honor." *American Mercury* July 1930: 268–74. *DRM*. *CS*. See Meriwether, *Literary Career* 173, 174, for the suggestion that "Point of Honor," submitted to *The Saturday Evening Post* on 7 Mar. 1930, is probably the same story.

"The Hound." *Harper's* Aug. 1931: 266–74. *DRM*. Incorporated in *H*, book 3, chapter 2. *US*. See *US* 688–89.

*Idyll in the Desert*. New York: Random, 1931. *US*. VA: 4-pp. ms.; 19-pp. ts.; 19-pp. ts. See *US* 701; *WFM 24* xii–xiii, xvii, 200–245.

"Indians Built a Fence." See "A Justice."

"Jealousy." New Orleans *Times-Picayune* 1 Mar. 1925, Sunday magazine section: 2. *NOS*. NYPL: 7-pp. ts. (entitled "Royal Street" with another title, "Bourbon Street," cancelled); 9-pp. ts. Running head on the 7-pp. ts. is "SINBAD IN NEW ORLEANS"; on the 9-pp. ts. "The Mirror of Chartres Street." See *WFM 24* viii–ix, xvi, 50–65.

"A Justice." *T13*. *CS*. A portion revised for *BW*. VA: 10-pp. ms. The original title of the story was apparently "Indians Built a Fence." See Meriwether, "Faulkner's Correspondence" 261–62; Putzel 312; *WFM 9* ix–x, xii, 215–27.

"The Kid Learns." New Orleans *Times-Picayune* 31 May 1925, Sunday magazine section: 2. *NOS*. NYPL: 1-p. ts. fragment. See *WFM 24* x, xvi, 91.

"The Kingdom of God." New Orleans *Times-Picayune* 26 Apr. 1925, Sunday magazine section: 4. *NOS*. NYPL: 8-pp. carbon ts. The running head on the ts. is "The Mirror of Chartres Street." See *WFM 24* ix, xvi, 74–81.

"Knight's Gambit." Title novella of *KG*. The novella is an expansion of an unpublished short story (29 ts. pp. on 23 sheets) at VA. At VA are also the following: 151-pp. ts. setting copy of the novella; 228-pp. carbon ts. on 157 sheets of the novella; and 80 miscellaneous ts. and carbon ts. pp. of both the novella and the short story on 50 sheets. See *WFM 18* x–xii, 109–644.

"Landing in Luck." *The Mississippian* 26 Nov. 1919: 2, 7. *EPP*.

"The Leg"; "Leg." *DRM*. *CS*. TX: 26-pp. ts. VA: 10-pp. ms.; 26-pp. carbon ts. (of TX ts.). In *DRM* the story is entitled "Leg," in the other versions, "The Leg." See Putzel 312–13; *WFM 11* xi, xiii, 251–86.

"A Letter"; "The Letter"; "A Letter to Grandmamma"; "A Letter to Grandmamma." Unpublished. In ROP there are 42 pp. of mss. and tss. of a number of different versions, all incomplete: 4-pp. ms., 7-pp. ts., 13-pp. ts. (all entitled "A Letter"); 3-pp. ms. and 8-pp. ms. (both entitled "The Letter"); 1-p. ms. ("A Letter to Grand-mamma"); and 6-pp. ts. ("A Letter to Grandmamma"). See Dasher 349–50. The 6-pp. ts. has E. Oldham's name at the top. The idea for the story was probably Estelle Faulkner's. See *FB* 1: 646; Skei, *Short Story Career* 39.

"The Liar." New Orleans *Times-Picayune* 26 July 1925, Sunday magazine section: 3, 6. *NOS*.

"Lion." *Harper's* Dec. 1935: 67–77. Revised and expanded for inclusion in *GDM* version of "The Bear." The latter, with the exception of part four, incorporated in *BW*. *US*. See *US* 690–91.

"Lizards in Jamshyd's Courtyard." *Saturday Evening Post* 27 Feb. 1932: 12–13, 52, 57. Incorporated in *H*, book 1, chapter 3, and book 4, chapter 2. *US*. ROP: 9-pp. ms.; four complete or nearly complete tss. (23-pp.; 21-pp., entitled "Omar's Eighteenth Quatrain"; 30-pp.; 25-pp.); numerous fragments and miscellaneous ts. pp.: (2-pp. carbon; 5-pp. carbon; 9-pp.; 1-p.; 1-p.; 8-pp.; 11-pp. carbon; 2-pp. carbon; 10-pp.; 1-p.; 13-pp. carbon; 1-p. carbon). See Putzel 304, 314; *WFM 15* 1: xv. For some additional sorting out of this material, see Skei, *Short Story Career* 63–64; and *US* 686–88.

"Lo!" *Story* Nov. 1934: 5–21. *CS*. ROP: 12-pp. ms.

"Love." *Missouri Review* 11 (1988): 123–50. VA: 13-pp. ms.; 5-pp. ms., miscellaneous; 49-pp. ts. (incomplete). ROP: 29-pp. ts., 5-pp. carbon ts. fragment. In ROP there are also various versions of a screen treatment of this material called "Beyond Love." See Putzel 314–15; *WFM 25* ix–xiii, 30–96.

*Mayday.* Notre Dame: U of Notre Dame P, 1977, 1980. TU: 43-pp. illustrated handbound booklet. See Putzel 315–16.

"The Mirror of Chartres Street." See "Mirrors of Chartres Street."

"Mirrors of Chartres Street." New Orleans *Times-Picayune* 8 Feb. 1925, Sunday magazine section: 1, 6. *NOS*. NYPL: 4-pp. ts. entitled "Chartres Street"; 5-pp. carbon ts. entitled "The Mirror of Chartres Street." The running head on the 4-pp. ts. is "SINBAD IN NEW ORLEANS." TU: 9-pp. ts. See Putzel 316; Skei, *Short Story Career* 21–23; *WFM 24* viii, xvi, 12–20.

"Mississippi." *Holiday* Apr. 1954: 33–47. A portion incorporated in *BW*. *ESPL*. PR: 40-pp. ts.; 38-pp. carbon ts.

*Miss Zilphia Gant.* Dallas: Book Club of Texas, 1932. *US*. TX: 23-pp. ts. VA: 9-pp. ms.; 18-pp. ts.; 23-pp. carbon ts. (of TX ts.). The probable order in which these versions were written is 18-pp. ts., ms., 23-pp. ts. See *US* 700; Putzel 316; *WFM 24* xii, xvii, 138–98; Pitavy.

"Mistral." *T13*. *CS*. VA: 17-pp. ms.; 46-pp. carbon ts. See *WFM 9* x–xi, xiv, 293–357.

"Monk." *Scribner's* May 1937: 16–24. *KG*. ROP: 3-pp. ts. fragment. See *WFM 18* ix, xi.

"Moonlight." *US*. VA: 16-pp. carbon ts. (incomplete); 13-pp. ts. The two versions of the story are very different. The 13-pp. version, apparently much later than the other, is used in *US*. See *US* 706; *WFM 25* x, xi, 1–29.

"Mountain Victory"; "A Mountain Victory." *Saturday Evening Post* 3 Dec. 1932: 6–7, 39, 42, 44, 45, 46 (entitled "A Mountain Victory"). Revised for *DRM*; that version in *CS*. VA: 18-pp. ms.; 42-pp. carbon ts. TX: 46-pp. ts. See "An Unpublished Episode from 'A Mountain Victory,'" *Mississippi Quarterly* 32 (1979): 481–83. See also *WFM 11* xi, xiii, 287–346.

"Mr. Acarius." *Saturday Evening Post* 9 Oct. 1965: 26–27, 28, 29, 30, 31. VA: 19-pp. carbon ts. entitled "Weekend Revisited." BC: two copies of 22-pp. carbon ts. entitled "Weekend Revisited"; 2-pp. ms.; 1-p. ts. JFSA: 19-pp. ts. See Gresset, "Weekend" 173n2; *US* 703; Meriwether, "Short Fiction" 304–5; *WFM 25* xi, xiii, 228–46.

"Mule in the Yard." *Scribner's* Aug. 1934: 65–70. *CS*. Incorporated in *T*, chapter 16. VA: 10-pp. ms.; 10-pp. ts. (incomplete). ROP: 1-p. ms. fragment. See *WFM 21* 1: ix–xi, 346–65.

"Music—Sweeter than the Angels Sing." Originally published in the University of Mississippi *The Freshman Theme Review* Apr. 1928, with the authorship credited to Katharine Hargis. Wells and Wells 868–71.

"My Grandmother Millard and General Bedford Forrest and the Battle of Harrykin Creek." *Story* Mar.–Apr. 1943: 68–86. *CS*. PR: 42-pp. ts. VA: 2 pp. ts. fragment and 2-pp. carbon ts. fragment; 43-pp. carbon ts. See *WFM 24* xiv, xviii, 351–412.

"A Name for the City." *Harper's* Oct. 1950: 200–214. Revised and entitled "The Courthouse (A Name for the City)" for the prologue to Act I of *RN*. See Meriwether, "Short Fiction" 305.

"Never Done No Weeping When You Wanted to Laugh." See "That Evening Sun."

"New Orleans." *Double Dealer* Jan.-Feb. 1925: 102–7. Consists of eleven sketches: "Wealthy Jew," "The Priest," "Frankie and Johnny," "The Sailor," "The Cobbler," "The Longshoreman," "The Cop," "The Beggar," "The Artist," "Magdalen," and "The Tourist." *NOS*. TX: *Royal Street: New Orleans*, a 26-pp. handlettered booklet Faulkner wrote and bound for Estelle Oldham Franklin in 1926, containing all the above sketches with the exception of "The Tourist," which is replaced by "Hong Li." See Polk, " 'Hong Li' and *Royal Street*"; and "William Faulkner's 'Hong Li.' " See also Skei, *Short Story Career* 24.

*Notes on a Horsethief*. Greenville, Miss.: Levee, 1951. Revised for *FAB* 151–89. Pp. 151–204 of the novel were published under the title "Notes on a Horsethief" in *Vogue* July 1954: 46–51, 101, 102, 103, 104, 105, 106. Original title "A Dangling Clause from Work in Progress"; see *FB* 2: 1374.

"Nympholepsy." *Mississippi Quarterly* 26 (1973): 403–9. *FM* 149–55. *US*. NYPL: 8-pp. ts. See Putzel 316; *US* 698; *WFM 24* vii, xvi, 1–8.

"An Odor of Verbena." *U*. VA: 23-pp. ms.; 54-pp. ts.

"The Old People." *Harper's* Sept. 1940: 418–25. Revised for *GDM*; that version in *BW*. *US*. VA: 17-pp. ts. See *US* 691–92; *WFM 16* 1: viii, xvi, 1–17.

"Omar's Eighteenth Quatrain." See "Lizards in Jamshyd's Courtyard."

"Once Aboard the Lugger (I)"; "Once Aboard the Lugger (II)." (The two stories are considered together here since most of the extant ms. and ts. versions include at least portions of both works. They were clearly originally intended to be parts of the same work and are linked by some unpublished transitional material. In *US* Blotner gave the stories the above titles.) "Once Aboard the Lugger (I)": *Contempo* 1 Feb. 1932: 1, 4. *US*. PC: 12-pp. ts. entitled "Once Aboard the Lugger—." (See Meriwether, "Short Fiction" 306.) "Once Aboard the Lugger (II)": *US*. ROP: mss. and tss. for both works, largely miscellaneous and fragmentary (20-pp. ts. and carbon ts.; 1-p. ms.; 24-pp. ts.; 4-pp. carbon ts.; 6-pp. ms.; 4-pp. ms.; 4-pp. ts.; 4-pp. ts.; 14-pp. ts.) The text of "Once Aboard the Lugger (II)" in *US* is apparently based on the latter ts. See *US* 699–700.

"Out of Nazareth." New Orleans *Times-Picayune* 12 Apr. 1925, Sunday magazine section: 4. *NOS*.

"Pantaloon in Black." *Harper's* Oct. 1940: 503–13. Revised for *GDM*. *US*. VA: 24-pp. carbon ts. See *US* 694; *WFM 16* 1: x, xvii, 124–48.

"The Peasants." See "Spotted Horses."

"Pennsylvania Station." *American Mercury* Feb. 1934: 166–74. *CS*. VA: 8-pp. ms.; 2-pp. ts. fragment; 1-p. ms. fragment; 4-pp. ts. fragment; 21-pp. ts. TX: 2-pp. ms. fragment entitled "Bench for Two." TU: 22-pp. carbon ts. On his sending schedule Faulkner apparently referred to the story as "Two on Bench." See Meriwether, *Literary Career* 175; Skei, *Short Story Career* 40–41; *WFM 24* xi–xii, xvi–xvii, 102–37.

"Per Ardua." See "All the Dead Pilots."

"Peter." *US*. NYPL: 7-pp. ts. (probably a rough draft). See *US* 705–6; *WFM 24* x, xvi, 95–101.

"Point of Honor." See "Honor."

"A Point of Law." *Collier's* 22 June 1940: 20–21, 30, 32. Revised for *GDM*, chapter one of "The Fire and the Hearth." *US*. VA: 21-pp. ts. See *US* 692–93; *WFM 16* 1: ix, xvi, 18–39.

"A Portrait of Elmer." *Georgia Review* 33 (1979): 534–64. *US*. VA: 58-pp. ts.; 4 sheets of miscellaneous ms. (one with material on verso) entitled "Growing Pains"; 4-pp. ts. fragment entitled "Portrait of Elmer Hodge." ROP: 2-pp. ms. fragment entitled "Growing Pains"; 33-pp. ts.; 9-pp. ts. fragment; 2-pp. ts. fragment. (It is difficult to establish in every case which of the mss. and tss. noted above are from the novel and which are from the story. See McHaney, "Elmer Papers"; Putzel 311, 317; *US* 710; *WFM 1* xxviii–xxxi, 138–95. See also *Elmer* (Northport, Ala.: Seajay, 1984).

"Portrait of Elmer Hodge." See "A Portrait of Elmer."

"The Priest." *Mississippi Quarterly* 29 (1976): 446–50. *US*. NYPL: 8-pp. carbon ts. See *US* 699; Putzel 317; *WFM 24* ix, xvi, 66–73.

"Race at Morning." *Saturday Evening Post* 5 Mar. 1955: 26–27, 103, 104, 106. Revised for *BW*. *US*. PR: 20-pp. ts. VA: 8-sheet galley proof of *Post* version. BC: 20-pp. ts. See *US* 696–97.

"Raid." *Saturday Evening Post* 3 Nov. 1934: 18–19, 72, 73, 75, 77, 78. Revised for *U*. *US*. ROP: 12-pp. ms.; 35-pp. ts. See *US* 682–83.

"Red Leaves." *Saturday Evening Post* 25 Oct. 1930: 6–7, 54, 56, 58, 60, 62, 64. Revised for *T13*; that version in *CS*. A portion revised for *BW*. VA: 12-pp. ms.; 36-pp. carbon ts. See Putzel 317; *WFM 9* ix, xii, 139–86.

"Resurgam Two Men Memphis Anecdote Episode." See "Dull Tale."

"Retreat." *Saturday Evening Post* 13 Oct. 1934: 16–17, 82, 84, 85, 87, 89. Revised for *U*. *US*. ROP: 32-pp. ts.; 10-pp. ms. See "Ambuscade" above for a note on an incorrect identification. See also *US* 682.

"A Return." *US*. VA: 9-pp. incomplete ms. entitled "Rose of Lebanon." ROP: 10-pp. ms. and 33-pp. ts. (both entitled "Rose of Lebanon"); 53-pp. ts. See *US* 708.

"Riposte in Tertio." See "The Unvanquished."

"The Rosary." New Orleans *Times-Picayune* 3 May 1925, Sunday magazine section: 2. *NOS*.

"A Rose for Emily." *Forum* Apr. 1930: 233–38. Revised for *T13*; that version in *CS*. VA: 6-pp. ms. (incomplete); 17-pp. carbon ts. See Putzel 317–18; *WFM 9* ix, xii–xiv, 188–214.

"Rose of Lebanon." See "A Return." This is a title for early versions of the story eventually published in *US* as "A Return." See Putzel 318; *WFM 25* xi, xii, 183–91.

"Royal Street." See "Jealousy."

*Royal Street: New Orleans.* See "New Orleans." See also Putzel 318.

"Salvage." See "Elly."

"Selvage." See "Elly."

"Sepulchre South: Gaslight." See "Sepulture South: Gaslight."

"Sepulchre South: in Gaslight." See "Sepulture South: Gaslight."

"Sepulture South: Gaslight." *Harper's Bazaar* Dec. 1954: 84–85, 140, 141. *US*. PR: 8-pp. ms. and ts. entitled "Sepulchre South: in Gaslight"; 1-p. ts. fragment; 5-pp. ts. fragment; 3-pp. ts. fragment, entitled "Sepulchre South: Gaslight." BC: ms. and ts. fragments. See Meriwether, "Unknown Short Stories"; and *US* 703–4.

"Shall Not Perish." *Story* July-Aug. 1943: 40–47. *CS*. VA: 16-pp. carbon ts. (incomplete); 4-pp. ts. fragment; 8-pp. carbon ts. (incomplete); 3-pp. carbon ts. (incomplete). See *WFM 24* xiv–xv, xviii–xix, 413–65.

"Shingles for the Lord." *Saturday Evening Post* 13 Feb. 1943: 14–15, 68, 70, 71. *CS*. VA: 21-pp. carbon ts. See *WFM 24* xv–xvi, xix, 499–530.

"Skirmish at Sartoris." *Scribner's* Apr. 1935: 193–200. Revised for *U*. *US*. ROP: 10-pp. ms. entitled "Drusilla"; 32-pp. ts. entitled "Drusilla." See *US* 683.

"Smoke." *Harper's* Apr. 1932: 562–78. *DRM. KG.* VA: 12-pp. ms.; 1-p. ts. fragment. See *WFM 11* ix–x, xii, 143–54; *WFM 18* viii–ix, xii, 1.

"Snow." *US*. VA: 4-pp. ts. fragment; 18-pp. carbon ts. JFSA: 18-pp. ts. See Meriwether, "Short Fiction" 316; Skei, *Short Story Career* 101; *US* 711–12; *WFM 25* xi, xii, 192–227.

"Spotted Horses." *Scribner's* June 1931: 585–97. Incorporated in *H*, book 4, chapter 1. *US*. (None of Faulkner's short stories poses greater textual-bibliographical problems than this one because of the many different versions of the material the writer composed and because of the difficulty in distinguishing between short-story versions and those composed for *H* and *FA*. In this regard see *US* 689–90; Skei, *Short Story Career* 43–47; Putzel 304, 320–21; *WFM 15* vii–xxii; *WFM 2* ix–xv. I cite here the versions known to me of the "Spotted Horses" material, whether they are projected short stories or fragments of a novel.) VA: 17-pp. carbon ts. entitled "As I Lay Dying"; 22-pp. carbon ts. entitled "As I Lay Dying"; 8-pp. incomplete ms. entitled "The Peasants"; 59-pp. carbon ts. entitled "The Peasants"; 16-pp. ts. entitled "Aria Con Amore"; 16-pp. carbon ts. of the preceding; unfinished 54-pp. ts. entitled *Father Abraham*; unfinished and incomplete 54-pp. carbon ts. entitled *Father Abraham*; 51-pp. unfinished carbon ts. entitled *Father Abraham*; 1-p. ts. fragment; 9-pp. incomplete ts. entitled *Father Abraham*; 4-pp. carbon ts.; 9-pp. ts. entitled "Abraham's Children"; 48-pp. unfinished ts. entitled "Abraham's Children"; 13 miscellaneous carbon ts. pp. of the preceding; 2 carbon ts. pp. of "Abraham's Children." ("As I Lay Dying," the 22-pp. carbon ts. at VA cited above, has been published in *Mississippi Quarterly* 39 (1986), 369–85.) NYPL: 24-pp. incomplete ms. entitled "Father Abraham." ROP: 18-pp. ts.

entitled "As I Lay Dying"; 1 untitled ms. p. See *WFM 15* 1: 1–123; *WFM 2* 1–204.

"Sunset." New Orleans *Times-Picayune* 24 May 1925, Sunday magazine section: 4, 7. *NOS*.

"The Tall Men." *Saturday Evening Post* 31 May 1941: 14–15, 95, 96, 98, 99. *CS*. VA: 18-pp. carbon ts. See *WFM 24* xiv, xviii, 333–50.

"That Evening Sun." *American Mercury* Mar. 1931: 257–67 (entitled "That Evening Sun Go Down"). Revised and entitled "That Evening Sun" for *T13*; that version in *CS*. Yale: 6-pp. ms. (incomplete) entitled "Never Done No Weeping When You Wanted to Laugh." VA: 26-pp. carbon ts. entitled "That Evening Sun Go Down." NYPL: 26-pp. ts. setting copy. See Manglavati; Putzel 321; Morrison; *WFM 9* x, xii, 228–56.

"That Evening Sun Go Down." See "That Evening Sun."

"That Will Be Fine." *American Mercury* July 1935: 264–76. *CS*. ROP: 10-pp. ms.; 11-pp. carbon ts. (incomplete); 1-p. carbon ts. fragment; 1-p. ts. fragment.

"There Was a Queen." *Scribner's* Jan. 1933: 10–16. *DRM*. *CS*. VA: 5-pp. ms. (incomplete); 8-pp. ms. entitled "An Empress Passed" and with cancelled title "Through the Window"; 25-pp. ts.; 25-pp. carbon ts. (of the preceding). See Putzel 321–22; *WFM 11* ix, xii, 105–42.

"This Kind of Courage." Lost. See Meriwether, "Faulkner's Correspondence" 279–80. One page may still exist; see Skei, *Short Story Career* 83. This was apparently an early version of *P*.

"Thrift." *Saturday Evening Post* 6 Sept. 1930: 16–17, 76, 82. *US*. VA: 5-pp. ms. (incomplete); 18-pp. ts. (incomplete). See *US* 700–701; *WFM 24* xiii, xviii, 297–319.

"Through the Window." See "There Was a Queen."

"Tomorrow." *Saturday Evening Post* 23 Nov. 1940: 22–23, 32, 35, 37, 38, 39. *KG*. VA: 20-pp. untitled ts. See *WFM 18* ix, xi, 64–85.

"Turnabout"; "Turn About." *Saturday Evening Post* 5 Mar. 1932: 6–7, 75, 76, 81, 83. Revised for *DRM*; that version in *CS*. VA: 16-pp. ms. All versions except the one in *CS* are entitled "Turn About." See *WFM 11* x, xiii, 155–70.

"Two Dollar Wife." *College Life* Jan. 1936: 8–10, 85, 86, 88, 90. *US*. VA: 3-pp. ms. entitled "The Devil Beats His Wife." PC: 3-pp. ms. and 5-pp. ts. or carbon ts., both entitled "Christmas Tree," with the canceled title "Whoopee" on the ms. (See Meriwether, "Short Fiction" 313–14). ROP: 15-pp. ms. and 1-p. ms. fragment, both entitled "Christmas Tree." See *US* 701–2; Meriwether, "Unknown Stories."

"Two on Bench." See "Pennsylvania Station."

"Two Soldiers." *Saturday Evening Post* 28 Mar. 1942: 9–11, 35, 36, 38, 40. *CS*.

"Uncle Willy." *American Mercury* Oct. 1935: 156–68. *CS*. ROP: 10-pp. ms. (incomplete); 5-pp. ts. (incomplete).

[Untitled fragment]. Beginning of possible short story. Repository is not identified in *WFM*, but it is probably NYPL. 3-pp. ts. See *WFM 24* xvi, 9–11.

"The Unvanquished." *Saturday Evening Post* 14 Nov. 1936: 12–13, 121, 122, 124, 126, 128, 130. Revised and entitled "Riposte in Tertio" for *U*. *US*. ROP: 13-pp. ms. See *US* 683.

"Vendée." *Saturday Evening Post* 5 Dec. 1936: 16–17, 86, 87, 90, 92, 93, 94. Revised for *U. US.* ROP: 12-pp. ms.; 34-pp. ts. See *US* 684.

"Victory." *T13. CS.* VA: 4-pp. ms. fragment; 5-pp. ms. fragment; 51-pp. ts.; 54-pp. ts. (incomplete). See Skei, *Short Story Career* 120n56; *FB* 1: *100–101;* Putzel 322. Both ts. versions contain the material that was later to become the separate story, "Crevasse." On p. 22 of the 51-pp. ts. the material that became that story is given that title. See *WFM 9* viii, xii, 3–116.

"Was." *GDM.* Original title "Almost." VA: 22-pp. untitled ts.; 6-pp. ts. (miscellaneous); material on versos of rejected pages of "The Fire and the Hearth." Collection of Carl Petersen: one leaf with typing on recto and verso. See Roth; Meriwether, "Short Fiction" 310; *WFM 16* 1: xi, xvii, 149–78, 250.

"Wash." *Harper's* Feb. 1934: 258–66. *DRM.* Incorporated in *AA,* chapter 7. *DRM* version in *CS.* BC: 8-pp. ms.; 12-pp. ms.; 22-pp. ts. See Brodsky, "Textual Development."

"Weekend Revisited." See "Mr. Acarius."

"Whoopee." See "Two Dollar Wife."

"Wild Palms." Unpublished. Incorporated in the first section of *WP.* ROP: 6-pp. ms.; 22-pp. ts. This was at one time probably intended for publication as a separate story.

*The Wishing Tree; The Wishing-Tree. Saturday Evening Post* 8 Apr. 1967: 48–49, 50, 51, 52, 53, 57, 58, 60, 61, 62, 63. *WT.* BC: 68-pp. typed text entitled *The Wishing Tree;* BC: 44-pp. carbon ts. entitled *The Wishing-Tree.* VA: 47-pp. carbon ts. entitled *The Wishing-Tree;* 47-pp. ts. entitled *The Wishing-Tree;* 43-pp. ts. entitled *The Wishing Tree* and its carbon, 42-pp. (incomplete); 44-pp. carbon ts. (identical to 44-pp. carbon ts. in BC). TX: 44-pp. carbon ts. entitled *The Wishing-Tree* (incomplete). See Putzel 322–23; Brodsky, "*Wishing Tree*"; Hamblin and Brodsky 107; *WFM 4* 207–350.

"With Caution and Dispatch." *US.* VA: 2-pp. ms. fragment; 47-pp. ts. (incomplete); miscellaneous pp. on versos of setting copy of *H,* 530–36, 535–36 [sic]. See Meriwether, *Literary Career* 87-88.

"Yo Ho and Two Bottles of Rum." New Orleans *Times-Picayune* 27 Sept. 1925, Sunday magazine section: 1, 2. *NOS.*

Note: Setting copies of the "story-novels" are still extant. There is a 211-pp. ts. of *The Unvanquished* in ROP; and a 414-pp. ts. of *Go Down, Moses* at VA. For the latter, see Meriwether, *Literary Career* 75; *WFM 16* 1: xviii; 2: 1–417.

# Notes

## Introduction

1. Because of problems of definition, no two scholars will agree on the exact number of works of short fiction Faulkner published during his lifetime, not to mention the many that have appeared since his death. Isn't "Mississippi," for example, even though it has fictional elements, primarily an essay? Should "Appendix: Compson 1699–1945" be counted as a separate work of short fiction? What are we to do with the many extracts from the novels that were separately published? Should different versions of essentially the same material under different titles—e.g., "The Big Shot" and "Dull Tale"—be counted as separate stories? And so on.
2. For example, the book-length studies by Olga Vickery, Adams, Slatoff, and Thompson. Even in Brooks's more or less systematic attempt to evaluate the total body of Faulkner's work in *Yoknapatawpha Country* and *Toward Yoknapatawpha* he ignores much of the short fiction.
3. A brief but interesting discussion of the story is Bradford, "Late Encounter." Hans Skei also devotes a considerable amount of attention to the story in "Beyond Genre? Existential Experience in Faulkner's Short Fiction," a paper not yet published as of this writing.
4. This should not be confused with Millgate's later far more elaborate and important *Achievement*.
5. Howe 260–62; Kazin 154–58; Waggoner 194.
6. See McHaney, "Tall Tale," for some interesting insights into several formative influences on Faulkner's narrative interests and strategies.
7. See Millgate, *Achievement* 287.
8. The term is used by Olga Vickery (306).
9. The assumption here seems to be that a book-length work of fiction must be either a novel or a collection of stories. But our century has, in fact, produced many significant hybrids besides Faulkner's works: *Dubliners, In Our Time, The Pastures of Heaven*, etc. See Ingram.
10. Blotner notes, e.g. (*FB* 1: 791), that Faulkner set out as early as 1932 to create "The Golden Book of Jefferson & Yoknapatawpha County." A five-page

fragment, largely concerned with the Sartorises, survives. See Meriwether, "*Golden Book.*"

11. See Millgate, *Achievement* 284–87.

12. Indeed, some of the most fascinating recent work on Faulkner has been in the area of "intertextual" criticism. Irwin's *Doubling and Incest/Repetition and Revenge*, in particular, has had a marked influence on Faulkner studies of the last decade.

13. My conclusions about the dating of the stories are heavily indebted to Meriwether, "Short Fiction"; the two editions of Blotner's biography of Faulkner; Skei, *Short Story Career*; and, especially, the introductions to the relevant volumes of *WFM*. Because my own speculations about dating are somewhat peripheral to the main arguments in the text of this study, those conjectures are largely confined to the notes.

CHAPTER 1
*The Career*

1. This chapter, in substantially its present form, was written a number of years before I read Skei's *Short Story Career*. There are some obvious resemblances between some of my own conclusions and those reached by Skei in his excellent textual-bibliographical study, but, except where I acknowledge my indebtedness to Skei, I reached those conclusions independently.

2. In *Short Story Career* 14–15, Skei also has a four-period categorization, but it is slightly different from mine.

3. See *FB* 1: 155, 160. One must bear in mind, however, that such sources are not always trustworthy.

4. This should not be confused with the very different "Moonlight" first published in *US*.

5. 31 (1978): 453–64.

6. There are a number of different ms. and ts. versions of "Love," most of them fragmentary. See *WFM* 25 x–xiii. Meriwether ("Short Fiction" 315) dates the writing of the story in about 1921, as does Blotner (*FB* 1: 322–23). Putzel, however, in *Genius of Place* (127–28, 314–15), suggests that "Love" may have been written much later. It seems likely that Faulkner worked on the story for brief periods of time for more than a decade. But I find it inconceivable, because the writing is so callow, that the earliest versions were written much later than 1921. That Faulkner continued to work so long on this dreadful material suggests a real critical blind spot.

7. Not all critics agree with this assessment. In his scholarly dissertation, *Sinbad in New Orleans*, Leland Cox makes an interesting case, which I don't find completely convincing, for the skill and cohesiveness of the New Orleans material.

8. However, Skei believes the vignette came first. See *Short Story Career* 22; *WFM* 25 x.

9. See Watson, "New Orleans" 215; Cox xx–xxvi.
10. However, Faulkner was not above using the simile of the bathtub drain even in *MOS* (12).
11. For example, "a voice as light and dry as an eggshell" (*US* 469) or "the tangled blackbirds slating down wind like scraps of burned paper" (471).
12. There are two typescript versions of the piece in the Alderman Library. I am referring to the ts. classified in Series IIA, 7b. See *WFM 9* xi.
13. See, e.g., his comments on the story in *FU* (22).
14. See *WFM 11* x–xi.
15. See *FB* 1: 502–3; Skei, *Short Story Career* 42–43.
16. Because of the pagination of the typescripts of three stories—those of "As I Lay Dying," (an early version of the spotted horses story), "Once Aboard the Lugger," and "Idyll in the Desert," another story that could have been composed at this time—Skei speculates that Faulkner might have intended to use them in such a collection. See Skei, *Short Story Career* 43.
17. See Meriwether, "Short Fiction" 310–11; *FB* 1: 541–42; Brodsky, *"Wishing Tree"* and *WFM 2* 207–12. I reached most of my conclusions about this story before reading the relatively small amount of commentary on it, some of which is partially in accord with my ideas. See Gidley; Gresset, "Faulkner féerique"; Davis; Ditsky.
18. The version of "Snow" first published in *US* can be dated in 1942. However, I think it reasonable to assume that Faulkner added the clumsy and xenophobic framing device to make the story more salable when the United States was at war with Germany. The style, symbolism, and theme of "Snow" are so similar to those of "Mistral" that I think it virtually certain that both stories were originally written at about the same time.
19. Blotner (*FB* 1: 72n) suggests the possibility of this influence. See also Shepherd.
20. See Schoenberg 20–23.
21. Here I seem to be at odds with much of the scholarly opinion today about the dating of the story, which favors the summer or early fall of 1930, two years after the completion of *SF*. See *FB* rev. 265, 733n16, chapter 29; Skei, *Short Story Career* 65–67; Putzel, *Genius of Place* 229–32, 321. On the other hand, in the original two-volume biography of Faulkner, Blotner speculates that "Never Done No Weeping When You Wanted to Laugh" may have been written before *SF*. He indicates that the handwriting in the two manuscripts is virtually the same, and he notes some of the arguments advanced by Leon Howard in an unpublished paper, "Three American Novels: A Genetic Approach," that the story precedes the novel. Howard argues that the absence of Benjy from the story and the fact that Quentin tells it at the age of twenty-four, although he commits suicide when he is twenty, suggests that an early version of the story precedes the novel (*FB* 1: 82n).

    I find the former argument more compelling than the latter because Faulkner was never very much concerned about consistency from work to work in the ages of his characters. Moreover, the framing device employing the mature

Quentin is not used in "Never Done No Weeping." But it is difficult to believe that, having created as memorable a character as Benjy for *SF*, Faulkner would not have at least alluded to him in "Never Done No Weeping," even though his presence in the story might very well have been distracting. Furthermore, if the composition of *SF* had preceded that of "Never Done No Weeping," I wonder if Dilsey would have been so passive and ineffectual in the latter.

It seems reasonable to assume that Faulkner revised the story in 1930 and added the frame at that time. If he already had on hand a manuscript of the work that antedated *SF*, he would have been less likely two years after the composition of the novel to be concerned about the inconsistencies I have noted. He would have been aware of them, but in his characteristically economical fashion he would have built on what he already had. But if he had started from scratch in 1930, he would surely have alluded to Benjy and created a stronger Dilsey. See also Manglavati; Pearson; and Morrison.

22. The idea for the story was suggested to Faulkner by Estelle. See *FB* 1: 604.

23. In *FB* 1 (493–94) and *FB* rev. (177) Blotner suggests that the story may have been written in 1926. See also his note in *US* (707). However, such a date seems too early. The first concrete evidence we have of the existence of the story is an entry on the sending schedule dated January 23, 1930.

24. See *US* 707–8.

25. See the chart in Skei's *Short Story Career* 36–37.

26. As Thomas L. McHaney has suggested in his review of the manuscript of this study, one of the reasons Faulkner devoted a considerable amount of attention to the Snopes material at this time was the interest in it expressed by magazines. See e.g., Meriwether, "Faulkner's Correspondence" 262–71.

27. See the discussion in the first section of this chapter.

28. Nevertheless, the volume may not be so casually structured as some have assumed it to be. See the first section of chapter 5, "Collecting Stories."

CHAPTER 2
*Patterns*

1. The most comprehensive treatment of this subject is in Broughton.

2. Others have called attention to the importance of this theme in Faulkner's works, e. g., Watson, "Short Story Structure."

3. Most notably, Irwin.

4. Bradford has referred to this tendency of Faulkner's characters in "Escaping Westward."

5. In "Chronicles of Children" Libby sees Faulkner as obsessively concerned with children and childlike characters in the short stories. Libby's dissertation is one of the best sustained pieces of writing on the short fiction that I have read. I will indicate in the notes that follow his influence on my thinking about some of these works. In a number of cases, however, we reached similar conclusions independently.

6. Faulkner discussed the genesis of the novel on a number of occasions. A useful summation is contained in *FB* 1: 566–79. See also Kinney, *Critical Essays*, which contains two introductions by Faulkner to *SF* and other valuable background material.

7. One of the few scholars who understands that the story involves Quentin's initiation is Pearson.

8. See, e.g., *LG* 146–47.

9. The best treatment of this subject is by Irwin.

10. I am somewhat indebted here to Libby, who has influenced my interpretation of the story. See also Grimwood 55–60.

11. Faulkner was fascinated throughout his career by lost, maimed, and injured limbs, which he refers to in such novels as *AILD* and *FAB* and in many stories: "The Tall Men," "Barn Burning," "Mountain Victory," and "Death Drag," among others. In Freudian terms, this preoccupation suggests the fear of castration.

12. Libby treats this subject extensively. See 122–73.

13. See Noel Polk's fascinating Freudian study, "The Dungeon Was Mother Herself."

14. See Libby 129.

15. In "Beyond," Faulkner's rather obscure and clumsy tale of the supernatural, there is an interesting variation on this archetype and on another pattern in his works. Here the father is searching for the son, but he gives up the quest because, unlike so many of Faulkner's characters, he prefers a weltanschauung in which injustice is rooted in the very nature of things. If he were to find the boy, life would make sense, would add up, and the old man would therefore have to deny everything he has lived for.

16. Libby has commented on this, 126–29.

17. For another striking example of this pattern of imagery, see the concluding page of the second version of "Moonlight" (*US* 503).

18. Several critics have commented on this aspect of the story. See, e.g., Libby 41–51; and Howell, "Inversion and the Female Principle" 308–14.

19. See Polk, "Dungeon."

20. Many critics have noted Faulkner's concern with this subject. See, e.g., Skei, "Trapped Female."

21. Libby devotes a great amount of attention to the influence of Southwestern humor on Faulkner's short fiction. See 4–22, 55–60, passim. See also McHaney, "Tall Tale"; and Schroeder. The most extensive analysis of the influence of folklore on Faulkner is Hoffman's *Faulkner's Country Matters*.

22. This was the original title of the piece, which was to become "Riposte in Tertio" in the book to which it gave its title.

23. The frame of "Snow" was obviously written after the onset of World War II, but this is probably a revision of the basic story, which was written much earlier. See n18, chapter 1 above.

24. Broughton's book is a full-length treatment of Faulkner's handling of the subject.

CHAPTER 3
*Point of View*

1. I will not, for example, be concerned, except tangentially, with purely stylistic considerations, although much important work could surely be done on the differences between the language of the novels and that of the short stories. Another subject of great interest to which I cannot, because of lack of space, devote any attention here is the use in the short stories of tableaux, of those "frozen moments" to which Karl Zink and others have called attention. If anything, they occur more frequently in the stories than in the novels, and they have about the same function in the short and long fiction.

2. The criticism of modern fiction has, of course, been largely dominated by the study of point of view in the classic work of James, Lubbock, Beach, and Booth. The most useful short study of the subject is Friedman's "Point of View." As my text reveals, I am heavily indebted to Friedman. Since writing this chapter I have also become acquainted with Ruppersburg's *Voice and Eye*, an impressive study that concentrates largely on point of view in the novels and is interesting because of its reassessment of the problem, particularly of the terminology employed in its discussion. However, I prefer to use the standard terminology, with certain modifications, because of its greater familiarity to most readers.

3. See my discussion in chapter 2 under "Initiation: Sexual and Otherwise."

4. Booth (308–9) raises some basic questions about this passage.

5. The reader should be reminded again that my terminology is different from that of Friedman. See my discussion in the section preceding this one.

6. In the original 29-pp. ts. Charles Weddell is the first-person narrator. In the miscellaneous 80-pp. ts. revisions in the Alderman Library there is a two-page segment in which Faulkner changes the phrase "Stevens and his nephew" to "Uncle Gavin and I" (*WFM 18* 621).

7. Of course, Faulkner treated the development of a sensibility—that of Joe Christmas—superbly in *Light in August*.

8. There is the same problem in "The Big Shot," an earlier version of much of the same material. In this piece Dal Martin tells the narrator, Don Reeves, the story of his early life. But since we know nothing about Reeves or about the relationship between the two men, in contrast to what we know about the relationship between Blount and Martin in "Dull Tale," it is perhaps a bit more likely that Martin might have imparted this information to Reeves. However, the handling of the problem in the earlier story still strains credibility.

    Problems of point of view bedeviled Faulkner in much of the Memphis material. The device of the confidant is most clumsily employed in ms. and ts. versions of "Rose of Lebanon" (10-pp. ms., 31-pp. ts., ROP).

9. See n18, chapter 1.

CHAPTER 4
*Form*

1. See Friedman, "Short Story."
2. In the manuscript this sentence is virtually illegible. I am grateful to Thomas L. McHaney for his suggestion of the probable reading, which strikes me as being almost certainly valid.
3. The term—as opposed to *sujet* or *sjuzhet,* the order in which the events of the story are presented—is often employed by formalist and structuralist critics in this sense. Several Faulkner scholars, notably Kuyk in his study of *Go Down, Moses,* use it. See also Culler.
4. Creighton briefly refers to this pattern (31).
5. The best general study of closure I have read is Torgovnik's impressive book. Kreiswirth has some most convincing things to say about Faulkner's handling of beginnings and endings.
6. Here and, more generally, in my discussion of Faulkner's "musical" techniques in the pages that follow, I am somewhat indebted to Calvin Brown's classic study, *Music and Literature,* especially 208–18.
7. See John B. Vickery for a discussion of this theme.
8. In these early versions the protagonist, who is named Harry, does not commit suicide. In one of them, at the end of the story, as Amy bemoans the loss of her baby, "He did not look at her. After a while he saw the poker in his hand again. He watched the poker prodding clumsily at the fire" (15-pp. ts.; ROP, 15). Earlier (12) Amy takes the poker from Harry and arranges the coals more skillfully!
9. Karl deals briefly (784) with the symbolism of chess and horses in the novella, but he does not note the problem caused by Faulkner's handling of the symbolism. A paper, not yet published as of this writing, that devotes some attention to this symbolism is John T. Irwin's fascinating "*Knight's Gambit*: Poe, Faulkner, and the Tradition of the Detective Story."
10. See, e.g., Leahy, Malbone, Merrill, Poindexter, Yarup, Zender.
11. In an article written after Leahy's, Merrill suggests that Faulkner simply botched his handling of the poker game. Merrill may well be right. But see also Anderson's excellent article.

CHAPTER 5
*Stories and Books*

1. See Millgate, *Achievement* 259–75; and Kinney, "Narrative Poetics."
2. The changes were made largely in order to restore the original text. See Manglavati.
3. Several years after arriving at my conclusions about Faulkner's use of tonal

counterpoint in his collections of short fiction, I read Bungert's "Faulkner's Humor," in which there is a single short paragraph (149) devoted to this technique in *Collected Stories*. Bungert reportedly deals more extensively with the subject in *humoristische Tradition*, which I have not read. See "Faulkner's Humor" 151n35.

4. Considering this technique of contrasting moods, it is interesting that Faulkner did *not* choose "Thrift," another story of World War I, for inclusion in *These 13*. But, as Hans Skei indicates, the protagonist of this work is so different from those of the other stories in the volume that the inclusion of "Thrift" would have been detrimental to the mood Faulkner was attempting to establish ("Sending Schedule" 69). The saga of MacWyrglinchbeath is too positive, its tonality too light for *These 13*. Skei is quite right in calling attention to the significance of the works that were *excluded* from the book.

5. See chapter 1, the section titled "The First Period."

6. He implied a fondness for "Lo!" by indicating in his letter to Malcolm Cowley of August 16, 1945, that he would find it difficult to choose for the proposed *Portable Faulkner* among that story, "Red Leaves," and "A Justice" (*SL* 197). At one time he maintained that "All the Dead Pilots" was the best story in *These 13* (*FB* 1: 731–32).

7. In the letter to Haas about the inclusion of stories in *Collected Stories*, Faulkner capitalized the word *YES* beside "Two Soldiers," something he did not do with any of the other stories to which he referred (*SL* 274).

8. However, at least two critics, Klinkowitz and Grimwood (187–222), have argued that *Knight's Gambit* is considerably more unified than a casual reading of the volume might indicate.

9. The most exhaustive study of the volume is Burggraf's dissertation. See also Johnson and Ragan.

10. Blotner has compiled a useful bibliography of works concerned with Faulkner's revisions of his short stories. See *US* 713–16.

11. Creighton notes some of these parallels (13–14).

12. See chapter 1, section titled "The Third Period."

13. See *GDM* 71.

14. See also Howe 90; and Libby 267–70.

15. In his remarkably close and perceptive review of the manuscript of this study, Thomas L. McHaney suggests that Sam does not fire because of the taint of slavery in his blood and hence his sense that he is unworthy to be the slayer of Old Ben. This is surely a valid interpretation. Nevertheless, the Sam of the first two sections of "The Bear" seems to me to have a very different function, to be a very different character from the Sam who trains Lion to kill Old Ben.

16. This inconsistency is noted in Millgate, *Achievement* 203; and Early 79.

17. The assessments of the different versions of these later works is complicated by the fact that the stories are likely to be segments of "works in progress." Faulkner extracted *Notes on a Horsethief*, e.g., from the ms. of *A Fable*.

18. For an excellent discussion of this chapter, see Torgovnik 157–75.

19. E.g., Strandberg (14–23).
20. For the latter, see especially Brooks, *Yoknapatawpha Country* 387–91.
21. The best brief discussion of this matter is in Brooks, *Yoknapatawpha Country* 436–40.

# Works Cited

Adams, Richard P. *Faulkner: Myth and Motion*. Princeton: Princeton UP, 1968.

Anderson, Carl L. "Faulkner's 'Was': 'A Deadlier Purpose than Simple Pleasure.'" *American Literature* 61 (1989): 414–28.

Beach, Joseph Warren. *The Twentieth-Century Novel: Studies in Technique*. New York: Century, 1932.

Blotner, Joseph. *Faulkner: A Biography*. 2 vols. New York: Random, 1974.

———. *Faulkner: A Biography*. One Volume Edition. New York: Random, 1984.

Booth, Wayne C. *The Rhetoric of Fiction*. Chicago: U of Chicago P, 1961.

Bradford, M. E. "Escaping Westward: Faulkner's 'Golden Land.'" *Georgia Review* 19 (1965): 72–76.

———. "A Late Encounter: Faulkner's 'Mountain Victory.'" *Mississippi Quarterly* 40 (1987): 373–81.

———. "That Other Patriarchy: Observations on Faulkner's 'A Justice.'" *Modern Age* 18 (1974): 266–71.

Brodsky, Louis Daniel. "The Textual Development of William Faulkner's 'Wash': An Examination of Manuscripts in the Brodsky Collection." *Studies in Bibliography* 37 (1984): 248–81.

———. "A Textual History of William Faulkner's *The Wishing-Tree* and *The Wishing Tree*." *Studies in Bibliography* 38 (1985): 330–74.

Brooks, Cleanth. *William Faulkner: The Yoknapatawpha Country*. New Haven: Yale UP, 1963.

———. *William Faulkner: Toward Yoknapatawpha and Beyond*. New Haven: Yale UP, 1978.

Broughton, Panthea Reid. *William Faulkner: The Abstract and the Actual*. Baton Rouge: Louisiana State UP, 1974.

Brown, Calvin S. *Music and Literature: A Comparison of the Arts*. Athens: U of Georgia P, 1948.

Bungert, Hans. "Faulkner's Humor: A European View." Fowler & Abadie 136–51.

———. *William Faulkner und die humoristische Tradition des amerikanischen Südens*. Heidelberg: Carl Winter Universitätsverlag, 1971.

Burggraf, David L. *The Genesis and Unity of Faulkner's Big Woods*. Diss. Ohio U, 1975. Ann Arbor: UMI, 1977. 76-8847.

Collins, Carvel. Introduction. *New Orleans Sketches*. By William Faulkner. Ed. Collins. New York: Random, 1958. xi–xxxiv.

Corwin, Ronald Lloyd. *The Development of Narrative Technique in the Apprenticeship Fiction of William Faulkner*. Diss. Brandeis U, 1976. Ann Arbor: UMI, 1977. 76-25, 298.

Cowley, Malcolm, ed. *The Portable Faulkner*. New York: Viking, 1946. Rev. ed. 1967.

Cox, Leland Holcombe, Jr. *Sinbad in New Orleans: Early Short Fiction by William Faulkner: An Annotated Edition*. Diss. U of South Carolina, 1977. Ann Arbor: UMI, 1977. 77-22404.

Creighton, Joanne V. *William Faulkner's Craft of Revision: The Snopes Trilogy, "The Unvanquished," and "Go Down, Moses."* Detroit: Wayne State UP, 1977.

Culler, Jonathan. "Fabula and Sjuzhet in the Analysis of Narrative." *Poetics Today* 3.1 (1980): 27–37.

Dasher, Thomas E. *William Faulkner's Characters: An Index to the Published and Unpublished Fiction*. New York: Garland, 1981.

Davis, Boyd. "Caddy Compson's Eden." *Mississippi Quarterly* 30 (1977): 381–94.

Ditsky, John. "William Faulkner's *The Wishing Tree*: Maturity's First Draft." *The Lion and the Unicorn* 2 (1978): 56–64.

Early, James. *The Making of 'Go Down, Moses'*. Dallas: Southern Methodist UP, 1972.

Fowler, Doreen, and Ann J. Abadie, eds. *Faulkner and Humor. Faulkner and Yoknapatawpha, 1984*. Jackson: UP of Mississippi, 1986.

Friedman, Norman. "Point of View in Fiction: The Development of a Critical Concept." *PMLA* 70 (1955): 1160–84.

———. "What Makes a Short Story Short." *Modern Fiction Studies* 4 (1958): 103–17.

Gidley, Mick. "Faulkner and Children." *Signal: Approaches to Children's Books* 3 (1970): 91–102.

Gold, Joseph. *William Faulkner: A Study in Humanism from Metaphor to Discourse*. Norman: U of Oklahoma P, 1966.

Gresset, Michel. *A Faulkner Chronology*. Tr. Arthur B. Scharff. Jackson: UP of Mississippi, 1985.

———. "Un Faulkner féerique." *Nouvelle Revue Française* 17 (1969): 437–40.

———. "Weekend, Lost and Revisited." *Mississippi Quarterly* 21 (1968): 173–78.

Grimwood, Michael. *Heart in Conflict: Faulkner's Struggles with Vocation*. Athens: U of Georgia P, 1987.

Hamblin, Robert W., and Louis Daniel Brodsky. *Selections from the William Faulkner Collection of Louis Daniel Brodsky: A Descriptive Catalogue*. Charlottesville: UP of Virginia, 1979.

Harrington, Evans B. "Technical Aspects of William Faulkner's 'That Evening Sun.'" *Faulkner Studies* 1 (1952): 54–59.

Hoffman, Daniel. *Faulkner's Country Matters: Folklore and Fable in Yoknapatawpha*. Baton Rouge: Louisiana State UP, 1989.

Howe, Irving. *William Faulkner: A Critical Study*. 3rd ed. Chicago: U of Chicago P, 1975.

Howell, Elmo. "Inversion and the 'Female Principle': William Faulkner's 'A Courtship.'" *Studies in Short Fiction* 4 (1967): 308–14.

————. "Sam Fathers: A Note on Faulkner's 'A Justice.'" *Tennessee Studies in Literature* 12 (1967): 149–53.

Hult, Sharon S. "William Faulkner's 'The Brooch': The Journey to the Riolama." *Mississippi Quarterly* 27 (1974): 291–305.

Ingram, Forrest L. *Representative Short Story Cycles of The Twentieth Century: Studies in a Literary Genre*. The Hague: Mouton, 1971. 106–42.

Irwin, John T. *Doubling and Incest/ Repetition and Revenge: A Speculative Reading of Faulkner*. Baltimore: Johns Hopkins UP, 1975.

————. "*Knight's Gambit*: Poe, Faulkner, and the Tradition of the Detective Story." The University of Mississippi Faulkner and Yoknapatawpha Conference: Faulkner and the Short Story, August 1, 1990.

James, Henry. *The Art of the Novel*. Ed. R. P. Blackmur. New York: Scribner's, 1934.

Johnson, Glen M. "*Big Woods*: Faulkner's Elegy for Wilderness." *Southern Humanities Review* 14 (1980): 249–58.

Karl, Frederick R. *William Faulkner: American Writer: A Biography*. New York: Weidenfeld & Nicolson, 1989.

Kazin, Alfred. *Contemporaries*. Boston: Little, 1962. 154–58.

Kinney, Arthur F. *Critical Essays on William Faulkner: The Compson Family*. Boston: Hall, 1982.

————. "Faulkner's Narrative Poetics and *Collected Stories*." *Faulkner Studies* 1 (1980): 58–79.

Kinney, Arthur F., and Doreen Fowler. "Faulkner's Rowan Oak Papers: A Census." *Journal of Modern Literature* 10 (1983): 327–34.

Klinkowitz, Jerome F. "The Thematic Unity of *Knight's Gambit*." *Critique* 11 (1969): 81–100.

Klotz, Marvin. "Procrustean Revision in Faulkner's *Go Down, Moses*." *American Literature* 37 (1965): 1–16.

Kreiswirth, Martin. "Centers, Openings, and Endings: Some Faulknerian Concepts." *American Literature* 56 (1984): 38–50.

Kuyk, Dirk, Jr. *Threads Cable-strong: William Faulkner's* Go Down, Moses. Lewisburg: Bucknell UP, 1983.

Leahy, Sharon L. "Poker and Semantics: Unraveling the Gordian Knot in Faulkner's 'Was.'" *American Literature* 57 (1985): 129–37.

Libby, Anthony P. *Chronicles of Children: William Faulkner's Short Fiction*. Diss. Stanford U, 1969. Ann Arbor: UMI, 1976. 69-17, 438.

Lubbock, Percy. *The Craft of Fiction*. 1926. New York: Compass-Viking, 1957.

McHaney, Thomas L. "The Elmer Papers: Faulkner's Comic Portraits of the Artist." *A Faulkner Miscellany*. Ed. James B. Meriwether. Jackson: UP of Mississippi, 1974. 37–69.

————. "What Faulkner Learned from the Tall Tale." Fowler & Abadie 110–35.

Malbone, Raymond G. "Promissory Poker in Faulkner's 'Was.'" *English Record* 22 (1971): 23–25.

Manglavati, Leo M. J. "Faulkner's 'That Evening Sun' and Mencken's 'Best Editorial Judgment.'" *American Literature* 43 (1972): 649–54.

Meriwether, James B., ed. *A Faulkner Miscellany*. Jackson: UP of Mississippi, 1974.

————. "Faulkner's Correspondence with *Scribner's Magazine*." *Proof* 3 (1973): 253–82.

————. *The Literary Career of William Faulkner: A Bibliographical Study*. 1961. Columbia: U of South Carolina P, 1971.

————. "The Novel Faulkner Never Wrote: His *Golden Book* or *Doomsday Book*." *American Literature* 42 (1970): 93–96.

————. "The Short Fiction of William Faulkner: A Bibliography." *Proof* 1 (1971): 293–329.

————. "Two Unknown Faulkner Short Stories." *Recherches Anglaises et Américaines* 4 (1971): 23–30.

Merrill, Robert. "Faulkner's Sleight of Hand: The Poker Game in 'Was.'" *Studies in Short Fiction* 25 (1988): 31–40.

Millgate, Michael. *The Achievement of William Faulkner*. 1966. Lincoln: Bison-U of Nebraska P, 1978.

————. *William Faulkner*. 1961. New York: Capricorn, 1971.

————. "William Faulkner: The Problem of Point of View." *Patterns of Commitment in American Literature*. Ed. Marston LaFrance. Toronto: U of Toronto P, 1967. 181–92.

Momberger, Philip. *A Critical Study of Faulkner's Early Sketches and Collected Stories*. Diss. Johns Hopkins U, 1970. Ann Arbor: UMI, 1976. 72-28, 967.

Morrison, Gail Moore, ed. "Never Done No Weeping When You Wanted to Laugh." By William Faulkner. *Mississippi Quarterly* 36 (1983): 461–74.

Pearson, Norman Holmes. "Faulkner's Three 'Evening Suns.'" *Yale University Library Gazette* 29 (1954): 61–70.

Pitavy, François L. "A Forgotten Faulkner Story: 'Miss Zilphia Gant.'" *Studies in Short Fiction* 9 (1972): 131–42.

Poindexter, Helen M. "Faulkner the Mississippi Gambler." *Journal of Modern Literature* 10 (1983): 334–38.

Polk, Noel. "'The Dungeon Was Mother Herself': Faulkner: 1927–1931." *New Directions in Faulkner Studies: Faulkner and Yoknapatawpha, 1983*. Eds. Doreen Fowler and Ann J. Abadie. Jackson: UP of Mississippi, 1984. 61–93.

————. "'Hong Li' and *Royal Street*: The New Orleans Sketches in Manuscript." *Mississippi Quarterly* 26 (1973): 393–95.

————. "William Faulkner's 'Carcassonne.'" *Studies in American Fiction* 12 (1984): 29–43.

————. "William Faulkner's 'Hong Li' on Royal Street." *The Library Chronicle of the University of Texas at Austin* No. 13 (1980): 27–30.

Putzel, Max. "Evolution of Two Characters in Faulkner's Early and Unpublished Fiction." *Southern Library Journal* 5.2 (1973): 47–63.

————. *Genius of Place: William Faulkner's Triumphant Beginnings*. Baton Rouge: Louisiana State UP, 1985.

Ragan, David Paul. "'Belonging to the Business of Mankind': The Achievement of Faulkner's *Big Woods*." *Mississippi Quarterly* 36 (1983): 301–17.

Reed, Joseph. *Faulkner's Narrative*. New Haven: Yale UP, 1973.

Roth, Russell. "The Brennan Papers: Faulkner in Manuscript." *Perspective* 2 (1949): 219–24.

Ruppersburg, Hugh M. *Voice and Eye in Faulkner's Fiction.* Athens: U of Georgia P, 1983.

Schoenberg, Estelle. *Old Tales and Talking: Quentin Compson in William Faulkner's* Absalom, Absalom! *and Related Works.* Jackson: UP of Mississippi, 1977.

Schroeder, Patricia R. "Ratliff's Descent from the Buckboard: Tall Tale Techniques in *The Hamlet. Faulkner Journal* 3.2 (1988): 2–11.

Shepherd, Allen. "Hemingway's 'An Alpine Idyll' and Faulkner's 'Mistral.'" *University of Portland Review* (1973): 63–68.

Skei, Hans H. "Beyond Genre? Existential Experience in Faulkner's Short Fiction." The University of Mississippi Faulkner and Yoknapatawpha Conference: Faulkner and the Short Story, July 30, 1990.

———. "The Trapped Female Breaking Loose: William Faulkner's 'Elly.'" *American Studies in Scandinavia* 11 (1979): 15–24.

———. "William Faulkner's Short Story Sending Schedule and His First Short Story Collection, *These 13*: Some Ideas." *Notes on Mississippi Writers* 11 (1979): 64–72.

———. *William Faulkner: The Short Story Career: An Outline of Faulkner's Short Story Writing from 1919 to 1962.* Oslo: Universitetsforlaget, 1981.

Slatoff, Walter J. *Quest for Failure: A Study of William Faulkner.* Ithaca: Cornell UP, 1960.

Strandberg, Victor. *A Faulkner Overview: Six Perspectives.* Port Washington: Kennikat, 1981.

Thompson, Lawrance. *William Faulkner: An Introduction and Interpretation.* 2nd ed. New York: Holt, 1967.

Torgovnik, Marianna. *Closure in the Novel.* Princeton: Princeton UP, 1981.

Vickery, John B. "Ritual and Theme in Faulkner's 'Dry September.'" *Arizona Quarterly* 18 (1962): 5–14.

Vickery, Olga. *The Novels of William Faulkner: A Critical Interpretation.* 1959. Baton Rouge: Louisiana State UP, 1964.

Waggoner, Hyatt W. *William Faulkner: From Jefferson to the World.* 1959. Lexington: U of Kentucky P, 1966.

Watkins, Floyd C. "The Structure of 'A Rose for Emily.'" *Modern Language Notes* 69 (1954): 508–10. Rpt. in *William Faulkner: A Rose for Emily.* Ed. M. Thomas Inge. The Merrill Literary Casebook Series. Columbus: Merrill, 1970. 46–47.

Watson, James G. "Faulkner: Short Story Structure and Reflexive Forms." *Mosaic* 11.4 (1978): 127–37.

———. "Faulkner's Short Stories and the Making of Yoknapatawpha County." *Fifty Years of Yoknapatawpha: Faulkner and Yoknapatawpha 1979.* Eds. Doreen Fowler and Ann J. Abadie. Jackson: UP of Mississippi, 1980. 202–25.

———. "New Orleans, *The Double Dealer*, and 'New Orleans.'" *American Literature* 56 (1984): 214–26.

Wells, Dean Faulkner, and Lawrence Wells. "The Trains Belonged to Everybody: Faulkner as Ghost Writer." *Southern Review* 12 (1976): 864–71.

Yarup, Robert L. "Faulkner's 'Was.'" *Explicator* 41 (1983): 43–45.

Zender, Karl F. "A Hand of Poker: Game and Ritual in Faulkner's 'Was.'" *Studies in Short Fiction* 11 (1974): 53–60.

Zink, Karl E. "Flux and the Frozen Moment: The Imagery of Stasis in Faulkner's Prose." *PMLA* 71 (1956): 285–300.

# Selected List of Additional Works Consulted

Because of limitations of space, it is impossible to list in these pages all the scholarly and critical works devoted entirely or in part to Faulkner's short fiction. Furthermore, much that has been written about the stories is of little or no value. The list below, together with the Works Cited section of this study, contains only about half of the secondary sources I have consulted in the research for this book.

Of the general studies of Faulkner's work, I cite here only those that include significant assessments of the stories or that are so interesting and perceptive that the insights they contain can be applied profitably to the short fiction. Of the shorter secondary sources, I have eliminated most of the very brief notes on the stories and a number of essays and articles that seem to me of dubious worth. Because of the great amount of scholarly and critical work devoted to the "story novels," *Go Down, Moses* and *The Unvanquished* (particularly the former), I have included only a few of the very best studies concerned with some aspects of these works.

For anyone who is seriously interested in the study of Faulkner's short fiction, the books and articles in this list, together with those in the Works Cited section, should constitute, I believe, a useful basic bibliography of secondary sources. Those who are interested in developing more comprehensive bibliographies should consult Skei's *William Faulkner: The Short Story Career* (see Works Cited); Bassett's two checklists and McHaney's *William Faulkner: A Reference Guide* (see below); and the excellent annual checklists in the Spring issues of the *Mississippi Quarterly*. Very useful also are the annual surveys of research and criticism in the Summer issues of that journal, which are devoted exclusively to Faulkner.

Ackerman, R. D. "The Immolation of Isaac McCaslin." *Texas Studies in Language and Literature* 16 (1974): 557–65.

Akin, Warren, IV. "The Norm of Human Feelings: An Interpretation of Faulkner's 'Pantaloon in Black.' " *Studies in Short Fiction* 15 (1978): 397–404.

Allen, Dennis W. "Horror and Perverse Delight in Faulkner's 'A Rose for Emily.'" *Modern Fiction Studies* 30 (1984): 685–96.

Alsen, Eberhard. "An Existential Reading of Faulkner's 'Pantaloon in Black.'" *Studies in Short Fiction* 14 (1977): 169–78.

Bache, William B. "Moral Awareness in 'Dry September.'" *Faulkner Studies* 3 (1954): 53–57.

Barbera, Jack. "Tomorrow and Tomorrow and *Tomorrow*." *Southern Quarterly* 19 (1981): 183–97.

Barnes, Daniel R. "Faulkner's Miss Emily and Hawthorne's Old Maid." *Studies in Short Fiction* 9 (1972): 373–77.

Barth, J. Robert, ed. *Religious Perspectives in Faulkner's Fiction: Yoknapatawpha and Beyond*. Notre Dame: U of Notre Dame P, 1972.

Bassett, John Earl. *Faulkner: An Annotated Checklist of Recent Criticism*. Kent: Kent State UP, 1983.

———. *William Faulkner: An Annotated Checklist of Criticism*. New York: Lewis, 1972.

Beck, Warren. *Faulkner: Essays*. Madison: U of Wisconsin P, 1976.

Bell, Haney H., Jr. "A Reading of Faulkner's *Sartoris* and 'There Was a Queen.'" *Forum* 4 (1965): 23–26.

Bennett, Ken. "The Language of the Blues in Faulkner's 'That Evening Sun.'" *Mississippi Quarterly* 38 (1985): 339–42.

Bethea, Sally. "Further Thoughts on Racial Implications in 'That Evening Sun.'" *Notes on Mississippi Writers* 6 (1974): 87–92.

Blotner, Joseph. *William Faulkner's Library: A Catalogue*. Charlottesville: UP of Virginia, 1964.

Bomze, Joann. "Faulkner's 'Mountain Victory': The Triumph of 'The Middle Ground.'" *CEA Critic* 46 (1983–84): 9–11.

Bond, Adrienne. "Eneas Africanus and Faulkner's Fabulous Racehorse." *Southern Literary Journal* 9 (1977): 3–15.

Bonner, Thomas, Jr. "'Once Aboard the Lugger'—An Uncollected Faulkner Story." *Notes on Modern American Literature* 3 (1978): Item 8.

Bowen, James K., and James K. Hamby. "Colonel Sartoris Snopes and Gabriel Marcel: Allegiance and Commitment." *Notes on Mississippi Writers* 3 (1971): 101–7.

Bradford, Melvin E. "An Aesthetic Parable: Faulkner's 'Artist at Home.'" *Georgia Review* 27 (1973): 175–81.

———. "All the Daughters of Eve: 'Was' and the Unity of *Go Down, Moses*." *Arlington Quarterly* 1 (1967): 28–37.

———. "The Anomaly of Faulkner's World War I Stories." *Mississippi Quarterly* 36 (1983): 243–62.

———. "Certain Ladies of Quality: Faulkner's View of Women and the Evidence of 'There Was a Queen.'" *Arlington Quarterly* 1 (1967–68): 106–39.

———. "Family and Community in Faulkner's 'Barn Burning.'" *Southern Review* 17 (1981): 332–39.

———. "Faulkner's 'A Courtship': An Accommodation of Cultures." *South Atlantic Quarterly* 80 (1981): 355–59.

———. "Faulkner and the Great White Father." *Louisiana Studies* 3 (1964): 323–29.

———. "Faulkner and the Jeffersonian Dream: Nationalism in 'Two Soldiers' and 'Shall Not Perish.'" *Mississippi Quarterly* 18 (1965): 94–100.

———. "Faulkner's 'Elly': An Exposé." *Mississippi Quarterly* 21 (1968): 179–87.

———. "Faulkner's 'Tall Men.'" *South Atlantic Quarterly* 61 (1962): 29–39.

———. "Faulkner's 'That Evening Sun.'" *CEA Critic* 28 (1966): 1, 3.

———. "Faulkner's 'Tomorrow' and the Plain People." *Studies in Short Fiction* 2 (1965): 235–40.

———. "The Knight and the Artist: Tasso's and Faulkner's 'Carcassonne.'" *South Central Bulletin* 41 (1981): 88–90.

———. "The Winding Horn: Hunting and the Making of Men in Faulkner's 'Race at Morning.'" *Papers on English Language and Literature* 1 (1965): 272–78.

Brodsky, Louis Daniel, and Robert W. Hamblin. *Faulkner: A Comprehensive Guide to the Brodsky Collection: Vol. 2: The Letters.* Jackson: UP of Mississippi, 1984.

Brooks, Cleanth. "The Image of Helen Baird in Faulkner's Early Poetry and Fiction." *Sewanee Review* 85 (1977): 218–34.

———. "A Note on Faulkner's Early Attempts at the Short Story." *Studies in Short Fiction* 10 (1973): 381–88.

———. *A Shaping Joy: Studies in the Writer's Craft.* New York: Harcourt, 1971.

———. *William Faulkner: First Encounters.* New Haven: Yale UP, 1983.

Broughton, Panthea Reid. "The Cubist Novel: Toward Defining the Genre." Fowler & Abadie, *Cosmos* 36–58.

———. "Faulkner's Cubist Novels." Fowler & Abadie, *Cosmos* 59–94.

Brown, Calvin S. "Faulkner's Manhunts: Fact into Fiction." *Georgia Review* 20 (1966): 388–95.

———. "Faulkner's Use of the Oral Tradition." *Georgia Review* 22 (1968): 160–69.

Brown, May Cameron. "Voice in 'That Evening Sun': A Study of Quentin Compson." *Mississippi Quarterly* 29 (1976): 347–60.

Brown, Suzanne Hunter. "Appendix A: Reframing Stories" [concerning "A Rose for Emily"]. *Short Story Theory at a Crossroads.* Ed. Susan Lohafer and Jo Ellyn Clarey. Baton Rouge: Louisiana State UP, 1989. 311–27.

Brylowski, Walter. *Faulkner's Olympian Laugh: Myth in the Novels.* Detroit: Wayne State UP, 1968.

Bunselmeyer, J. E. "Faulkner's Narrative Styles." *American Literature* 53 (1981): 424–82.

Cackett, Kathy. "'Barn Burning': Debating the American Adam." *Notes on Mississippi Writers* 21.1 (1989): 1–17.

Callen, Shirley. "Planter and Poor White in *Absalom, Absalom!*, 'Wash,' and *The Mind of the South.*" *South Central Bulletin* 23.4 (1963): 24–36.

Cambon, Glauco. "Faulkner's 'The Old People': The Numen-Engendering Style." *Southern Review* 1 (1965): 94–107.

Cantrell, Frank. "Faulkner's 'A Courtship.'" *Mississippi Quarterly* 24 (1971): 289–95.

———. "An Unpublished Faulkner Short Story: 'Snow.'" *Mississippi Quarterly* 26 (1973): 325–30.

————. *Faulkner's Late Short Fiction*. Diss. U of South Carolina, 1970. Ann Arbor: UMI, 1976. 71–9709.

Carey, Glenn O. "Social Criticism in Faulkner's 'Dry September.'" *English Record* 15 (1964): 27–30.

Carothers, James B. "Faulkner's Short Stories: 'And Now What's to Do.'" *New Directions in Faulkner Studies: Faulkner and Yoknapatawpha, 1983*. Eds. Doreen Fowler and Ann J. Abadie. Jackson: UP of Mississippi, 1984. 202–27.

————. *William Faulkner's Short Stories*. Ann Arbor: UMI, 1985.

Castille, Philip. "'There Was a Queen' and Faulkner's Narcissa Sartoris." *Mississippi Quarterly* 28 (1975): 307–15.

Chittick, Kathryn. "Telling It Again and Again: *Notes on a Horsethief*." *Mississippi Quarterly* 32 (1979): 423–35.

Ciardi, John. "Faulkner and Child, Faulkner and Negro." *Harper's* May 1967: 114.

Clark, Charles C. "'Mistral': A Study in Human Tempering." *Mississippi Quarterly* 21 (1968): 195–204.

Cleman, John L. "'Pantaloon in Black': Its Place in *Go Down, Moses*." *Tennessee Studies in Literature* 22 (1977): 170–81.

Collins, Carvel. "A Note on the Conclusion of 'The Bear.'" *Faulkner Studies* 2 (1954): 58–60.

Comprone, Joseph. "Literature and the Writing Process: A Pedagogical Reading of William Faulkner's 'Barn Burning.'" *College Literature* 9 (1982): 1–21.

Cowley, Malcolm. *The Faulkner-Cowley File: Letters and Memories, 1944–1962*. New York: Viking, 1966.

Crane, John K. "But the Days Grow Short: A Reinterpretation of Faulkner's 'Dry September.'" *Twentieth Century Literature* 31 (1985): 410–20.

Creighton, Joanne Vanish. "Revision and Craftsmanship in 'The Fire and the Hearth.'" *Studies in Short Fiction* 11 (1974): 161–72.

————. "Revision and Craftsmanship in the Hunting Trilogy of *Go Down, Moses*." *Texas Studies in Language and Literature* 15 (1973): 577–92.

Crigler, John Payton, III. *Faulkner's Early Short Story Career*. Diss. Yale U, 1976. Ann Arbor: UMI, 1977. 76–29, 827.

Cullen, John B. *Old Times in the Faulkner Country*. In collaboration with Floyd C. Watkins. 1961. Baton Rouge: Louisiana State UP, 1975.

Dabney, Louis M. *The Indians of Yoknapatawpha: A Study in Language and Literature*. Baton Rouge: Louisiana State UP, 1974.

————. "'Was': Faulkner's Classic Comedy of the Frontier." *Southern Review* 8 (1972): 736–49.

Davis, Scottie. "Faulkner's Nancy: Racial Implications in 'That Evening Sun.'" *Notes on Mississippi Writers* 5 (1972): 30–32.

Day, Douglas. "The War Stories of William Faulkner." *Georgia Review* 15 (1961): 385–94.

Dessner, Lawrence Jay. "William Faulkner's 'Dry September': Decadence Domesticated." *College Literature* 11 (1984): 151–62.

Díaz-Diocaretz, Myriam. "Faulkner's Hen House: Woman as Bounded Text." Fowler & Abadie, *Women* 235–69.

Dickerson, Mary Jane. "Faulkner's Golden Steed." *Mississippi Quarterly* 31 (1978): 369–80.

———. "The Magician's Wand: Faulkner's Compson Appendix." *Mississippi Quarterly* 28 (1975): 317–37.

Dillon, Richard T. "Some Sources for Faulkner's Version of the First Air War." *American Literature* 44 (1973): 629–37.

Dowling, David. *William Faulkner*. New York: St. Martins, 1989.

Dunlap, Mary Montgomery. "William Faulkner's 'Knight's Gambit' and Gavin Stevens." *Mississippi Quarterly* 23 (1970): 223–39.

Dussinger, Gloria R. "Faulkner's Isaac McCaslin as Romantic Hero Manqué." *South Atlantic Quarterly* 68 (1969): 377–85.

Duvall, John N. "Silencing Women in 'The Fire and the Hearth' and 'Tomorrow.' " *College Literature* 16 (1989): 75–82.

Fant, Joseph L., and Robert Ashley. *Faulkner at West Point*. New York: Random, 1964.

Faulkner, Howard J. "The Stricken World of 'Dry September.' " *Studies in Short Fiction* 10 (1973): 47–50.

Faulkner, John. *My Brother Bill: An Affectionate Reminiscence*. New York: Trident, 1963.

Fetterley, Judith. *The Resisting Reader: A Feminist Approach to American Fiction*. Bloomington: Indiana UP, 1978. 34–45.

Fisher, Marvin. "The World of Faulkner's Children." *University of Kansas City Review* 27 (1960): 13–18.

Folks, Jeffrey J. "Honor in Faulkner's Short Fiction." *Southern Review* 18 (1982): 506–16.

———. "William Faulkner's 'The Rosary' and Florence L. Barclay." *Studies in Short Fiction* 18 (1981): 445–47.

Ford, Arthur L. "Dust and Dreams: A Study of Faulkner's 'Dry September.' " *College English* 24 (1962): 219–20.

Foster, Thomas C. "History, Private Consciousness, and Narrative Form in *Go Down, Moses*." *Centennial Review* 28 (1984): 61–76.

Fowler, Doreen, and Ann J. Abadie, eds. *A Cosmos of My Own: Faulkner and Yoknapatawpha 1980*. Jackson: UP of Mississippi, 1981.

———. *Faulkner and Women: Faulkner and Yoknapatawpha 1985*. Jackson: UP of Mississippi, 1986.

Franklin, Phyllis. "Sarty Snopes and 'Barn Burning.' " *Mississippi Quarterly* 21 (1968): 189–93.

French, Warren. "William Faulkner and the Art of the Detective Story." *The Thirties: Fiction, Poetry, Drama*. Deland, Fla.: Everett Edwards, 1967. 55–62.

Frey, Leonard H. "Irony and Point of View in 'That Evening Sun.' " *Faulkner Studies* 2 (1953): 33–40.

Funk, Robert W. "Satire and Existentialism in Faulkner's 'Red Leaves.' " *Mississippi Quarterly* 25 (1972): 339–48.

Gage, Duane. "William Faulkner's Indians." *American Indian Quarterly* 1 (1974): 27–33.

Garrison, Joseph M. "Bought Flowers in 'A Rose for Emily.' " *Studies in Short Fiction* 16 (1979): 341–44.

————. "Faulkner's 'The Brooch': A Story for Teaching." *College Teaching* 36 (1974): 51–57.

————. "The Past and the Present in 'That Evening Sun.' " *Studies in Short Fiction* 13 (1976): 371–73.

Gibb, Robert. "Moving Fast Sideways: A Look at Form and Image in *The Unvanquished*." *Faulkner Journal* 3.2 (1988): 40–47.

Gidley, Mark. "Beyond 'Beyond': Aspects of Faulkner's Representation of Death." Hönnighausen 234–41.

————. "Elements of the Detective Story in William Faulkner's Fiction." *Journal of Popular Culture* 7 (1973): 97–123.

Greiner, Donald J. "Universal Snopesism: The Significance of 'Spotted Horses.' " *English Journal* 57 (1968): 1133–37.

Gresset, Michel. "Faulkner's 'The Hill.' " *Southern Literary Journal* 6 (1974): 3–18.

————. "From Vignette to Vision: The 'Old, Fine Names of France' or Faulkner's 'Western Front' from 'Crevasse' to *A Fable*." *Faulkner: International Perspectives: Faulkner and Yoknapatawpha, 1982*. Eds. Doreen Fowler and Ann J. Abadie. Jackson: UP of Mississippi, 1984. 97–120.

Griffin, William J. "How to Misread Faulkner: A Powerful Plea for Innocence." *Tennessee Studies in Literature* 1 (1956): 27–34.

Grimwood, Michael. " 'Delta Autumn': Stagnation and Sedimentation in Faulkner's Career." *Southern Literary Journal* 16 (1984): 93–106.

————. "Faulkner's 'Golden Land' as Autobiography." *Studies in Short Fiction* 23 (1986): 275–80.

————. "Mr. Faulkner and Ernest V. Trueblood." *Southern Review* 21 (1985): 361–71.

Guerard, Albert J. *The Triumph of the Novel: Dickens, Dostoevsky, Faulkner*. New York: Oxford UP, 1976.

Hamblin, Robert W. "Before the Fall: The Theme of Innocence in Faulkner's 'That Evening Sun.' " *Notes on Mississippi Writers* 11 (1979): 86–94.

————. " 'Carcassonne': Faulkner's Allegory of Art and the Artist." *Southern Review* 15 (1979): 355–65.

Hamilton, Gary D. "The Past in the Present: A Reading of *Go Down, Moses*." *Southern Humanities Review* 5 (1971): 171–81.

Harrington, Evans, and Ann J. Abadie, eds. *Faulkner, Modernism, and Films: Faulkner and Yoknapatawpha 1978*. Jackson: UP of Mississippi, 1979.

Harter, Carol Clancey. "The Winter of Isaac McCaslin: Revisions and Irony in Faulkner's 'Delta Autumn.' " *Journal of Modern Literature* 1.2 (1970): 209–25.

Haynes, Jane Isbell. "Faulkner's Verbena." *Mississippi Quarterly* 33 (1980): 355–62.

Hays, Peter L. "Who is Faulkner's Emily?" *Studies in American Fiction* 16 (1988): 105–10.

Heller, Terry. "The Telltale Hair: A Critical Study of William Faulkner's 'A Rose for Emily.' " *Arlington Quarterly* 28 (1972): 301–18.

Hendricks, William O. " 'A Rose for Emily': A Syntagmatic Analysis." *PTL: A Journal for Descriptive Poetics and Theory of Literature* 2 (1977): 257–95.

Hermann, John. "Faulkner's Heart's Darling in 'That Evening Sun.' " *Studies in Short Fiction* 7 (1970): 320–23.

Hiles, Jane. "Kinship and Heredity in Faulkner's 'Barn Burning.'" *Mississippi Quarterly* 38 (1985): 329–37.

Hinkle, James. "Reading Faulkner's *The Unvanquished*." *College Literature* 13 (1986): 217–39.

Hochberg, Mark R. "The Unity of *Go Down, Moses*." *Tennessee Studies in Literature* 21 (1976): 58–65.

Hoffman, David. "Faulkner's 'Was' and Uncle Adam's Cow." Fowler & Abadie, *Humor* 57–78. (See my Works Cited section.)

Hogan, Patrick G. "Faulkner's New Orleans Idiom: A Style in Embryo." *Louisiana Studies* 5 (1966): 171–81.

Holland, Norman. "Fantasy and Defense in Faulkner's 'A Rose for Emily.'" *Hartford Studies in Literature* 4 (1972): 1–35.

———. *5 Readers Reading*. New Haven: Yale UP, 1975.

Holmes, Edward M. *Faulkner's Twice-Told Tales: His Re-Use of His Material*. The Hague: Mouton, 1966.

Hönnighausen, Lothar, ed. *Faulkner's Discourse: An International Symposium*. Tubingen: Niemeyer, 1989.

Houghton, Donald E. "Whores and Horses in Faulkner's 'Spotted Horses.'" *Midwest Quarterly* 11 (1970): 361–69.

Howell, Elmo. "Colonel Sartoris Snopes and Faulkner's Aristocrats: A Note on 'Barn Burning.'" *Carolina Quarterly* 11 (1959): 13–19.

———. "Faulkner's Country Church: A Note on 'Shingles for the Lord.'" *Mississippi Quarterly* 21 (1968): 205–10.

———. "Faulkner's Enveloping Sense of History: A Note on 'Tomorrow.'" *Notes on Contemporary Literature* 3 (1973): 5–6.

———. "Faulkner's Wash Jones and the Southern Poor White." *Ball State University Forum* 8 (1967): 8–12.

———. "William Faulkner and *Pro Patria Mori*." *Louisiana Studies* 5 (1966): 89–96.

———. "William Faulkner and Tennessee." *Tennessee Historical Quarterly* 21 (1962): 251–62.

———. "William Faulkner and the Andrews Raid in Georgia." *Georgia Historical Quarterly* 49 (1965): 187–92.

———. "William Faulkner and the Concept of Honor." *Northwest Review* 5 (1962): 51–60.

———. "William Faulkner and the Mississippi Indians." *Georgia Review* 21 (1967): 386–96.

———. "William Faulkner's Chickasaw Legacy: A Note on 'Red Leaves.'" *Arizona Quarterly* 26 (1970): 293–303.

———. "William Faulkner's General Forrest and the Uses of History." *Tennessee Historical Quarterly* 29 (1970): 287–94.

Hunt, John W. "The Disappearance of Quentin Compson." *Critical Essays on William Faulkner: The Compson Family*. Ed. Arthur F. Kinney. Boston: Hall, 1982. 366–80.

———. *William Faulkner: Art in Theological Tension*. 1965. New York: Haskell, 1973.

Hurt, Lester E. "Mysticism in 'Go Down, Moses.'" *English Record* 15 (1964): 17–22.

Ilacqua, Alma A. "The Place of the Elect in Three Faulkner Narratives." *Christian Scholar's Review* 12.2 (1983): 126–38.

Inscoe, John C. "Faulkner, Race, and Appalachia." *South Atlantic Quarterly* 86 (1987): 244–53.

Isaacs, Neil D. "Götterdämmerung in Yoknapatawpha." *Tennessee Studies in Literature* 8 (1963): 47–55.

Johnston, Kenneth G. "Time of Decline: Pickett's Charge and the Broken Clock in Faulkner's 'Barn Burning.'" *Studies in Short Fiction* 11 (1974): 434–36.

———. "The Year of Jubilee: Faulkner's 'That Evening Sun.'" *American Literature* 46 (1974): 93–100.

Jones, Leonidas M. "Faulkner's 'The Hound.'" *Explicator* 15 (1957): Item 37.

Kartiganer, Donald M. *The Fragile Thread: The Meaning of Form in Faulkner's Novels.* Amherst: U of Massachusetts P, 1979.

Kenner, Hugh. "Faulkner and Joyce." Harrington and Abadie 20–33.

———. "Faulkner and the Avant-Garde." Harrington and Abadie 182–96.

Kerr, Elizabeth. "William Faulkner and the Southern Concept of Women.'" *Mississippi Quarterly* 15 (1962): 1–16.

———. *Yoknapatawpha: Faulkner's "Little Postage Stamp of Native Soil".* New York: Fordham UP, 1969.

Kinney, Arthur F. "Faulkner and the Possibilities for Heroism." *Southern Review* 6 (1970): 1110–25.

———. *Faulkner's Narrative Poetics: Style as Vision.* Amherst: U of Massachusetts P, 1978.

Knieger, Bernard. "Faulkner's 'Mountain Victory,' 'Doctor Martino,' and 'There Was a Queen.'" *Explicator* 30 (1972): Item 45.

Kohn, Sheldon Scott. "Ira Ewing, Jr., and His 'Monument': Architecture in Faulkner's 'Golden Land.'" *Notes on Mississippi Writers* 15 (1983): 79–86.

Kreiswirth, Martin. "Learning as He Wrote: Re-Used Materials in *The Sound and the Fury.*" *Mississippi Quarterly* 34 (1981): 281–98.

———. *William Faulkner: The Making of a Novelist.* Athens: U of Georgia P, 1983.

Kuyk, Dirck, Jr., et al. "Black Culture in William Faulkner's 'That Evening Sun.'" *Journal of American Studies* 20 (1986): 33–50.

Lang, Béatrice. "*Dr. Martino*: The Conflict of Life and Death." *Delta* 3 (1976): 23–33.

———. "An Unpublished Faulkner Story: 'The Big Shot.'" *Mississippi Quarterly* 26 (1973): 312–24.

Langford, Beverly Y. "History and Legend in William Faulkner's 'Red Leaves.'" *Notes on Mississippi Writers* 6 (1973): 19–24.

Lee, Jim. "The Problem of Nancy in Faulkner's 'That Evening Sun.'" *South Central Bulletin* 21 (1961): 49–50.

Levitt, Paul. "An Analogue for Faulkner's 'A Rose for Emily.'" *Papers on Language and Literature* 9 (1973): 91–94.

Limon, John. "The Integration of *Go Down, Moses.*" *Critical Inquiry* 12 (1986): 422–38.

Lind, Ilse Dusoir. "The Language of Stereotype in 'Death Drag.'" Hönnighausen 127–31.

Lisca, Peter. "*The Hamlet*: Genesis and Revisions." *Faulkner Studies* 3 (1954): 5–13.

Longley, John Lewis. *The Tragic Mask: A Study of Faulkner's Heroes.* Chapel Hill: U of North Carolina P, 1963.

McDermott, John V. "Faulkner's Cry for a Healing Measure: 'Dry September.'" *Arizona Quarterly* 32 (1976): 31–34.

McHaney, Thomas L. *William Faulkner: A Reference Guide.* Boston: Hall, 1976.

MacMillan, Duane J. "Fictional Facts and Factual Fiction." *Faulkner Journal* 2.2 (1987): 47–54.

Martin, Jay. "'The Whole Burden of Man's History of His Impossible Heart's Desire': The Early Life of William Faulkner." *American Literature* 53 (1982): 607–29.

Massey, Linton R., comp. *"Man Working," 1919–1962: William Faulkner: A Catalogue of the William Faulkner Collections at the University of Virginia.* Charlottesville: UP of Virginia, 1968.

Matthews, John T. *The Play of Faulkner's Language.* Ithaca: Cornell UP, 1982.

Mellard, James M. "The Biblical Rhythm of *Go Down, Moses.*" *Mississippi Quarterly* 20 (1967): 135–47.

———. "Faulkner's Miss Emily and Blake's 'Sick Rose': 'Invisible Worm,' *Nachträglichkeit,* and Retrospective Gothic." *Faulkner Journal* 2.1 (1986): 37–45.

Memmott, A. James. "Sartoris *Ludens*: The Play Element in *The Unvanquished.*" *Mississippi Quarterly* 29 (1976): 375–88.

Meriwether, James B. "Faulkner's Correspondence with *The Saturday Evening Post.*" *Mississippi Quarterly* 30 (1977): 461–75.

———. "Faulkner's 'Mississippi.'" *Mississippi Quarterly* 25 (1972), supplement: 15–23.

———. "The Place of *The Unvanquished* in William Faulkner's Yoknapatawpha Series." Diss. Princeton U, 1958.

Mickelsen, David. "The Campfire and the Hearth in *Go Down, Moses.*" *Mississippi Quarterly* 38 (1985): 311–27.

Millgate, Jane. "Short Story into Novel: Faulkner's Reworking of 'Gold Is Not Always.'" *English Studies* 45 (1964): 310–17.

Milum, Richard A. "Faulkner's 'Carcassonne': The Dream and the Reality." *Studies in Short Fiction* 15 (1978): 133–38.

———. "Ikkemotubbe and the Spanish Conspiracy." *American Literature* 46 (1974): 389–91.

Miner, Ward L. *The World of William Faulkner.* 1952. New York: Cooper Square, 1963.

Minter, David. *William Faulkner: His Life and Work.* Baltimore: Johns Hopkins UP, 1980.

Mitchell, Charles. "The Wounded Will of Faulkner's Barn Burner." *Modern Fiction Studies* 11 (1965): 185–89.

Momberger, Philip. "Faulkner's 'The Village' and 'That Evening Sun': The Tale in Context." *Southern Literary Journal* 11 (1978): 20–31.

———. "A Reading of Faulkner's 'The Hill.'" *Southern Literary Journal* 9 (1977): 16–29.

Morell, Giliane. "Prisoners of the Inner World: Mother and Daughter in *Miss Zilphia Gant.*" *Mississippi Quarterly* 28 (1975): 299–305.

Morrison, Gail M. "The Composition of *The Sound and the Fury.*" *William Faulkner's The Sound and the Fury: A Critical Casebook.* Ed. André Bleikasten. New York: Garland, 1982. 33–64.

———. "Faulkner's Priests and Fitzgerald's 'Absolution.'" *Mississippi Quarterly* 32 (1979): 461–65.

———. "'Time, Tide, and Twilight.': *Mayday* and Faulkner's Quest Toward *The Sound and the Fury.*" *Mississippi Quarterly* 31 (1978): 337–57.

Mortimer, Gail L. *Faulkner's Rhetoric of Loss.* Austin: U of Texas P, 1983.

Moses, W. R. "Victory in Defeat: 'Ad Astra' and *A Farewell to Arms.*" *Mississippi Quarterly* 19 (1966): 85–89.

Muller, Gilbert H. "The Descent of the Gods: Faulkner's 'Red Leaves' and the Garden of the South." *Studies in Short Fiction* 11 (1974): 243–49.

Myres, W. V. "Faulkner's Parable of Poetic Justice." *Louisiana Studies* 8 (1969): 224–30.

Noble, Donald R. "Faulkner's 'Pantaloon in Black': An Aristotelian Reading." *Ball State University Forum* 14 (1973): 16–19.

O'Brien, Frances Blazer. "Faulkner and Wright: Alias S. S. Van Dine." *Mississippi Quarterly* 14 (1961): 101–7.

O'Connor, William Van. *The Tangled Fire of William Faulkner.* Minneapolis: U of Minnesota P, 1954.

Owens, Tony J. "Faulkner, Anderson, and 'Artist at Home.'" *Mississippi Quarterly* 32 (1979): 393–412.

Paddock, Lisa. "'Trifles with a tragic profundity': The Importance of 'Mistral.'" *Mississippi Quarterly* 32 (1979): 413–22.

Page, Sally R. *Faulkner's Women: Characterization and Meaning.* Deland: Everett Edwards, 1972.

Peavy, Charles D. "An Early Casting of Benjy: Faulkner's 'The Kingdom of God.'" *Studies in Short Fiction* 3 (1966): 347–48.

———. "The Eyes of Innocence: Faulkner's 'The Kingdom of God.'" *Papers on Language and Literature* 2 (1966): 178–82.

Perluck, Herbert A. "'The Heart's Driving Complexity': An Unromantic Reading of 'The Bear.'" *Accent* 20 (1960): 23–46.

Perrine, Laurence. "'That Evening Sun': A Skein of Uncertainties." *Studies in Short Fiction* 22 (1985): 295–307.

Perry, Menakhem. "Literary Dynamics: How the Order of a Text Creates Its Meanings [With an Analysis of Faulkner's 'A Rose for Emily']." *Poetics Today* 1 (1979): 35–64, 311–61.

Petry, Alice Hall. "Double Murder: The Women of Faulkner's 'Elly.'" Fowler & Abadie, *Women* 220–34.

Pilkington, John. "'Strange Times' in Yoknapatawpha." *Fifty Years of Yoknapatawpha: Faulkner and Yoknapatawpha 1979.* Eds. Doreen Fowler and Ann J. Abadie. Jackson: UP of Mississippi, 1980. 71–89.

Pitavy, François. [Note on *Idyll in the Desert*]. *Nouvelle Revue Française* 40 (1972): 69–70.

Pitcher, E. W. "Motive and Metaphor in Faulkner's 'That Evening Sun.'" *Studies in Short Fiction* 18 (1981): 131–35.

Pryse, Marjorie. "Miniaturizing Yoknapatawpha: *The Unvanquished* as Faulkner's Theory of Realism." *Mississippi Quarterly* 33 (1980): 343–54.

———. "Race: Faulkner's 'Red Leaves.'" *Studies in Short Fiction* 12 (1975): 133–38.

Putzel, Max. "Faulkner's Memphis Stories." *Virginia Quarterly Review* 59 (1983): 254–70.

———. "Faulkner's Short Story Sending Schedule." *Papers of the Bibliographical Society of America* 71 (1977): 98–105.

Ragan, David Paul. "The Evolution of Roth Edmonds in *Go Down, Moses.*" *Mississippi Quarterly* 38 (1985): 295–309.

Richardson, H. Edward. *William Faulkner: The Journey to Self-Discovery.* Columbia: U of Missouri P, 1969.

Rollyson, Carl E., Jr. "Faulkner into Film: 'Tomorrow' and 'Tomorrow.'" *Mississippi Quarterly* 32 (1979): 437–52.

Ross, Stephen. "Lying Beneath Speech: Preliminary Notes on the Representation of Thought in 'Carcassonne.'" Hönnighausen 159–69.

Ryan, Steven T. "'Mistral' and 'Evangeline': The Gothic Derivation of *Absalom, Absalom!*" *Kentucky Review* 5 (1983): 56–71.

Samway, Patrick, S. J. "Gavin Stevens as Uncle-Creator in *Knight's Gambit.*" *Faulkner and Idealism: Perspectives from Paris.* Eds. Michel Gresset and Patrick Samway. Jackson: UP of Mississippi, 1983. 144–63.

Sanders, Barry. "Faulkner's Fire Imagery in 'That Evening Sun.'" *Studies in Short Fiction* 5 (1967): 69–71.

Sartoris, Brenda Eve. "*Cornbote*: Feudal Custom and Faulkner's 'Barn Burning.'" *Studies in American Fiction* 11 (1983): 91–94.

Scherting, Jack. "Emily Grierson's Oedipus Complex: Motif, Motive, and Meaning in Faulkner's 'A Rose for Emily.'" *Studies in Short Fiction* 17 (1980): 397–405.

Schlepper, W. E. "Truth and Justice in *Knight's Gambit.*" *Mississippi Quarterly* 37 (1984): 365–75.

Sederburg, Nancy B. "'A Momentary Anesthesia of the Heart': A Study of the Comic Element in Faulkner's *Go Down, Moses.*" Fowler & Abadie, *Humor* 79–96. (See my Works Cited section.)

Selzer, John L. "'Go Down, Moses' and *Go Down, Moses.*" *Studies in American Fiction* 13 (1985): 89–96.

Simpson, Hassell A. "Wilbur Daniel Steele's Influence on Faulkner's Revision of 'Beyond.'" *Mississippi Quarterly* 34 (1981): 335–39.

Skei, Hans H. "Faulkner's *Knight's Gambit*: Detection and Ingenuity." *Notes on Mississippi Writers* 13.2 (1981): 79–83.

———. "A Forgotten Faulkner Story: 'Thrift.'" *Mississippi Quarterly* 32 (1979): 453–60.

———. "Inadequacies of Style in Some of William Faulkner's Short Stories." Hönnighausen 234–41.

———. *William Faulkner: The Novelist as Short Story Writer: A Study of William Faulkner's Short Fiction.* Oslo: Universitetsforlaget, 1985.

Slabey, Robert M. "Quentin Compson's Lost Childhood." *Studies in Short Fiction* 1 (1964): 173–83.

Smith, Raleigh W. "Faulkner's 'Victory': The Plain People of Clydebank." *Mississippi Quarterly* 23 (1970): 241–49.

Solery, Marc. " 'Black Music' ou la Métamorphose du Regard." *Delta* 3 (1976): 35–43.

Spatz, Jonas. *Hollywood in Fiction: Some Versions of the American Myth.* The Hague: Mouton, 1969. 116–19.

Stein, William Bysshe. "Faulkner's Devil." *Modern Language Notes* 76 (1961): 731–32.

Stephens, Rosemary. "Ike's Gun and Too Many Novembers." *Mississippi Quarterly* 23 (1970): 279–87.

———. "Mythical Elements of 'Pantaloon in Black.' " *University of Mississippi Studies in English* 11 (1970): 45–51.

Stewart, Jack F. "Apotheosis and Apocalypse in Faulkner's 'Wash.' " *Studies in Short Fiction* 6 (1969): 586–600.

———. "The Infernal Climate of Faulkner's 'Dry September.' " *Research Studies: A Quarterly Publication of Washington State University* 47 (1979): 238–43.

———. "Structure, Language, and Vision in Faulkner's 'The Old People.' " *Ball State University Forum* 22 (1981): 51–57.

Stone, Edward. "Usher, Poquelin, and Miss Emily: The Progress of Southern Gothic." *Georgia Review* 14 (1960): 434–43.

———. "William Faulkner's Two Little Confederates." *Ohio University Review* 4 (1962): 5–18.

Stoneback, H. R. "Faulkner's Blues: 'Pantaloon in Black.' " *Modern Fiction Studies* 21 (1975): 241–45.

Stonum, Gary Lee. *Faulkner's Career: An Internal Literary History.* Ithaca: Cornell UP, 1979.

Strozier, Robert. "Some Versions of Faulkner's Pastoral." *Forum* (Houston) 5 (1967): 35–40.

Sullivan, Ruth. "The Narrator in 'A Rose for Emily.' " *Journal of Narrative Technique* 1 (1971): 159–78.

Sultan, Stanley. "Call Me Ishmael: The Hagiography of Isaac McCaslin." *Texas Studies in Literature and Language* 3 (1961): 50–66.

Sunderman, Paula. "Speech Art Theory and Faulkner's 'That Evening Sun.' " *Language and Style* 14 (1981): 304–14.

Sundquist, Eric J. *Faulkner: The House Divided.* Baltimore: Johns Hopkins UP, 1983.

Taylor, Nancy Dew. "Moral Housecleaning and Colonel Sartoris's Dream." *Mississippi Quarterly* 37 (1984): 353–64.

Taylor, Walter. "Faulkner's Pantaloon: The Negro Anomaly at the Heart of *Go Down, Moses.*" *American Literature* 44 (1972): 430–44.

———. "Horror and Nostalgia: The Double Perspective of Faulkner's 'Was.' " *Southern Humanities Review* 8 (1974): 74–84.

Tick, Stanley. "The Unity of *Go Down, Moses.*" *Twentieth-Century Literature* 8 (1962): 67–73.

Tucker, Edward L. "Faulkner's Drusilla and Ibsen's Hedda." *Modern Drama* 16 (1973): 157–61.

Tuso, Joseph F. "Faulkner's 'Wash.'" *Explicator* 27 (1968): Item 17.

Utley, Francis Lee, Lynn Z. Bloom, and Arthur F. Kinney. *Bear, Man and God: Eight Approaches to William Faulkner's "The Bear."* 2nd ed. New York: Random, 1971.

Volpe, Edmond L. "'Barn Burning': A Definition of Evil." *Faulkner: The Unappeased Imagination.* Ed. Glenn O. Carey. Troy. N.Y.: Whitson, 1980. 75–82.

———. "'Dry September': Metaphor for Despair." *College Literature* 16 (1989): 60–65.

———. "'Elly': Like Gunpowder in a Flimsy Vault." *Mississippi Quarterly* 42 (1989): 273–80.

———. "Faulkner's 'Knight's Gambit': Sentimentality and the Creative Imagination." *Modern Fiction Studies* 24 (1978): 232–39.

———. "Faulkner's 'Monk': The Detective Story and the Mystery of the Human Heart." *Faulkner Studies* 1 (1980): 22–47.

———. "Faulkner's 'Red Leaves': The Deciduation of Nature." *Studies in American Fiction* 3 (1975): 121–31.

———. "Faulkner's 'Uncle Willy': A Childhood Fable." *Mosaic* 12.1 (1978): 177–81.

———. *A Reader's Guide to William Faulkner.* 1964. New York: Octagon-Farrar, 1974.

Walker, David. "Out of the Old Time: 'Was' and *Go Down, Moses.*" *The Journal of Narrative Technique* 9 (1979): 1–11.

Walker, William E. "*The Unvanquished*: The Restoration of Tradition." *Reality and Myth: Essays in American Literature in Memory of Richard Croom Beatty.* Eds. William E. Walker and Robert L. Welker. Nashville: Vanderbilt UP, 1964. 275–97.

Watkins, Floyd C., and Thomas Daniel Young. "Revisions of Style in Faulkner's *The Hamlet.*" *Modern Fiction Studies* 5 (1959): 327–36.

Watson, James G. "Literary Self Criticism: Faulkner in Fiction on Fiction." *Southern Quarterly* 20 (1981): 46–63.

———. "Short Story Fantasies and the Limits of Modernism." *Faulkner Studies* 1 (1980): 80–85.

Weiss, Daniel. "William Faulkner and the Runaway Slave." *Northwest Review* 6 (1963): 71–79.

West, Ray B. *The Short Story in America 1900–1950.* Chicago: Regnery, 1952.

Whicher, Stephen E. "The Compsons' Nancies: A Note on *The Sound and the Fury* and 'That Evening Sun.'" *American Literature* 26 (1954): 253–55.

Williams, David. *Faulkner's Women: The Myth and the Muse.* Montreal: McGill-Queen's UP, 1977.

Wilson, Gayle Edward. "Being Pulled Two Ways: The Nature of Sarty's Choice in 'Barn Burning.'" *Mississippi Quarterly* 24 (1971): 279–88.

Winchell, Mark Ryder. "William Faulkner's 'Golden Land': Some Time in Hell." *Notes on Mississippi Writers* 14.1 (1981): 12–17.

Winn, James A. "Faulkner's Revisions: A Stylist at Work." *American Literature* 41 (1969): 231–250.

Winslow, Joan D. "Language and Destruction in Faulkner's 'Dry September.'" *CEA Journal* 20 (1977): 380–86.

Wittenberg, Judith Bryant. *Faulkner: The Transfiguration of Biography*. Lincoln: U of Nebraska P, 1979.

Wolfe, Ralph Haven, and Edgar F. Daniels. "Beneath the Dust of 'Dry September.'" *Studies in Short Fiction* 1 (1964): 158–59.

Wright, Austin McGiffert. *The American Short Story in the Twenties*. Chicago: U of Chicago P, 1961.

Zender, Karl. F. "Character and Symbol in 'Barn Burning.'" *College Literature* 16 (1989): 48–59.

# Index

Because Faulkner's characterizations are not a central concern of this book, the index does not include the names of his characters. Reading notes have been indexed but not reference notes, parenthetical citations within the text, and the various bibliographies. (For additional information about the short fiction, including variant titles, see the "Bibliography of Faulkner's Short Fiction," pp. 187–98.) Where appropriate, the standard abbreviations for Faulkner's books have been employed. (See "Abbreviations for Faulkner's Texts," pp. xv–xvii.) "WF" has been used throughout the index to identify William Faulkner.

**DATE DUE**

*Faulkner's Short Fiction* was designed by Dariel Mayer,
composed by Tseng Information Systems, Inc., and printed
by Cushing/Malloy, Inc. The book is set in Fournier
and printed on 50-lb. Glatfelter Natural.